THE DUDE DIET

THE
DUDE DIET

Clean(ish) Food
for People Who Like to Eat Dirty

Serena Wolf

Photographs by Matt Armendariz

HARPER

An Imprint of HarperCollinsPublishers

THE DUDE DIET. Copyright © 2016 by Serena Wolf. Photographs © Matt Armendariz Photography. All rights reserved. Printed in the United States of America. No part of this book may be used or reproduced in any manner whatsoever without written permission except in the case of brief quotations embodied in critical articles and reviews. For information, address Harper-Collins Publishers, 195 Broadway, New York, NY 10007.

HarperCollins books may be purchased for educational, business, or sales promotional use. For information, please e-mail the Special Markets Department at SPsales@harpercollins.com.

FIRST EDITION

Designed by Leah Carlson-Stanisic

Library of Congress Cataloging-in-Publication Data has been applied for.

ISBN 978-0-06-242438-9

16 17 18 19 20   RRD   10 9 8 7 6 5 4 3 2 1

To

LOGAN.

Your body is a wonderland.

CONTENTS

INTRODUCTION

Almost four years ago, I was roused from a Saturday-morning snooze by several loud bangs and a sound I can only describe as reminiscent of a dying bear. Alarmed, I sprinted down the hall to find my boyfriend, Logan, stepping on and off the bathroom scale in all his naked glory, occasionally stopping to reset the thing by banging it aggressively on the tiled floor. "This scale is broken!!!" he raged. When I gently informed him that the scale was brand new and in perfect working condition, his eyes glazed over with panic. Many expletives and a few "are you shitting me?!"s later, Logan took a deep breath, put his hands on his (still very naked) hips, and declared, "I'm going on a diet."

I'm going on a diet. Five beautiful and completely unexpected words that changed both of our lives forever.

But let's back up for a second. In order to fully appreciate the gravity of the above statement, you need to understand a few things about Logan Smith Unland. First and foremost, the dude loves food more than any human being I have ever known. He lives for "epic sandos," lights up at the mere mention of BBQ and pizza, and regularly finds himself embroiled in heated debates over the best cheesesteak spot in Philly or where to order Chinese food in NYC. If you ask him what he's thinking about, nine times out of ten the response is "Mac and cheese!" (or if he's feeling particularly creative, "Mac and cheese! With hot dogs!!!"). Logan also fancies himself quite the epicure. As he will tell anyone who asks and those who don't, "Daddy does not fuck around" when it comes to food. (At some point, Logan began referring to himself as "Daddy." No explanation.)

Don't even get me started on what it's like to attend weddings, cocktail parties, and other social events with the dude. Let's just say that I've spent a lot of time reenacting the scene from *My Best Friend's Wedding* where Julia Roberts chases Dermot Mulroney (who she's in love with), who's chasing Cameron Diaz (who he's in love with) across a giant lawn. In these scenarios, I'm Julia, Logan is Dermot, and Cameron is a poor, unsuspecting server with a tray of pigs in a blanket.

Since I was enrolled in culinary school when we first met, Logan's intense love of food was one of the things that initially drew me to him. And in the early days of our relationship, I saw only the endearing, humorous side of his unbridled passion for all things "dank." Sure, I was shocked by some of his larger feasts, but basking in Logan's food-based joy was one of my favorite activities—there's nothing quite like the contact high from watching him ecstatically crush a hoagie—and I figured he definitely ate some nutritious stuff on his own time. It was only when we moved in together and I became privy to his day-to-day choices, that I began to worry about Logan's health and fitness.

The dude's diet was straight-up *terrifying.*

At twenty-nine, Logan was still eating like a college athlete—which in his mind, he still was—rather than a deskbound adult male who exercised sporadically at best. His primary food groups were meat, cheese, and white bread, and he counted several of the local pizza and Chinese deliverymen as close personal friends. Food was inhaled (rather than chewed and swallowed in the traditional fashion) with no regard for its nutritional value, a behavior that appeared to fuel a rather serious antacid addiction. Worst of all, Logan regularly gave himself the "meat sweats." (In case you're not familiar, the meat sweats are exactly what they sound like—sweating caused by your body's inability to process an outrageous amount of animal protein. They're usually accompanied by a stomachache, insomnia, and extreme irritability.)

Like most guys I know, Logan had packed on a few extra lbs since college, but the dude's weight was the least of my concerns. Based on his obsession with all things cheesy, Buffalo-flavored, and deep-fried, I legitimately feared he didn't have many years left to live (which was only mildly melodramatic). As I'd grown pretty attached to Logan by this point and hoped to keep him around past the age of thirty-five, I'd occasionally mention that he should try eating a little bit better. Unfortunately, the dude dismissed these suggestions with derogatory comments about vegetables and blanket refusals to eat "weird vegan shit." A few times, he actually screamed, "I do what I want!!" before skipping across the street to Chipotle.

As much as I wanted to, I knew deep down that I could never force Logan to change his ways. So I backed off, praying that he'd come around to the idea of a healthier lifestyle on his own one day. Since I wasn't exactly holding my breath, you can imagine my surprise when that day came much sooner than anticipated. (Logan's fateful Saturday weigh-in took place mere weeks after I'd resigned myself to his batshit crazy eating habits!) Thrilled that longevity was still an option for the dude, I offered my full support, promising to help Logan revamp his diet come hell or high water.

THE DUDE DIET IS BORN

Clearly, overhauling the eating habits of someone who comes precariously close to having an excitement seizure in the vicinity of finger food and who regularly trips over himself while running to the door to get his Domino's wouldn't be easy, but I love a challenge (and Logan) and was wholeheartedly committed to the job. I've been a healthy eater my whole life, am known for my excellent common sense, and have killer chef skills courtesy of Le Cordon Bleu Paris, so I felt more than qualified to act as the dude's nutritional spirit guide.

From the get-go, there were two major barriers to Logan's dieting success. The first was that he understood absolutely nothing about nutrition. Despite his incredible intelligence, Logan couldn't identify a balanced meal or healthy snack to save his life. He had also internalized random concepts from various popular diets, applying them as needed to justify his ridiculous food choices. He'd eat a handful of greens topped with fried chicken fingers and smothered in ranch dressing and then demand congratulations for ordering a "green salad." An Italian hero became instantly slimming on a low-carb wrap, and mac and cheese was good for him because "it's vegetarian." Anything labeled "gluten-free" or "vegan" was also calorie-free, and things like sweet potato fries and onions rings were considered vegetables. You get the point. Logan was, to put it bluntly, a nutritional idiot, and even when he tried to eat healthy, he often missed the mark. (By a lot.)

The second stumbling block was the fact that Logan harbored a deep-seated bias against all "health food." He was convinced that anything nutritious was either flavorless or gross, wrongly assuming that eating well meant restricting himself to a miserable regimen of lettuce, tofu, and nonfat yogurt. With an outlook like this, all dieting efforts were doomed from the start.

Taking these issues into account, I set to work tailoring a healthy lifestyle program to Logan's specific needs, which I affectionately dubbed "The Dude Diet." ("The Common Sense Diet" just didn't have quite the same ring to it.) After breaking down nutrition basics for the dude in a way he could comprehend (/didn't bore him to tears) and emphasizing the importance of mindfulness, moderation, and portion control, I developed an arsenal of wholesome recipes designed to help Logan change his grim view of nutritious food. My goal was not to create meals that were simply "healthy," but rather feasts that the dude was downright psyched to eat. This was a tall order—Logan has surprisingly high standards for someone who used to subsist primarily on pizza and sandwiches—but like I said, I was committed.

The Dude Diet's early days weren't exactly smooth sailing, but on the whole, some very impressive strides were made. Logan paid more attention to the things he put in his mouth and willingly(!) ingested more vegetables, lean meats, and whole grains. These small changes noticeably improved his mood, energy levels, and physique, and people began to take notice, complimenting the dude wherever we went on how happy and svelte he looked. It was obviously too early to bank on The Dude Diet's long-term success, but the future of Logan's health seemed shockingly bright.

THE BLOG

For better or worse, by focusing so closely on Logan's diet, I became hyperaware of the eating habits of the other men in my life. The amount of overlap was disturbing. Many of these individuals, including my brother and some of my best friends, also appeared to suffer from nutritional confusion, indicating that Logan's food-related behavior was the rule rather than the exception in the dude community. Troubled by this realization, I decided to document Logan's story on my blog, Domesticate-Me.com, in the hope that it might encourage a dude or two to get his shit together. Everyone loves a good "health journey," right?

So, on September 19, 2012, I wrote a short piece simply titled "The Dude Diet." In it, I summarized Logan's fetish for insanely fattening fare, the nagging fear that his diet would send him to an early grave, and my plan to improve his health by teaching him the fundamentals of nutrition and an appreciation for nourishing, whole foods. (I also shared a poorly depicted recipe for lightened-up osso buco as an example of the hearty deliciousness being used to keep the dude on the nutritional straight and narrow.) The post was honest and informative, but it was meant to be a one-off. A cathartic exercise, if you will.

Needless to say, I was taken aback when I received a flood of phone calls, texts, and e-mails from friends and readers regarding that post. They were intrigued. Was Logan really on a diet? *Damn straight.* What exactly did this diet entail? *Moderation and being less of an idiot.* Should they go on the same diet? *Definitely. I might be a genius.* Was Logan going to break up with me because I had outed his wayward dietary habits on the Internet? *I certainly hoped not. We had just become roommates!*

There were so many Dude Diet–related questions, and people seemed intent on me providing them with answers. So I decided to give the "masses" what they wanted, and The Dude Diet became a regular series on the blog.

From portion control and snacking to post-workout meals and responsible boozing, each Dude Diet installment targeted a specific area of nutritional confusion and included a straightforward recipe for a healthy, dude-friendly meal. With these posts, I systematically debunked common misconceptions about both health and health food, while encouraging dudes to take control of their diets and learn how to cook for themselves. Knowing that the cooking part would be a source of contention, I made sure that each recipe was as simple as possible and required only easily accessible ingredients and basic kitchen tools, so that even the most culinary-challenged individuals would be able to pull them off.

THE RESPONSE

"As a dude in LA fighting against vegans and Paleo dieters, you're making my life way better. I can't believe I bought tofu today, and I'm afraid of it, but it's all your fault and likely to be seriously delicious."

—Random Dude (via e-mail)

The response to this series was far more enthusiastic than I could have ever imagined. The Dude Diet seemed to fill a gap in the highly saturated diet market, appealing to men who wanted to clean up their act but couldn't fathom counting things like calories and carbs, and who would rather die than give up entire food groups altogether (especially meat, grains, and dairy). These men responded well to The Dude Diet's "tough love" approach to nutrition, and the idiotproof nature of the recipes empowered many of them to conquer their culinary fears.

I regularly received e-mails (like the one on the previous page) from dudes that appreciated an alternative to restrictive mainstream diets, as well as hilarious thank-you notes directed toward Logan himself—the dude community appeared to be endlessly grateful to him for inspiring such epic creations as Dude Diet Philly Cheesesteaks (page 90), Cauliflower Mac and Cheese with Chicken Sausage (page 64) and Buffalo Chicken Tenders with Yogurt Ranch (page 108). Logan had inadvertently become a healthy-eating hero, and it warmed my dude-loving heart.

But it wasn't just men that were digging The Dude Diet. Hordes of women reached out to say that they had been relying on Dude Diet recipes to feed their picky, health food–fearing boyfriends, husbands, dads, and sons. Not only were they relieved that their dudes were eating more nutritious meals, they were excited to discover recipes that they could enjoy alongside the men they loved without sacrificing their own health and waistlines. A growing number of women were also personally embracing The Dude Diet to satisfy their Logan-esque comfort food cravings, a trend I strongly encouraged. (I've been on The Dude Diet for years!)

In short, what had started as a low-maintenance healthy lifestyle for my boyfriend had grown into a movement that transcended gender, age, and nutritional understanding. Thanks to The Dude Diet, people were grabbing their health (and the health of their loved ones) by the balls, making smarter food choices, cooking more, and turning their bodies into wonderlands. I was ~~a genius!!!~~ humbled and overjoyed.

My next move? Take The Dude Diet mainstream.

THE NFL EFFECT

I always knew a high-profile dude would eventually legitimize The Dude Diet and help bring it to the masses; I just wasn't clear on exactly how or when. I mostly envisioned getting my hands on a pre-weight-loss Seth Rogan type, putting him on The Dude Diet in secret for a couple of months, and then unveiling his sexy new bod to the world in some grand fashion. When Jimmy Kimmel inevitably asked how this dude had slimmed down, he would sing The Dude Diet's many praises (and maybe carry me around on his newly muscled shoulders as I high-fived the crowd). Said celebrity would then star in national ad campaigns with Logan, and The Dude Diet would become the new Weight Watchers.

That is not what happened. But I did become the private chef for two young NFL players, which is close enough. (For now.)

How was I able to recruit kick-ass professional athletes as Dude Diet disciples? The short answer is *fate*. The long answer is that I was put in touch with a regional NFL team's nutritionist who needed a private chef for two of her clients. I was hired based on my dedication to super-satisfying healthy fare, and the rest is Dude Diet history. I spent two seasons cooking nutritious, flavor-packed meals for these dudes, one of whom actually lost 10 pounds in just two months and claimed he felt significantly faster and stronger. No joke.

If you're wondering who these NFL players are, I'm not going to tell you (because I can't). Trust me, it's better that way. Not knowing gives you the freedom to picture your favorite player—preferably one with an enviable athletic physique—and use that image as incentive to get with The Dude Diet program. (Imagining yourself or someone you love with a Tom Brady eight-pack? It could happen!) After all, if The Dude Diet can make professional athletes harder/better/faster/stronger, imagine what it can do for the average man or woman!

FORWARD AND ONWARD

The Dude Diet has come a long way in just three short years, but after countless blog posts, recipes, success stories, high fives from NFL players, and a lot of laughs, I'm most rewarded by the transformation of its unlikely ambassador. I respect the actual poundage Logan has lost, but I'm far more proud of how much he's learned about nutrition in the process. Slowly but surely, The Dude Diet's teachings seem to have sunk in. Logan makes more informed choices, spends less money on Zantac, and rarely hates on healthy food these days. Yes, he gets weird with a double cheeseburger or an obscene amount of barbecue from time to time, but that's to be expected. I take solace in the fact that when these things happen, Logan wipes the meat sweat from his brow, asks me to sew the seam on the jeans that he split up the crotch, and climbs right back on The Dude Diet wagon. It's nothing short of a miracle.

Logan's continuous progress is a constant source of inspiration, reminding me daily of The Dude Diet's potential and my newfound purpose. Everyone has a calling, and I've realized that mine is to arm dudes and the people that love them with the information and skills they need to lead healthier, happier lives. That's why I wrote this book.

Packed with nutritional guidance, culinary tips, and more than 125 drool-worthy recipes, the following pages aim to demystify healthy eating and prove that meals made with nutrient-dense whole foods can be every bit as mind-blowingly awesome as your favorite fattening feasts. From badass breakfasts and sexy sides to game-day eats and slimmed-down versions of classic comfort foods, the recipes in this book will satisfy your many cravings while helping you feel better and look hotter. So whether you're looking to ditch your man boobs by beach season, get your meat sweats under control, or you simply want to "crush dank shit" without feeling like crap, The Dude Diet has your back.

Get on board.

THE DUDE DIET COMMANDMENTS

1 I resolve to be less of a nutritional idiot. I shall think before I put things in my mouth, especially pizza, burritos, and other foods that are larger than my head.

2 I shall eat more fish, poultry, and lean pork. Red meat is an indulgence, not a diet staple.

3 Excluding my birthday and barbecue festivals to which I have purchased a ticket, I shall not eat any type of meat in quantities large enough to give me the meat sweats. Not even on No-Calorie Sunday.

4 If it's white, I shall always think twice. I will limit my consumption of white bread, rice, and pasta, and eat more whole grains, which are surprisingly delicious.

5 I shall curb my refined sugar habit because it makes me fat, sick, and unhappy.

6 I shall crush less dairy. Cream, butter, cheese, and ice cream will be eaten sparingly.

7 I shall not clog my arteries with large quantities of fried food. There are many healthier cooking methods, and I will learn to appreciate them.

8 I shall make an effort to consume at least five servings of vegetables a day and three servings of fruit. This will provide me with essential nutrients and leave me too full to eat junk.

9 I shall pay attention to sauces, dressings, and condiments, many of which are filled with a shocking amount of calories, fat, and scary additives. I will eat fresh, flavor-packed foods so that I am not tempted to douse them in ranch.

10 I shall exercise portion control. I will not eat to the point that I feel ill, require medication, or am unable to move.

11 I shall eat at a reasonable pace. Eating more slowly will give my body a chance to recognize when it's full. It is also more civilized.

12 I shall exercise on a regular basis. Such exercise will break a sweat. Sitting in a steam room or sauna does not count.

13 I shall drink alcohol responsibly (most of the time) and keep my beer belly in check.

14 My body is a wonderland. I commit myself to The Dude Diet in the hope that other people will agree with this statement.

THE DUDE DIET

CHAPTER

DUDE DIET 101

The Keys to Success

The Dude Diet is pretty straightforward, and if you internalize its simple commandments and work the recipes in this book, you'll be well on your way to a wonderland body and excellent long-term health. With that said, I'd like to draw your attention to a few key directives that will help you kick-start your leaner lifestyle, avoid common pitfalls, and maximize your overall Dude Diet success. Learn them. Live them. Love them.

KICK YOUR REFINED CARBOHYDRATE HABIT. STAT.

From pizza to Snickers bars, refined carbohydrates are the average dude's kryptonite, and moderating your consumption should be at the top of your Dude Diet to-do list. To be clear, not *all* carbohydrates are bad. There's a huge difference between nutritious carbohydrates like whole grains, fruits, vegetables, and beans, and refined carbohydrates like white flour, white rice, white sugar, and corn syrup. While the former are a great source of nutrients and sustained energy, the latter have been subjected to the refining process, which breaks down, and in some cases completely removes, the whole-grain component of a food, stripping it of all the "good stuff" (i.e., essential vitamins, minerals, and fiber). As a result, refined carbs have close to zero nutritional value.

And while eating refined carbs provides an initial burst of energy, you may have noticed that just an hour or two after your bagel-and-smear breakfast or vending-machine snack, you start to crash. That's because eating shit like white bread and candy causes your blood sugar to skyrocket. Yes, refined carbs give you an instant high, but it's short-lived, and that blood sugar spike wreaks havoc on your body—complete with unattractive and potentially embarrassing consequences (i.e., unintentional dirt naps, decreased ability to control your appetite, and crazy mood swings).

Eating processed carbs is also an easy way to pack on pounds. When you eat foods that cause your blood sugar to soar, your body is forced to produce more insulin to bring your blood sugar back to a normal level. Insulin is a fat storage hormone, dudes. With higher levels of insulin in your bloodstream, your body converts refined carbs into sugars that get stored as body fat. In simple terms:

DEEP-DISH PIZZA ➡ **INSULIN SPIKE** ➡ **MAN BOOBS**

In other bad news, the more refined grains and sugars you consume, the more you crave them, and this vicious cycle can have far scarier consequences than man boobs and a jelly belly in the long run. Studies show that ingesting large quantities of refined carbs significantly increases your risk of developing insulin resistance, heart disease, diabetes, cancer, obesity, depression, and Alzheimer's. I'm guessing you'd like to avoid those things?

I'm not asking you to give up refined grains and sugars altogether (and you'll still find them used occasionally in Dude Diet recipes), but scaling back is clearly vital, and I promise that when you do, the immediate change in your well-being will blow your mind. Once Logan got over the withdrawal hump (and stopped claiming that The Dude Diet was "ruining his life!"), the dude was amazed by his higher energy levels, mental clarity, and newfound ability to sit down without unbuttoning his pants. You, too, can experience these wonders!

Cravings Decoded

Why You "Need" Refined Carbohydrates and How to Kick the Habit

TO KICK YOUR REFINED CARBOHYDRATE HABIT AND JUMP-START YOUR DUDE DIET PROGRESS. PLEASE CONSULT THE FOLLOWING CHART. WHICH OUTLINES THE MENTAL AND PHYSICAL CAUSES FOR YOUR CRAVINGS AND HOW BEST TO TACKLE THEM.

The Cause	The Fix
YOU WANT TO FEEL HAPPY. Sugar releases serotonin and endorphins that calm you down and make you feel good.	NATURAL SUGARS RELEASE THE SAME AMOUNTS OF "HAPPY" BRAIN CHEMICALS WITHOUT ALL THE NASTY SIDE EFFECTS. Try eating some fruit or a piece of whole-grain toast with peanut or almond butter when a craving strikes. You know what else boosts serotonin and endorphin levels? Exercise. Try some of that.
YOU HAVE AN IMBALANCE OF "BOWEL FLORA." If you regularly experience bloating. gas. diarrhea. constipation. or exhaustion. your gut bacteria could be out of whack. A bacterial imbalance can cause yeast to build up in your body. and since yeast thrives on sugar. yeast overgrowth could be (partially) responsible for your insatiable sweet tooth.	A GOOD PROBIOTIC SHOULD HELP BALANCE YOUR FLORA. Talk to your doctor and/or the friendly peeps at your local health food store.
YOU ARE EATING TOO MUCH SALT. Find yourself craving sweets after polishing off a bag of chips or a carton of Chinese food? This is because when you eat a lot of salt. the body naturally craves sugar to balance it out.	STOP EATING SO MUCH SALT! Not only will eating less sodium decrease your sugar cravings. it will also help you de-bloat by shedding water weight. You'll be surprised how fast your double chin disappears when you cut back.
YOU ARE STRESSED. When you're fatigued. depressed. or under chronic stress. your body craves quick sources of energy. which refined carbohydrates provide.	CHILL OUT. Do activities that relax you. Talk to your partner. friend. family member. or roommate. (Do not call Domino's. They can't help you.)
YOU LIKE THE TASTE OF REFINED GRAINS AND SUGARS. You really like it. Always have. always will. You crave these things because they are delicious and that's that.	GET IT TOGETHER. Everyone likes pizza and candy. but part of being a responsible human being is learning to exercise self-control. (Did you not read the paragraph where I said that eating too many refined carbs gives you man boobs and diabetes?)
YOU ARE LITERALLY A SUGAR "ADDICT." Studies have shown that a diet high in refined sugars stimulates the dopamine pathway. which is the pleasure-sensing area of the brain. Over time. the brain will crave more of the things that light up that pathway. (Soda! Cupcakes! Ice cream!) Eating sugar becomes a learned behavior that is extremely difficult to break.	THIS ISN'T AN EASY FIX, DUDES. You could ditch refined sugars cold turkey. but I suggest weaning yourself for safety reasons. It will be unpleasant—withdrawal always is—but in as little as 48 to 72 hours. your cravings will be noticeably less intense as your blood sugar levels balance out. Please warn your loved ones.

UNDERSTAND AND EXERCISE PORTION CONTROL

This may come as a shock, but eating healthy food is only half The Dude Diet battle. To slim down, you don't just need to eat well, you also need to eat LESS. "Healthy" is not synonymous with "calorie-free," and the fact that something is nutritious doesn't give you a hall pass to eat it in mass quantities. Portion control is crucial. Respect the serving sizes indicated for the recipes in this book (they're there for a reason), and when it comes to all other meals, do your best to adhere to the following portion size guidelines:

Dude Diet Portion Size Guidelines

- **MEAT, FISH, AND POULTRY:** 6 to 8 ounces, which is roughly the size of your hand. Unless you have freakishly large hands, there's no excuse for eating giant hunks of meat.

- **PASTA, RICE, QUINOA, AND OTHER WHOLE GRAINS:** ¾ cup cooked grains as a side dish, 1½ cups as a main course. As a point of reference, 1 cup is about the size of a teacup, not a Big Gulp.

- **FRUIT:** 1 medium whole fruit (i.e., apple, orange, banana), ½ large whole fruit (i.e., grapefruit, cantaloupe, mango), or 1 cup chopped fruit or berries. Aim to eat three servings a day.

- **VEGETABLES:** 1 cup of raw, leafy greens and ½ cup of other vegetables. The goal is five servings a day, but feel free to eat more if you like. (Do not smother them in ranch dressing, butter, or cheese!)

- **CHEESE:** 1½ ounces. This is the size of 1 string cheese (or your pointer finger).

- **NUTS:** ¼ cup of raw nuts, which is about a handful, or 2 tablespoons of nut butter.

I know these portion sizes may seem disconcertingly small, but I swear I'm not trying to starve you here, dudes. In fact, The Dude Diet's portions are far more generous than those dictated by the American Heart Association. (God knows you'd burn this book if I suggested limiting yourself to 3 ounces of meat or ½ cup of grains at any given meal.) There will likely be an uncomfortable adjustment period as you overcome your portion distortion, but the sooner you embrace reasonable serving sizes, the sooner you'll reset your body's "appetite thermostat" and begin to feel satisfied with less food.

To state the obvious, portion control also applies to snacks, so be mindful of the things you put in your mouth between meals—office baked goods and casual slices of pizza will derail your Dude Diet efforts faster than you can say "dad bod."

AVOID THE POST-WORKOUT BINGE

I'm not going to insult your intelligence by listing the many reasons why exercise is a critical component of The Dude Diet lifestyle. You already know working out chisels your muscles, helps you de-stress, and reduces your risk of disease, and that you should do it as often as you possibly can. Instead, I want to clear up a couple of common workout-related delusions that could sabotage your success.

Let's start with the fact that food does not become magically fat-and-calorie-free when you physically exert yourself. You might be starving after an aggressive sweat sesh and tempted to go on an eating rampage in your blissful, endorphin-filled haze, but try to keep it together. Your post-workout meals and snacks should refuel and repair your muscles, not flood your system with insane amounts of fat and sugar. Remember the importance of portion control, and keep this one simple rule in mind: *If it isn't time for a meal, don't have one.* Contrary to Taco Bell's ad campaigns, "fourth meal" isn't actually a thing, and taking down four large meals a day is unacceptable Dude Diet behavior. Instead, have a filling snack—preferably one that combines wholesome carbs and protein—to keep you happy and energized until your next legitimate feeding.

I also regret to inform you that the effects of exercise do not last multiple days. If you go for a run on Monday, you're not still burning calories from that same run on Friday. Monday's workout cannot be used to rationalize a box of hump-day doughnuts or a weeklong meatball sub bender. Sad, but true.

Finally, I'd like to briefly touch on the rampant abuse of sports drinks in the dude community. If you're participating in an Ironman triathlon or spending the majority of your day at the gym, by all means, feel free to go to town on a case of Gatorade, but chugging a quart of artificially flavored sugar-water after a twenty-minute jog is a bit overzealous. Please switch to good old H_2O.

EMBRACE THE DUDE DIET LONG TERM

Back in The Dude Diet's early days, Logan bet a friend that he could lose 6 percent of his body weight in a single month. It seemed like a long shot, but the dude is nothing if not competitive, and after 30 days of uncharacteristically clean eating and exercise, he had dropped the 14 pounds necessary to win this wager. Victory was sweet. Unfortunately, it was also fleeting.

Watching Logan admire his newly svelte physique in the mirror, I could see the wheels turning in his nutritionally challenged brain. He said nothing, but I knew he was imagining all the delicious, artery-clogging things he could consume now that he was "the skinniest dude alive!" My fears were quickly confirmed when Logan sprinted out the door to get a sausage, egg, and cheese sandwich because he looked "too fucking sexy" and deserved to celebrate after "starving to death for a month." Despite my warnings that he would not stay "skinny" if he continued to attack fattening foods like a competitive eater, Logan only went further off the rails. The next few days were a blur of Domino's, cheesesteaks, and Mexican feasts, and when he finally emerged from this tailspin, Logan found himself right back at his pre-wager weight.

As Logan learned the hard way, your health and hot body require constant maintenance, and you're never "done" when it comes to eating well. The Dude Diet is a lifestyle, not a monthlong emergency weight-loss program, and reverting to old habits as soon as you start to "feel good" or hit your goal weight is a recipe for disaster. It's also inefficient. Why go through the trouble of getting healthy and fit multiple times, when you could just do it once?

While the concept of eating healthily *forever* may sound daunting, remember that The Dude Diet is anti-restriction, and nothing is off-limits as long as you exercise moderation and portion control. The key to maintaining a healthy lifestyle long term is ensuring that you never get to the point where you feel excessively deprived. The Dude Diet needs no martyrs, and I actually encourage you to go ham on a deep-dish pizza or a pile of extra hot wings every once in a while. After all, that's what No-Calorie Sunday is for.

CELEBRATE NO-CALORIE SUNDAY

No-Calorie Sunday is the one day a week when you can throw caution to the wind and fulfill your wildest food-based fantasies without undoing your Dude Diet progress. You'll find that the promise of this weekly "holiday" makes it easier to stick to your guns throughout the week by giving you a psychological break and satisfying your more outlandish cravings. It also provides a friendly reminder of why you've chosen to lead a healthier lifestyle, usually in the form of severe heartburn and/or the meat sweats. So go ahead and wave that food freak flag, dudes! Come Monday, you'll be more than ready to get right back on the healthy eating horse.

(Needless to say, No-Calorie Sunday doesn't have to fall on a Sunday, but it's most effective when celebrated on the same day every week. And don't even think about celebrating a No-Calorie Sunday and Monday consecutively because "they're part of two different weeks.")

DON'T GO IT ALONE

The transition to The Dude Diet lifestyle is guaranteed to have its ups and downs, and you're going to need all the support you can get. I'm obviously with you in spirit, but a flesh-and-blood buddy to gently remind you that chili-cheese fries aren't the best side choice, or that it's time to switch from Bud Heavy to Bud Light, is a lifesaver. Whether it's your significant other, your best friend, your mom (no judgment), or a fellow Dude Dieter, make yourself accountable to at least one other person in your life. Hell, tell everyone you know you're on The Dude Diet! As a wise man once said, "Teamwork makes the dream work," and the more eyes a dude has on his diet, the better. It takes a village.

CHAPTER

THE DUDE DIET KITCHEN

Get Your Shit Together

Now that you've got a handle on The Dude Diet's basic principles, it's almost time to talk food. But before we dive headlong into the recipes, I'd like you to take a good, hard look at the state of your kitchen. If you happen to have a pantry brimming with spices and oils and nice, neat stacks of cookware in your cabinets, go ahead and move right along, you unicorn of a man! As for the rest of you, please take a few minutes to study the following pages, which detail the ingredients and equipment necessary to build a Dude Diet–friendly kitchen from the ground up. A little blocking and tackling when it comes to your setup goes a long way toward ensuring culinary wins. Let's do this.

PANTRY ESSENTIALS

Having a variety of essential ingredients on hand exponentially increases your chances of opting for a Dude Diet recipe over Hot Pockets or delivery on any given day. It also makes cooking a more pleasant experience by helping to mitigate grocery lists and avoid those devastating moments when you've already started plowing through a recipe and realize you're missing something simple yet vital to its success. Like olive oil. Or kosher salt.

The following pages contain a list of the ingredients that you'll find used over and over again throughout this book. Don't be intimidated by its length, dudes—there's no need to rush out and purchase every single item right away. Start by investing in the flavors that appeal to you most, and go from there. Spice addict? Make sriracha sauce and crushed red pepper flakes a priority. Into Asian-inspired awesomeness? Pick up some low-sodium soy sauce and rice vinegar, stat. If you collect a few staples every time you hit the market, you'll have a well-stocked pantry in no time. (I use the term "pantry" loosely here. For years my pantry was a giant plastic box next to the front door.)

The majority of the following ingredients are available in any supermarket, but some may be hidden in unexpected places. So before you give up on an ingredient and storm home cursing the obscurity of The Dude Diet's recipes, take 30 seconds to ask an employee if the store carries the item, and if so, where you can find it. I know many dudes are against asking for directions, but I beg you to swallow your pride in the name of delicious food and Dude Diet success. (My local market changes the location of the chipotles in adobo sauce with rage-inducing frequency, but the peppers are always there.) And on the off chance you can't track down an ingredient? I hear there's a little site called Amazon.com that can magically fulfill all your pantry needs in just 24 hours . . .

Oils

Extra-virgin coconut oil

Extra-virgin olive oil

Dark sesame oil

Light sesame oil

Vinegars

Apple cider vinegar

Balsamic vinegar

Distilled white vinegar

Sherry vinegar

Unseasoned rice vinegar

Whole-Grain Goodness

Brown rice

Farro (pearled or semi-pearled)

Old-fashioned rolled oats

Quinoa

Whole-wheat or brown rice pasta

Whole-wheat flour

Whole-wheat panko bread crumbs

Pantry Staples

Baking soda

Baking powder

Brown sugar (light and dark)

Canned beans (Stock your favorites; I like black, Great Northern, cannellini, and chickpeas.)

Canned tomatoes (crushed, diced, and pureed)

Chia seeds

Chipotles canned in adobo sauce

Cornstarch

Fresh garlic (Store it in a cool, dry place.)

Granulated pure cane sugar

Honey

Low-sodium chicken broth

Low-sodium soy sauce

No-stick cooking spray (I recommend canola oil spray.)

No-sugar-added nut butter (such as almond or peanut butter)

Onions (red and yellow)

Pure maple syrup

Pure vanilla extract

Raw nuts (such as almonds, cashews, walnuts, and pecans)

Sriracha sauce

Tomato paste

Tahini

Spice Cabinet Favorites

Black pepper (I recommend purchasing a small grinder with whole peppercorns.)

Cayenne pepper

Chili powder

Crushed red pepper flakes (aka red chili flakes)

Curry powder

Dried oregano

Fine-grain sea salt

Garlic powder

Ground cinnamon

Ground cumin

Ground dried ginger

Ground nutmeg

Kosher salt

Onion powder

Smoked paprika

Fridge Staples

Chicken or turkey sausage links

Dijon mustard

Eggs

Ezekiel bread

Lacinato kale

Lemons

Milk (regular or non-dairy)

Nonfat plain Greek yogurt

Parmesan cheese (Buy a wedge, and grate it as needed.)

Whole-grain tortillas (whole wheat, sprouted grain, or brown rice)

Let's take a closer look at the ingredients that may have left you scratching your head.

Extra-Virgin Coconut Oil

Known for its many health benefits, this increasingly popular oil is now widely available. Coconut oil is great for baking, but it's also awesome in stir-fries and salad dressings, and when added to smoothies for an extra energy boost. It has a slight tropical sweetness to it, but the coconut flavor is very subtle, so even coconut haters shouldn't find this oil offensive. Unlike olive oil, there is no difference between coconut oil labeled "extra virgin" and "virgin." They're interchangeable.

Just a heads-up, coconut oil is a solid at room temperature! To liquefy it, simply microwave the oil in its own container or a heat-resistant bowl for about 30 seconds until completely melted.

Dark Sesame Oil

Sometimes labeled "toasted sesame oil," you can find small bottles of this stuff in the Asian section of most supermarkets, and its unique toasted flavor jazzes up everything from stir-fries and noodles to marinades and salad dressings. A little bit goes a long way, so a single bottle should last you several months.

Unseasoned Rice Vinegar

Also labeled "rice wine vinegar," this mildly acidic, subtly sweet vinegar is made from rice. (Shocker.) You'll find it in the Asian section of most supermarkets, usually next to the soy sauce. (Marukan is the most common brand.) If you're craving a recipe that calls for unseasoned rice vinegar but don't have any on hand, white wine vinegar and apple cider vinegar are your best substitution options.

Farro

Nutty in taste and slightly chewy in texture, farro is a pure form of wheat that's considered the oldest cultivated grain on the planet. It's absurdly high in fiber and rich in cyanogenic glucosides, which sound scary but actually stimulate the immune system, regulate blood sugar levels, and lower cholesterol. Farro is also a good source of protein, and it's packed with B vitamins, antioxidants, and essential minerals.

The tricky thing about this grain is that there are multiple varieties. Farro can be whole/unpearled, semipearled, or pearled based on how much of the exterior bran and germ have been removed from the grain itself. More confusing still is the fact that some farro labeled "whole" is actually semipearled. Don't panic, dudes. The best way to distinguish between types of farro is simply to look at the cooking time stated on the package: 15 minutes or less = pearled, 30 minutes = semipearled, and 50+ minutes = whole. For the recipes in this book, you'll want to use either pearled or semipearled farro.

Quinoa

Pronounced "keen-wah," this ancient grain (technically a seed, but whatever) is all the rage these days, and it's now stocked in most supermarkets—usually between the rice and couscous. It's an excellent source of fiber, iron, and protein, and it's delicious as a simple side dish or added to a variety of recipes like Epic Meat Loaf (page 71) and Cheeseburger Quinoa Bake (page 86). Because quinoa has a natural coating called saponin that tastes bitter and soapy, the grains need to be rinsed and drained before cooking. I recommend buying quinoa labeled "pre-washed" from brands like Ancient Harvest to eliminate this annoying step.

Chia Seeds

Packed with vitamins, minerals, protein, and omega-3 fatty acids, chia is the definition of a "superfood." The coolest thing about these funky little seeds is that they can absorb up to ten times their own weight in liquid, and their gelling capability is ideal for making nutrient-rich jams and puddings. They can even be used as a binder in meatballs! Many supermarkets now carry chia seeds, as do all health food stores. (Chia seeds come in black and white varieties, but the difference is purely aesthetic.)

Chipotles Canned in Adobo Sauce

These are dried and smoked jalapeños canned in a sweet and tangy red sauce. Found in the Mexican section of most supermarkets—usually next to the canned jalapeños and beans—these peppers add serious heat and killer smoky flavor to any dish, making them one of The Dude Diet's most treasured pantry staples. You'll only need a pepper or two and a little adobo sauce per recipe, so store what's left of the can in an airtight container in the fridge for up to two months.

Cornstarch

A fine, powdery starch made from the endosperm of corn kernels, cornstarch is primarily used as a thickener for sauces, gravies, and pie or crumble fillings. You'll find it in the baking aisle of your supermarket. As long as it's tightly sealed and stored in a cool, dry place, a single container should last you a very, very long time. (I'm talking years, dudes.)

Whole-Wheat Panko Bread Crumbs

These are flaky Japanese bread crumbs with a particularly light and crispy texture. Panko is perfect for breading oven-fried foods like Buffalo Chicken Tenders with Yogurt Ranch (page 108), and it makes an epic crunchy topping for casseroles. I urge you to seek out 100 percent whole-wheat panko (Kikkoman brand is my favorite), which is less processed than white.

Kosher Salt

KOSHER SALT IS EVERYTHING! Sorry for yelling, but kosher salt is actually the most important ingredient in any pantry, and it will be used in 99 percent of the recipes in this book. There are a couple of things that set kosher salt apart from regular table salt. First, it has a cleaner taste due to its lack of additives like iodine. Second, it has larger, more irregular flakes. These flakes are easier to pinch than fine table salt crystals, giving you more control over the quantity of salt that you add to a dish. They also adhere better to the surface of meat, poultry, and fish. Kosher salt is available in every single grocery store everywhere and will run you all of $2 for a giant box, so please buy some ASAP (if you haven't already). If you must substitute table salt for kosher salt in a recipe, start with about half the amount called for and slowly add more to taste.

Pure Maple Syrup

This is the only type of syrup you should have in your pantry. Unlike the viscous squeeze-bottle stuff you may be used to, pure maple syrup has no added sugar, high-fructose corn syrup, or artificial flavorings. Its pronounced maple flavor is obviously delightful on pancakes and French toast, but it's also a great sweetener for oatmeal, smoothies, sauces, salad dressings, and more.

Smoked Paprika

Made from smoked pimiento peppers, this deep red spice is Hungarian paprika's sexy Spanish cousin. It's mild and slightly sweet with a unique smokiness that adds depth and complexity to a variety of savory recipes. It's now stocked in most supermarkets right next to the regular paprika, but if you can't find it, I recommend ordering a jar online. It's life-changing. (Yes, you can sub regular paprika for smoked in a pinch, but the resulting dish won't have quite the same oomph.)

Sriracha Sauce

This addictive red chile sauce is a personal favorite, and it's an incredibly versatile Dude Diet staple. The blend of chile peppers, garlic, vinegar, salt, and sugar gives sriracha a tang and slight sweetness that sets it apart from your run-of-the-mill hot sauce, and I support its use in and on everything from scrambled eggs to meatballs. I'm partial to the traditional "rooster sauce" made by Huy Fong Foods, but feel free to indulge your inner hipster and experiment with one of the many artisanal sriracha sauces on the market.

Tahini

This is a paste made from ground hulled sesame seeds. It's commonly used in hummus, salad dressings, and sauces, as well as soups and baked goods, and you'll find it in the ethnic section of most supermarkets and at all health food stores. Tahini has a tendency to separate in the jar, so make sure to mix it well before adding it to a recipe.

Ezekiel Bread

Produced by the Food for Life brand, Ezekiel bread is made entirely from sprouted grains rather than flour, and it boasts some serious health benefits. Not only does it have more protein, vitamins, and fiber than your average whole-grain bread, it's also much easier for your body to digest (and God knows you've probably tortured your digestive system enough). The texture takes a little getting used to—it's denser than your typical loaf—so I suggest eating it toasted. Because sprouted grains are highly perishable, most markets stock Ezekiel bread in the frozen foods section, and you'll need to store it in your fridge or freezer at home as well.

Lacinato Kale

Also called "dinosaur kale," this is the type of kale with big, flat leaves. It's milder and less grassy than curly kale (which is why I recommend it to kale newbies), and it's literally bursting with essential vitamins and minerals. Unlike most leafy greens, kale can last for up to 2 weeks in the fridge, so even if you just add a little bit to a smoothie or scramble here and there, it's a smart staple to have on hand. Make sure you always wash your kale before eating it and remove the center ribs, dudes—they're tough and gross.

EQUIPMENT ESSENTIALS

If you've ever been "lucky" enough to hang out at Williams-Sonoma or spend a nice little Saturday at Bed, Bath & Beyond with your significant other (or mom), you've probably been exposed to the infinite array of cookware and tools on the market. While the sight of skillets stacked to high heaven and entire walls devoted to specialty spatulas makes me giddier than Logan at a Chinese buffet, I recognize that it can be overwhelming for the average dude. Especially those outfitting their kitchens from scratch. To make choosing the right equipment as painless as possible, I've compiled a comprehensive list of everything you could possibly need to pull off the recipes in this book—right down to the parchment paper you'll bake your party mix on.

The Cookware

LARGE (12- TO 14-INCH) OVENPROOF SKILLET: A large skillet is your ride-or-die pan, and if you only buy one piece of cookware, this should be it. The sloping sides make for easy sautéing, but you'll also find it useful for baking things like casseroles and cornbread. I love cast iron (which only becomes better and more nonstick with use), but a stainless-steel or traditional nonstick skillet will serve you just as well.

NONSTICK SKILLET: When it comes to eggs, fish, and other items that have a tendency to stick to the pan, a true nonstick skillet is a lifesaver. I recommend a 10-inch skillet for your basic needs, but a large one also comes in very handy if you've got the space.

SAUTÉ PAN: Like a skillet, but with higher, straight sides instead of sloping, this pan is perfect for cooking larger volume dishes, especially those with a lot of liquid. I recommend a medium (3-quart) size.

GRILL PAN: This genius pan helps fill the void for dudes who love grilling but don't have access to an actual grill. It's also ideal for the colder months, when outdoor grilling just isn't an option. Both cast-iron and nonstick grill pans perform equally well, but a nonstick is easier to clean.

SAUCEPANS (AKA POTS): When it comes to simmering sauces, cooking grains, blanching vegetables, and even boiling pasta, a saucepan is the man for the job. I recommend a small (1- to 2-quart) and medium (3-quart) saucepan.

A 4- TO 6-QUART ENAMELED DUTCH OVEN OR HEAVY-BOTTOMED SOUP POT: Soup, chili, braised meats, and other big batch items cook best in a Dutch oven or heavy-bottomed soup pot, which distributes heat more evenly and prevents scorching. You can also cook pasta and even roast a chicken in one of these things.

The Bakeware

9 X 13-INCH BAKING DISH (CERAMIC OR GLASS): All your dankest casseroles (i.e., lasagna, enchiladas, etc.) will be made in this dish.

9 X 9-INCH OR 7 X 11-INCH BAKING DISH (CERAMIC OR GLASS): This is ideal for smaller casseroles, and it doubles as a serving dish for your favorite sides.

2 LARGE, RIMMED BAKING SHEETS: You probably know these as "cookie sheets," but you'll use them for far more than sweet treats. Baking sheets are crucial for oven-fried delicacies like Chicken Parmesan (page 68) and Chipotle Chicken Taquitos (page 130), as well as for baking, roasting and broiling meat, fish, and vegetables. You can't live without them. (If you have a tiny oven, be sure to buy baking sheets that will fit its dimensions.)

WIRE RACKS: While these are traditionally used for cooling baked goods, they also make a huge difference when oven-frying. Baking food on a wire rack set on top of a baking sheet allows 360-degree air circulation and ensures all-over crisping.

MUFFIN TIN: Should you ever have a craving for muffins or cupcakes, a good old muffin tin will come in handy. I recommend a nonstick tin so you don't have to mess with liners.

8 X 4-INCH LOAF PAN: Essential for quick breads, cakes, and the occasional meat loaf.

The Electronics

FOOD PROCESSOR: From whipping up a silky smooth hummus to pureeing cauliflower, a food processor makes quick work of countless kitchen tasks. If you're short on space, you can make almost every recipe in this book with a 4-cup processor, which is small, cheap, and works like a charm. (Cuisinart makes an excellent model.)

HIGH-SPEED BLENDER: Your best bet for making smoothies and pureeing soups is a high-speed blender, which can also handle many of the same tasks as a food processor. If you only plan to invest in one of the two, a blender is the way to go.

The Tools

KNIVES: You really don't need a fancy knife set, dudes—especially since most culinary tasks can be accomplished with just two basic knives, an 8- to 10-inch chef's knife and a medium serrated knife. You'll use your chef's knife for almost everything, but a serrated knife's scalloped, toothlike edge is helpful when slicing things with a hard exterior and a soft interior (i.e., bread, cake, tomatoes, and citrus). There's no need to break the bank, but a good chef's knife is worth investing in. And always make sure to keep it sharp! Not only is a dull knife a pain in the ass to work with, it's also dangerous. (If you're afraid of sharpening your knife and don't want to get it professionally sharpened, consider going the ceramic route.)

Most chefs and cookbooks will tell you that you also need a paring knife, but the truth is, you can survive without it. Yes, it comes in handy for more detail-oriented tasks like peeling and sectioning fruit or slicing a single clove of garlic, but you can also do these things with a chef's knife.

CUTTING BOARDS: Always use your knives on a cutting board, NEVER on a plate, paper towel, or straight on the counter. I recommend getting two cutting boards, one for meat and another for everything else. (Plastic is best for meat because it's easier to sanitize.) If you happen to splurge on a good-looking wooden cutting board, know that it can easily double as a cheese board or rustic serving platter. Boom.

MIXING BOWLS: From tossing salads to mixing meatballs, you'll find yourself reaching for these bowls on the reg. At the bare minimum, you need one large and one medium mixing bowl (glass, metal, ceramic, and plastic are all great), but I suggest springing for some smaller sizes as well.

MEASURING CUPS (DRY AND LIQUID): You can't follow a recipe without measuring cups! Unfortunately, dry and liquid measurements are slightly different, so you'll need a set of measuring cups for dry goods like grains, flour, vegetables, etc., *and* a plastic or glass measuring cup with a spout for liquids. Sorry, but this is non-negotiable.

MEASURING SPOONS: Again, you need these to successfully follow a recipe. Duh.

FINE-MESH COLANDER: A colander is a must-have for draining pasta, grains, and vegetables, but you can also put it to use in a variety of unexpected ways. It happens to work quite well as a MacGyver flour sieve, cocktail strainer, and steamer basket.

SILICONE SPATULA: This bad boy will get the most play in your kitchen, hands down. Its heatproof coating makes it the ultimate all-purpose tool for everything from sautéing vegetables to stirring soups and sauces. For the record, whenever a recipe asks you to "fold in" an ingredient, you should always use a spatula.

FLEXIBLE THIN METAL SPATULA: A thin spatula easily slides under even the most delicate foods, making tasks like flipping pancakes, turning fish or meat, and transferring cookies to a cooling rack completely stress-free.

WHISK: Only a whisk will get you fluffy scrambled eggs and omelets, clump-free sauces, and a good salad dressing.

KITCHEN TONGS: Much more than just a grilling tool, tongs do you all kinds of favors in the kitchen. Use them to turn meat, toss stir-fries and pastas, serve salads, and in place of a meat fork when carving or slicing meat. (They can also be used to snag items on high shelves. Just throwing that out there.)

VEGETABLE PEELER: In addition to peeling vegetables (which you should be eating a lot of), you can also use a vegetable peeler to shave things like hard cheeses and chocolate.

COARSE GRATER: Since pre-shredded cheese is only available in a handful of varieties, you'll need a coarse grater to grate/shred many of the cheeses in this book.

MICROPLANE GRATER-ZESTER: This tool, which allows you to zest citrus and grate hard cheeses like a pro, and puree garlic and ginger almost instantly, will seriously up your culinary game. Whenever you see "grated fresh ginger" or "grated garlic" in a recipe, it refers to Microplane grating.

CAN OPENER: Your cans aren't going to open themselves.

PARCHMENT PAPER: Parchment paper is a godsend. It keeps food from sticking to your pans (whether that be roasted vegetables or cookies), can be used to fashion an awesome steamer pouch, and makes for super-easy cleanup. Keep a roll in your kitchen at all times.

ALUMINUM FOIL: Foil performs many of the same duties as parchment paper, but you can also use it as a makeshift lid for pots, pans, and casserole dishes, and there's nothing better for keeping food warm or storing leftovers.

IDIOTPROOF COOKING TIPS

1. READ THE ENTIRE RECIPE, DAMMIT! Reading through the entire recipe from start to finish prior to shopping or cooking is nonnegotiable. Figure out the ingredients and tools you'll need, the prep work required, and the timing for each step of the process. Taking a few extra minutes to make a game plan and get psyched up will make the cooking process much more pleasant (and prevent all manner of disasters).

2. PREP, PREP, PREP. Before you even think about doing any actual cooking, make sure you have your ingredients ready to go—vegetables chopped, spices measured, etc.—and all necessary equipment handy. There's nothing more devastating than burning a good steak or a lovingly assembled quesadilla while you turn your kitchen upside down to find a spatula.

3. GET FRIENDLY WITH YOUR STOVETOP AND OVEN. Unfortunately, every stovetop is a little different and ovens can be fickle beasts. Whether one burner runs extra hot or your oven takes a little longer to preheat than most, these things will impact timing and how you interpret a recipe. The more you use these appliances, the more you'll understand them, and you'll be able to adjust accordingly. For example, you'll know that recipe instructions to cook something over medium heat actually translates to medium-low on your extra-hot burner.

4. MEASURE HERBS PROPERLY. Always read herb measurements very carefully. If a recipe calls for "¼ cup fresh cilantro leaves, chopped," measure the leaves themselves *before* chopping them. However, if it calls for "¼ cup chopped fresh cilantro leaves," measure the herbs once chopped.

5. UNDERSTAND THAT SEASONING IS SUBJECTIVE. I've done my best to pinpoint a crowd-pleasing amount of salt in each recipe, and to warn you when a dish is particularly fiery, but everyone has a different tolerance for salt and spice, and you may need to alter things slightly to please your palate. Always taste your dishes as you cook and make tweaks when necessary.

6. YOU DO YOU—WITHIN REASON. Many recipes can and should be adapted based on your personal preferences (see above) and the ingredients you have on hand, and you'll often find substitution suggestions in the "You Do You" sidebars throughout this book. With that said, don't go switching up or leaving out major ingredients and expecting the same awesome results. (No, the lasagna won't work if you sub vanilla yogurt for ricotta cheese and leave out all the vegetables.) Exercise common sense.

7. BE PATIENT. Cutting corners in a recipe to speed things up will only screw you in the long run, dudes. Waiting for a skillet to heat or a piece of meat to rest may seem like time wasted, but these instructions aren't thrown in just to mess with you—they're critical to a recipe's success (and the food's deliciousness).

8. DON'T PANIC. If a recipe starts to go south, take a deep breath, pull yourself together, and calmly tackle the situation at hand. Most culinary disasters can be salvaged with a clear head and a little creativity, and excessive sweating, screaming, smoke alarm destruction, and running with knives will only make matters worse. In the unlikely event the meal can't be saved, chalk it up to a learning experience, crack a light beer, and make Grown-Up Beans on Toast (page 273).

CHAPTER

3

BADASS
BREAKFASTS

I hate to burst your bacon-egg-and-cheese bubble, dudes, but crushing breakfast sandos, pastries, bagels, and other such moob-inducing, gut-expanding items on the daily is slowly shaving years off your life. These beloved breakfast foods are packed with saturated fat and refined sugar, two leading contributors to pretty much every scary disease in the book (I'm talking heart disease, cancer, and diabetes), and starting every day with them is basically playing Russian roulette with both your short- and long-term health.

Feeling smug right now because you "don't really eat breakfast"? You're in trouble, too. Skipping the most important meal of the day leaves you feeling lethargic, moody, and unmotivated. Worse, it tends to cause reckless bingeing at lunch, which is completely unnecessary (and gross). Don't do it.

So, whether you're consuming multiple McMuffins first thing or skipping your A.M. feeding, please get it together on the breakfast front, stat. A balanced morning meal has the power to jump-start your metabolism, help you focus, and keep you feeling full and energized for hours at a time. Studies have also shown that what you eat for breakfast sets the nutritional tone for your entire day, so making solid choices is essential to Dude Diet success.

Good news! This chapter is full of badass options that will have you rising and shining like never before. To those of you rolling your eyes and claiming that you "don't have time" for a homemade breakfast, I'm calling bullshit on your busy and important ass. Many of these recipes can be prepped the night before and grabbed on your way out the door, while others require less than 10 minutes of cook time. I've seen Logan take longer to button his shirt in the morning. No excuses.

There will obviously be some mornings when you forgot to prep the night before or legit don't have a spare minute to assemble your morning meal. On those occasions, I urge you to make alternative breakfast selections with the following guidelines in mind.

The Dude Diet Breakfast Guidelines

- **PROTEIN AND FIBER IS THE ULTIMATE BREAKFAST POWER COUPLE.** Eating a good balance of the two helps boost your body's fat burning capabilities and keeps you full for long periods of time. Look to eggs, lean meats, and yogurt for your morning protein, and work in some whole-grain bread, oats, or fruit for a fiber boost.

- **A BAGEL AND CREAM CHEESE IS NOT YOUR FRIEND.** Remember when I said, "If it's white, think twice?" This combo is literally 100 percent white. Shut it down.

- **OATMEAL IS GOOD FOR YOU.** However, topping it with a fistful of dried fruit and a cup of brown sugar defeats the purpose. Try to restrain yourself. Stick to fresh fruit, a sprinkling of raw nuts, and a drizzle of honey or pure maple syrup.

- **MUFFINS ARE CUPCAKES.** Except larger and without frosting. For the record, vegan muffins (and other baked goods) are not "healthy" just because they're vegan. "Vegan" simply means that there are no animal products involved. The eggs in muffins are not making you fat, dudes. It's the sugar and white flour. Now you know.

- **AN OMELET OR SCRAMBLE IS A GREAT IDEA!** Until you add every kind of breakfast meat, cheese, and potatoes. Try to limit yourself to vegetables, lean meat, and minimal cheese.

- **BEWARE THE FRUIT AND GRANOLA PARFAIT.** It's deceptively fattening, especially since it usually involves a triple serving of sugar-laden granola and a large amount of full-fat, sweetened yogurt. Opt for a container of plain Greek yogurt and dress it up with fresh fruit, a handful of raw nuts, or a little bit of honey and cinnamon.

- **PUT DOWN THE GREASY BREAKFAST SANDWICHES AND BURRITOS.** Put them down, and run away from them. Seriously.

BUTTERNUT SQUASH AND BRUSSELS SPROUT HASH WITH CHICKEN SAUSAGE

6 ounces chicken apple sausage (2 standard links), meat diced

2 tablespoons extra-virgin olive oil

1 small butternut squash, peeled, seeded, and cut into ½-inch cubes (about 3½ cups cubed squash)

½ pound Brussels sprouts (about 12 medium sprouts), thinly sliced

½ medium yellow onion, diced

2 teaspoons smoked paprika

¼ teaspoon freshly ground black pepper

2 tablespoons low-sodium soy sauce

Kosher salt

6 large eggs

Hot sauce of your choice (optional)

When I first met Logan, he had full-blown celebrity status at the local diner. His entrance was greeted by literal whoops of excitement and high fives from the entire staff, who then hurried to present the dude with his usual order: a mountain of hash and eggs with a side of assorted breakfast meats and a cream cheese–slathered bialy. Logan would happily inhale said feast, fist bump his army of adoring fans on the way out, and then enjoy a short-lived meat and potato high before descending into a world of pain and morning meat sweats. It was ugly.

After wasting one too many weekends in post-diner recovery, Logan has finally come to appreciate the wonders of a more wholesome homemade hash like this one. Packed with veggies and plenty of lean chicken sausage, it's a sweet and savory skillet meal that's guaranteed to thrill even the most die-hard hash lover. No Zantac or post-brunch nap necessary.

1. Heat a large skillet over medium-high heat. When hot, add the chicken sausage and cook for 5 to 6 minutes or until nicely browned. Remove from the pan and set aside.

2. In the same skillet, heat the olive oil over medium heat. When the oil is hot and shimmering, add the butternut squash, Brussels sprouts, and onion. Cook until very tender and lightly browned in spots, 18 to 20 minutes. (It's cool if the squash starts to fall apart in the pan, dudes. It's called hash for a reason.) Stir in the paprika and pepper and cook for 1 minute. Return the sausage to the pan and add the soy sauce. Taste the hash and season with a little kosher salt if necessary. Reduce the heat to medium-low.

3. Using a spatula (or the back of a spoon), make 6 small indentations in the hash. Crack the eggs into the indentations, cover with a lid, and cook for 8 to 10 minutes or until the whites have set but the yolks are still runny. (Keep in mind that the eggs will continue to cook once you remove them from the heat—be careful not to overcook them.)

4. Divide the hash among plates or bowls and serve with your finest hot sauce, if desired.

APPLE PIE OVERNIGHT OATS

SERVES 2 GENEROUSLY

If you're into sweet breakfasts that are easily consumed on the go, please give your daily doughnut/Pop-Tart/muffin habit a rest and take these pie-inspired oats for a spin. Just whip them up before bed, let the mixture hang out in the fridge while you get your beauty sleep, and grab them on your way out the door in the morning. No muss, no fuss.

It's natural to be a little weirded out by the thought of cold oatmeal, but I need you to keep an open mind here. The combo of caramelized apples, cinnamon, and cool, creamy oats is simultaneously hearty and refreshing. I'm 100 percent confident that once you try this overnight awesomeness, you'll be hooked.

1. Heat the coconut oil in a small skillet over medium heat. When the oil is hot and shimmering, add the diced apple, maple syrup, cinnamon, and salt. Cook for 5 to 6 minutes, stirring occasionally or until the apple has softened and caramelized. Remove from the heat and let cool slightly.

2. In a medium bowl, combine the oats, almond milk, yogurt, chia seeds (if using), and vanilla. Stir in the cooled apple mixture.

3. Cover the bowl with plastic wrap and refrigerate for at least 4 hours or overnight. (You can also portion the oats into individual airtight containers before refrigerating to save yourself time in the A.M.)

4. When you're ready to dig in, give the cold oats a good stir. (They will be pretty thick, so feel free to add an extra splash of almond milk before serving if you prefer looser oats.) Top each serving with 2 tablespoons chopped pecans (if using), and an extra sprinkling of cinnamon if you like spice.

1 teaspoon extra-virgin coconut oil

1 apple, peeled, cored, and diced (I like Golden Delicious for this.)

2 tablespoons pure maple syrup

1 teaspoon ground cinnamon, plus extra for serving

Pinch of kosher salt

¾ cup old-fashioned rolled oats (Not the quick-cooking kind, dudes! The hearty stuff.)

1 cup unsweetened almond milk, plus extra if you prefer

¼ cup nonfat plain Greek yogurt

1 tablespoon chia seeds (optional)

½ teaspoon pure vanilla extract

¼ cup chopped pecans (optional)

KNOWLEDGE BOMB: OATS ARE AN EXCELLENT WHOLE-GRAIN SOURCE OF ANTIOXIDANTS AND FIBER. AND EATING THEM CAN HELP REDUCE CHOLESTEROL AND PREVENT HEART DISEASE AND DIABETES. PLUS, THEY BALANCE YOUR BLOOD SUGAR TO KEEP YOU FULL AND ENERGIZED FOR HOURS AT A TIME. BOOYAH.

ULTIMATE BreaKFAST QUeSaDILLa

½ cup water

1 cup finely chopped broccoli florets

2 links (6 to 8 ounces) sweet Italian turkey sausage, casings removed

4 large eggs, beaten

2 medium (8- to 10-inch) whole-grain tortillas

2 teaspoons hot sauce (I like Cholula for this.)

2 scallions, white and light green parts only, finely chopped

¼ cup grated sharp cheddar cheese

FOR SERVING (OPTIONAL)
Salsa of your choice

Jump up and down if you want a sausage, egg, and cheese! Now keep jumping for an hour, dudes, because it'll take at least that long to burn the ridiculous amount of fat and empty calories in your beloved breakfast sandwich. OR you could simply indulge your craving responsibly with this leaner (but equally boss) alternative.

Filled with turkey sausage, eggs, sharp cheddar, and a well-disguised serving of green vegetables, this crispy 'dilla kills it on the flavor and nutrition fronts. Plus, it comes together in about 15 minutes, which is definitely shorter than the weekend wait at your favorite deli . . .

1. Pour the water into a large nonstick skillet. Bring to a boil over medium-high heat, then add the broccoli florets. Cover the pan with a lid and cook for 2 minutes or until the florets are bright green and tender (but not mushy!). Drain immediately and set aside.

2. Wipe out the skillet and return it to the stovetop over medium-high heat. Add the sausage and cook for 4 to 5 minutes, stirring and breaking up the meat with a spatula or until no longer pink. Return the broccoli florets to the skillet.

3. Reduce the heat to medium and pour in the eggs. Cook for 1 to 2 minutes, stirring in large sweeping motions or until the eggs are *just* set. Immediately transfer to a plate. (The eggs will continue cooking after you remove them from the pan, so be careful not to overcook them!)

4. Arrange half of the scramble on one half of each tortilla. Drizzle each with hot sauce, and sprinkle with scallions and cheddar. Fold the empty half of each tortilla over the filling to close your 'dillas.

5. Wipe out the skillet a second time and return it to the stovetop over medium heat. When hot, add the quesadillas to the pan and cook for 2 to 3 minutes or until the underside of each tortilla is lightly browned and crispy. Flip them carefully and cook for another 2 minutes on the opposite side.

6. Transfer the quesadillas to a cutting board and slice each one into 3 triangles. Serve with salsa if that's your style.

JUST THE TIP: THESE QUESADILLAS CAN BE FULLY ASSEMBLED. WRAPPED TIGHTLY IN PLASTIC WRAP. AND KEPT IN THE FRIDGE FOR 3 TO 4 DAYS. SIMPLY MICROWAVE EACH 'DILLA FOR ABOUT A MINUTE TO WARM IT UP. COOK IT IN A PAN AS DIRECTED. AND ENJOY A WARM WEEKDAY FEAST IN 6 MINUTES FLAT.

CHOCOLATE CHIP
Banana Pancakes

SERVES 2 — 3

Taking down a stack of fluffy pancakes is pretty sweet. The aftermath? Not so much. That's why you need this epic recipe in your A.M. rotation. Brimming with whole-grain goodness and studded with antioxidant-rich dark chocolate chips, these banana bad boys are guaranteed to fulfill your wildest short stack fantasies without requiring the usual pants-free snooze. Game changer.

1. Mash the banana in a medium bowl with a fork. You want to get it pretty smooth, dudes, but a few small lumps are fine.

2. Add the egg, almond milk, vanilla, and salt to the bowl and whisk to combine. Add the cinnamon, flour, and baking powder and whisk just until incorporated. Again, a few lumps are cool.

3. Heat a couple of teaspoons of coconut oil in a large nonstick skillet over medium heat. When the oil is hot and shimmering (but not smoking!), ladle ¼-cup measures of batter into the skillet, and sprinkle each pancake with a few chocolate chips. (I recommend cooking 2 to 3 pancakes at a time, so you don't crowd the pan or get overwhelmed.) Cook until you see small bubbles appear on the top surface of each pancake, about 1 minute. Carefully flip the pancakes with a thin spatula and cook until the undersides are lightly browned, another minute or so.

4. Transfer the pancakes to a plate, add a little more oil to the skillet, and repeat the cooking process with the remaining batter.

5. Serve the pancakes warm, topped with sliced bananas and a drizzle of maple syrup.

1 ripe banana

1 large egg

⅔ cup unsweetened almond milk (or milk of your choice)

1 teaspoon pure vanilla extract

¼ teaspoon kosher salt

¼ teaspoon ground cinnamon

⅔ cup whole-wheat flour

2 teaspoons baking powder

Extra-virgin coconut oil for cooking

3 tablespoons dark chocolate chips

FOR SERVING (OPTIONAL)
1 banana, sliced

Pure maple syrup

YOU DO YOU: DON'T DO CHOCOLATE CHIPS AT BREAKFAST? TRY WALNUTS (FOR EXTRA PROTEIN) OR BLUEBERRIES (FOR AN ANTIOXIDANT BOOST) IN THEIR PLACE.

SIMPLE SHAKSHUKA

1 tablespoon extra-virgin olive oil

½ medium yellow onion, finely chopped

1 red bell pepper, seeded and diced

1 small jalapeño, finely chopped (If you're sensitive to heat, seed that bad boy first.)

8 ounces (2 or 3 links) Italian turkey sausage, casings removed (I like to use spicy sausage, but you do you.)

2 garlic cloves, minced

1 teaspoon smoked paprika

½ teaspoon ground cumin

¼ teaspoon kosher salt

One 28-ounce can whole peeled tomatoes

½ teaspoon honey

6 large eggs

2 ounces feta cheese, crumbled (about ½ cup)

2 tablespoons fresh cilantro leaves, chopped (optional)

In case you've never experienced the joys of shakshuka, allow me to enlighten you: it's a super-festive and flavorful Israeli dish featuring eggs poached in a spicy tomato sauce. This nontraditional version incorporates browned turkey sausage and plenty of crumbled feta cheese, resulting in a hearty one-skillet wonder that's significantly easier to make than it is to say.

1. Heat the olive oil in a large skillet or sauté pan over medium-high heat. When the oil is hot and shimmering (but not smoking!), add the onion, bell pepper, and jalapeño. Cook for 6 to 7 minutes or until the vegetables have softened. (It's totally cool if they get lightly browned in spots.)

2. Crumble the sausage meat into the pan. Cook for 5 to 6 minutes, stirring and breaking it up with a spatula, until no longer pink.

3. Reduce the heat to medium and stir in the garlic, paprika, cumin, and salt. Cook for 1 minute or until the spices are toasted and fragrant.

4. Add the tomatoes to the pan, breaking them up into smaller pieces with your spatula. Stir in the honey and cook for 10 to 12 minutes or until the sauce has thickened slightly.

5. Reduce the heat to low, so that the sauce is *just* simmering (aka bubbling very gently), and crack the eggs on top of the sauce. Cover the pan with a lid and cook for 8 to 10 minutes, or until the whites are just set but the yolks are still runny. Keep a close eye on them during the last few minutes—the yolks can go from perfectly runny to hard really fast. (Obviously, if you dig more solid yolks, feel free to cook your eggs longer.)

6. Sprinkle the whole shebang with feta and cilantro and serve immediately. Shakshuka your moneymaker!

YOU DO YOU: SHAKSHUKA IS THE ULTIMATE SHAREABLE WEEKEND BREAKFAST/BRUNCH. BUT IT'S ALSO GREAT FOR DINNER WITH A SIMPLE SALAD AND SOME WARM WHOLE-GRAIN PITA.

AMPED-UP AVOCADO TOAST

SERVES 1

2 slices turkey bacon

1 small Roma tomato, halved from pole to pole

½ teaspoon extra-virgin olive oil

½ ripe avocado

¼ teaspoon crushed red pepper flakes

Kosher salt

1 large egg

1 slice Ezekiel bread (or 100 percent whole-grain bread of your choice)

Avocado toast has been enjoying a very long moment in the sun, and for good reason. Not only does it taste bomb, the combo of heart-healthy fat, fiber, and carbohydrates is very effective when it comes to keeping hunger at bay. With that said, most dudes require slightly more than fruit on toast to fire on all cylinders (fun fact: avocado is a fruit), so I've amped things up with some crispy turkey bacon, charred tomatoes, and a runny egg for your feasting pleasure. Think of it as avocado toast in Beast Mode.

1. In a large skillet, cook the turkey bacon over medium heat until browned and crispy, about 4 to 5 minutes per side.

2. Halfway through the bacon's cooking time, place the tomato halves, cut side down, in the same skillet. Cook, undisturbed, for 4 to 5 minutes, until softened slightly. Don't move the tomatoes, dudes! You want them to develop a nice char. Remove the bacon and the tomatoes from the skillet and set aside.

3. Scoop the avocado flesh from its skin and place it in a small bowl. Add the red pepper flakes and mash with a fork. Season with salt to taste.

4. Moving on to the egg! Heat a small nonstick skillet over medium heat. When hot, add the egg and cook for 3 to 4 minutes or until the whites are set but the yolk is still runny. (If the white isn't setting, pop a lid on the pan for a minute or so to help it along.)

5. While the egg is cooking, toast your bread. Top the toast with the mashed avocado, turkey bacon, charred tomatoes, and the sunny-side-up egg. Get after it.

> JUST THE TIP: CRUNCHED FOR TIME? SKIP THE TOAST AND WRAP EVERYTHING UP IN A WHOLE-GRAIN TORTILLA FOR A MORE PORTABLE BREAKFAST OPTION.

Quinoa Crunch Granola

2½ cups old-fashioned rolled oats (Do not use quick-cooking oats! The granola will taste chalky.)

¾ cup chopped pecans

¾ cup sliced almonds

⅓ cup uncooked quinoa, rinsed and drained

2 teaspoons ground cinnamon

¼ teaspoon fine-grain sea salt

⅓ cup liquid extra-virgin coconut oil

½ cup pure maple syrup

Whether you sprinkle it on yogurt or fruit, drown it in milk, or eat it by the handful, this nutritious granola is a pantry staple that you'll want to keep in stock. I've toyed with countless recipes over the years, but this addictively crunchy, maple-tinged version stands head and shoulders above the rest, earning the nickname "crack granola" from some of my most discerning taste testers.

Why take the time to make granola at home when you could simply buy a giant bag at the grocery store? (I knew you'd go there.) The answer is twofold. First, most packaged varieties contain scary amounts of canola oil and refined sugar, whereas this stuff is made with a modest amount of extra-virgin coconut oil and pure maple syrup. Second, *the smell*. As Logan once shrieked, "The air smells like pancakes and snickerdoodles at the same time!!!"

You deserve to breathe that air, dudes.

1. Preheat the oven to 300°F. Line a large baking sheet with parchment paper.

2. In a medium bowl, combine the oats, nuts, quinoa, cinnamon, and salt.

3. In a separate bowl, whisk together the coconut oil and maple syrup.

4. Pour the wet ingredients over the dry ingredients and stir until well combined.

5. Spread the oat mixture on the prepared baking sheet in an even layer. Using the bottom of a glass, gently press the mixture to pack it down. (This will give you killer granola chunks later on.)

6. Transfer the granola to the preheated oven and bake for 40 to 45 minutes or until golden brown. (Keep an eye on it during the last 10 minutes of cooking time to make sure it doesn't get too dark.)

7. Let cool on the baking sheet for at least 30 minutes before breaking up into pieces.

8. Store the granola in an airtight container for up to 2 weeks.

YOU DO YOU: WANT A FLAKIER GRANOLA? REMOVE IT FROM THE OVEN EVERY 10 TO 15 MINUTES AND GIVE IT A STIR.

Green God Smoothie

Bright and tangy with the slightest hint of coconut, I like to think of this as a starter smoothie for those with deep-seated fears of "drinking a salad." Despite the Hulk-like hue, I swear it doesn't taste remotely green, and sipping this tropic thunder on a regular basis will work some serious magic on both your brain and your bod.

Please don't panic when you see avocado in the ingredient list. It provides necessary omega-3s and makes the smoothie awesomely thick and creamy, but the flavor is very subtle. (Read: It doesn't taste like guacamole.)

1. Place the coconut milk, spinach, avocado, and chia seeds in a blender. Blend until smooth. Add the diced mango and pineapple and blend again. (Pureeing the greens first ensures that you don't have any chewy greens in your smoothie.) Taste. If you have a sweet tooth, feel free to add 1 to 2 teaspoons honey or agave.

2. Pour your smoothie into a glass and drink immediately, or refrigerate in a sealed jar/container for up to 3 days.

1 cup light coconut milk (Almond milk also works well.)

1 cup baby spinach (If it's not pre-washed, make sure to wash it well.)

¼ ripe avocado, pitted and peeled

1 tablespoon chia seeds

¾ cup frozen diced mango

¾ cup frozen pineapple chunks

1 to 2 teaspoons honey or agave syrup (optional)

YOU DO YOU: IF YOU'RE SOMEONE THAT NEEDS SOLID FOOD AT EVERY MEAL, TRY A SMOOTHIE BOWL. REDUCE THE AMOUNT OF MILK IN THE RECIPE TO ²/₃ CUP, AND THEN POUR THE EXTRA-THICK SMOOTHIE INTO A BOWL. TOP WITH ANY COMBINATION OF SLICED FRUIT, NUTS, SEEDS, AND GRANOLA YOU LIKE, AND GRAB A SPOON.

DUDE DIET HUEVOS RANCHEROS

1 teaspoon plus
1 tablespoon extra-
virgin olive oil,
divided

2 links (6 to
8 ounces) spicy
turkey sausage,
casings removed

1 teaspoon smoked
paprika

½ teaspoon ground
cumin

½ medium yellow
onion, finely
chopped

2 medium tomatoes,
diced (or one
15-ounce can diced
tomatoes, drained)

One 15-ounce can
black beans, drained
and rinsed

Juice of ½ lime

Kosher salt

8 large eggs

4 corn tortillas

½ cup grated pepper
Jack cheese

½ ripe avocado,
pitted, peeled, and
diced

¼ cup fresh cilantro
leaves, finely
chopped

Hangovers are The Dude Diet's kryptonite. Whether you spent the night aggressively tailgating, pounding beers at the bar, or simply imbibed one too many c-tails on your couch, the morning after misery will test your will to live, let alone your commitment to keeping it tight. It's natural to crave a greasy feast in this vulnerable state, but the truth is, eating something extra fatty will only push you deeper into the hurt locker. *No bueno.*

So the next time you rip it a little too hard, please consider a more responsible recovery breakfast like these ultrasatisfying Huevos Rancheros. A warm corn tortilla topped with killer black bean and sausage fiesta sauce, melted pepper Jack cheese, and runny eggs is just what you need to get normal without completely falling off the wagon. Stay strong, dudes.

1. Heat 1 teaspoon of the olive oil in a medium skillet or sauté pan over medium heat. When the oil is hot and shimmering, crumble the turkey sausage meat into the pan and cook for 6 to 7 minutes, stirring and breaking it up with a spatula or until lightly browned.

2. Add the paprika and cumin and cook for 1 minute until toasted and fragrant. Stir in the onion, tomatoes, and black beans and cook for 4 to 5 minutes or until your "fiesta sauce" thickens slightly. Stir in the lime juice. Taste and season with a little salt if needed. Cover with a lid and keep warm while you cook your eggs.

3. Heat ½ tablespoon of olive oil in a medium skillet over medium heat. When hot, crack 4 eggs into the pan and cook for 3 to 4 minutes or until the whites are set but the yolks are still runny. (If your whites are having trouble setting, pop a lid on the pan for a minute or so.) Transfer the eggs to a plate, and add the remaining ½ tablespoon oil to the skillet. Cook the second batch of 4 eggs.

4. Warm each of the tortillas in a skillet or directly on a gas burner for 10 to 15 seconds per side.

5. Assembly time! Spread each warm tortilla with one-quarter of the fiesta sauce and sprinkle with 2 tablespoons of the cheese. Top with 2 eggs, one-quarter of the diced avocado and chopped cilantro, and serve immediately. Feel free to get your favorite hot sauce involved.

JUST THE TIP: THE SAUCE KEEPS WELL IN THE FRIDGE FOR 2 TO 3 DAYS. SO IF YOU MAKE THESE HUEVOS FOR A WEEKEND BRUNCH. SAVE THE LEFTOVER SAUCE (OR DOUBLE THE RECIPE) FOR WEEKDAY FIESTAS.

Bacon and Egg Quinoa Bowl

SERVES 2 GENEROUSLY

⅔ cup uncooked quinoa, rinsed and drained

1 cup low-sodium vegetable broth (or water)

6 slices bacon (preferably with no added nitrates), sliced crosswise into ½-inch strips

1 large shallot, finely chopped

3 garlic cloves, minced

1 teaspoon peeled and grated fresh ginger

5 ounces baby arugula, roughly chopped (You can also use baby spinach or kale if you prefer.)

2½ teaspoons low-sodium soy sauce

1 teaspoon sriracha sauce, plus extra for serving

2 large eggs

Important announcement: Bacon is allowed on The Dude Diet.

Don't abuse the privilege, dudes. I'm obviously not condoning reckless bacon consumption, but a few pieces here and there are totally fine, particularly in the context of a nutritious dish like this quinoa bowl. Loaded with protein, fiber, and plenty of greens, this supercharged breakfast is a badass flavor party that will help you power through your day like a champ.

The recipe requires a little prep, so do yourself a favor and whip up a batch (or two) of the quinoa base on Sunday, or whenever you have a little extra time on your hands. With the grunt work done, all you'll have to do in the A.M. is pop a serving in the microwave, fry an egg, and dig in. It's also great for dinner, and you can always ditch the egg and serve it as a side dish.

1. Combine the quinoa and vegetable broth in a small saucepan and bring to a boil. Reduce to a simmer, cover the saucepan with a lid, and cook for 14 minutes or until all the liquid has been absorbed. Let the quinoa rest, covered, for 5 minutes, then fluff with a fork.

2. Meanwhile, heat a large nonstick skillet over medium-high heat. When hot, add the sliced bacon and cook for 5 to 6 minutes or until lightly brown and crisp. Pour off all but about 1 tablespoon of the bacon grease from the skillet and return the skillet with the bacon to the stovetop. Reduce the heat to medium.

3. Add the shallot, garlic, and ginger to the skillet, and cook for 2 minutes or until the shallot has softened slightly. Add the greens (it will seem like a lot, but they'll cook down!), and cook for about 1 minute until they're dark green and just wilted.

4. Stir in the quinoa, soy sauce, and sriracha sauce and cook for 1 minute more. Divide the quinoa mixture between two bowls.

5. Wipe out your skillet and place it over medium heat. (If you do not have a nonstick skillet, add a teaspoon of extra-virgin olive oil

to the pan.) When hot, add the eggs, making sure to leave plenty of space between them. Cook for 3 to 4 minutes or until the whites are just set but the yolks are still runny. (If your eggs aren't setting, cover the skillet with a lid for a minute or so to help them along.)

6. Top each quinoa bowl with an egg. Serve warm with extra sriracha if you can handle it.

JUST THE TIP: THE QUINOA PACKAGE DIRECTIONS LIE! ALWAYS COOK QUINOA WITH A 1:1.5 QUINOA TO LIQUID RATIO FOR PERFECT, FLUFFY GRAINS.

Raspberry Chia Jam

12 ounces fresh or frozen raspberries

3 tablespoons honey

½ teaspoon pure vanilla extract

2 tablespoons chia seeds (I prefer white chia seeds for aesthetic purposes, but black will also do.)

Let's talk about chia seeds, dudes. Harvested from a desert plant grown in Mexico, they were a staple in the diets of the ancient Mayans and Aztecs. Soldiers reportedly crushed chia on the battlefield, and the seeds were thought to have magical powers based on their ability to increase stamina over long periods of time. (I'll give you a minute to get any stamina jokes out of your system.)

Chia seeds may not actually be magic, but they're pretty damn close. In addition to their high protein and fiber content, chia seeds are the best plant-based source of omega-3 fatty acids *on the planet*.

While making traditional jam is a finicky process, chia jam is a total no-brainer. All you have to do is cook some raspberries with a touch of vanilla extract and honey, stir in the chia, and wait 15 minutes. The seeds will plump up and take on a gel-like quality, leaving you with a fresh, nutrient-rich jam that you can use to jazz up everything from whole-grain toast and waffles to yogurt and oatmeal.

1. Combine the raspberries, honey, and vanilla in a small saucepan and place over medium heat. Bring the mixture to a boil, then reduce the heat to a simmer and cook for 3 to 4 minutes, mashing the berries with a spatula until the fruit has broken down completely.

2. Remove from the heat and stir in the chia seeds. Let cool for at least 15 minutes to allow the seeds to gel.

3. Serve immediately or store your jam in an airtight container in the fridge for up to 1 week.

YOU DO YOU: THIS JAM CAN EASILY BE MADE WITH ANY BERRY (OR BERRY MEDLEY) OF YOUR CHOICE. STRAWBERRIES AND BLUEBERRIES ARE NATURALLY SWEETER. SO IF YOU DECIDE TO USE ONE OF THEM. START WITH SLIGHTLY LESS HONEY AND SLOWLY BUILD UP TO YOUR PERFECT LEVEL OF SWEETNESS.

ENGLISH MUFFIN FRENCH TOAST WITH BERRY COMPOTE

2 large eggs

⅓ cup unsweetened almond milk

2 tablespoons pure maple syrup

½ teaspoon ground cinnamon

Pinch of kosher salt

3 whole-wheat English muffins, split in half

2 teaspoons extra-virgin coconut oil

Powdered sugar for serving (optional)

FOR THE BERRY COMPOTE
1½ cups mixed berries (I like a combo of strawberries, raspberries, and blueberries, but you do you.)

2 teaspoons pure maple syrup

1 tablespoon water

Say *bonjour* to your new go-to French toast. This delicious and nutritious treat also happens to be really, really, ridiculously good-looking, so I recommend it for weekend mornings when you've got somebody to impress (or simply don't want to brave the brunch lines). No need to fear compote— it's just a fancy word for dank fruit sauce. You got this.

1. In a large shallow baking dish, whisk together the eggs, almond milk, maple syrup, cinnamon, and salt until well combined.

2. Add the English muffin halves to the egg mixture. Turn to coat each side, and then press down gently to help the muffins absorb the liquid. Let soak for 10 minutes. Flip the muffins, pressing down gently again, and soak for another 10 minutes. You want the muffins to be good and saturated.

3. While the muffins are soaking, get to work on the berry compote. Bring the berries, maple syrup, and water to a boil in a medium saucepan. Reduce to a simmer and cook for about 4 minutes, stirring occasionally, until the berries are very soft but not completely broken down. Remove from the heat and set aside to cool for 4 to 5 minutes.

4. Time to cook the French toast! (You're going to do this in two batches, dudes.) Heat 1 teaspoon of the coconut oil in a large skillet over medium heat. When the oil is hot and shimmering (but not smoking!), add 3 soaked muffin halves and cook for 2 to 3 minutes per side or until golden brown. (If the oil starts smoking, stay calm, lower the heat and carry on.) Transfer to a plate. Add the remaining 1 teaspoon coconut oil to the skillet and repeat with the remaining 3 muffin halves.

5. Serve your French toast topped with the warm compote. Powdered sugar is allowed—just make sure it's a light dusting versus an avalanche.

JUST THE TIP: TO SAVE TIME IN THE A.M., PREP THE VEGGIES THE NIGHT BEFORE. WITH THE CHOPPING DONE, THE SCRAMBLE COMES TOGETHER IN LESS THAN 10 MINUTES.

Big Green Scramble

I'm pleased to report that this scramble was tested by a number of extremely picky dudes, and every single one of them gave it two very enthusiastic thumbs up.

Since each portion boasts a hefty serving of green vegetables and a minimal amount of cheese, I consider the widespread love for this vegetarian delight (and lack of "Where's the meat?!!" meltdowns) to be one of my crowning achievements. It's a Dude Diet miracle.

A couple of quick notes before you get cracking. For a light and fluffy scramble, you need to (a) whisk the eggs like you mean it, and (b) make sure to take them off the heat when they're *just* set. The eggs will keep cooking even after they hit the plate, so you want to get the scramble out of the pan while it's still a little softer than you'd like.

1. Crack the eggs into a medium bowl and whisk vigorously until pale yellow and slightly frothy. Set the eggs aside.

2. Heat the olive oil in a medium nonstick skillet over medium heat. When the oil is hot and shimmering, add the zucchini, spinach/kale, leek, and garlic. Sprinkle with a generous pinch of kosher salt and a few cranks of black pepper, and cook for 5 to 6 minutes, stirring periodically, until the vegetables are good and tender. Be careful not to burn the garlic! If it starts to brown, reduce the heat slightly and carry on. (If you like your veggies with a little crunch, simply reduce the cooking time by a couple of minutes.)

3. Reduce the heat to medium-low and add the beaten eggs. Cook, stirring in big sweeping motions to form large curds, until the eggs are just set. This will take 1 to 2 minutes max, so please have your plates handy.

4. Divide the eggs between two plates and top with the Parmesan cheese.

4 large eggs

1 tablespoon extra-virgin olive oil

1 small zucchini, diced

1 cup baby spinach or baby kale, finely chopped

1 leek, white and light green parts only, halved lengthwise and thinly sliced

1 garlic clove, minced

Kosher salt

Freshly ground black pepper

2 tablespoons freshly grated Parmesan cheese

THE CLASSICS

The very first time I cooked for Logan, I decided to surprise him with bacon mac and cheese. It was early in our relationship, but having already eaten several meals with the dude, I'd gleaned enough insight into his food preferences to know that I couldn't go wrong with cheese, bacon, and pasta. Sure, I expected him to be excited—Logan's a generally effusive guy—but nothing could have prepared me for his reaction . . .

When I set the mac in front of him, Logan whooped so loudly that I almost dropped my own bowl in shock. He then performed a drumroll on the floor with his feet before attacking the piping hot pasta like it was his last meal. There was ecstatic grunting, complimentary expletives, and multiple high fives, all of which culminated in him dubbing me a "culinary genius." I'd never seen anything quite like it. (We hadn't dropped L-bombs at that point, but it's very possible that bacon mac and cheese sealed the deal for Logan.)

Over time, I realized that while Logan was enthusiastic about food in general, there were only a handful of things that elicited the type of extreme reaction described above—burgers, cheesesteaks, enchiladas, and meatballs, to name a few. Needless to say, Logan is not alone in his love of these particular items. These meaty, cheesy "classics" are the stars of most dudes' food porn fantasies, and they are perpetual sources of Dude Diet concern.

Because I'd never deny dudes the meals that bring them such profound joy, I've given all of the best-loved comfort foods a nutritious makeover. They may be lightened up with lean meats, whole grains, and fresh vegetables, but you can take solace in the fact that I used the aforementioned bacon mac and cheese hysteria as my benchmark for success. No recipe made it into this chapter without causing a similar excitement freakout, and while it was exhausting at times, the rigorous testing was totally worth it. My life is richer for having seen the dude lose his shit over a bowl of Cheeseburger Quinoa Bake (page 86) and do a Victor Cruz–esque salsa dance with a Killer Cuban Sandwich (page 88) in hand.

Full disclosure, the following dishes are slightly more involved than you'll find elsewhere in this book, but don't let the longer recipes psych you out. As long as you read through them beforehand and stay organized while you cook, they're much less intimidating than they seem. So treat yourself to some background ESPN and a prep beer, and step up your culinary game, dudes. You got this.

CAULIFLOWER MAC AND CHEESE
WITH CHICKEN SAUSAGE

SERVES 4

½ head cauliflower, cored and broken into florets (about 3 cups florets)

2 cups water

2 cups skim milk, divided

8 ounces whole-wheat medium shells (Penne or fusilli also work well.)

1 teaspoon Dijon mustard

½ teaspoon kosher salt

¼ teaspoon cayenne pepper

1 cup grated sharp cheddar cheese, divided

1 cup grated provolone cheese, divided

¼ cup grated Parmesan cheese

3 links spicy chicken sausage, diced

FOR THE TOPPING
3 tablespoons whole-wheat panko bread crumbs

1½ tablespoons grated Parmesan cheese

¼ teaspoon smoked paprika

If you appreciate a good mac even half as much as Logan does, you're going to be all over this cheesy casserole, which gets a nutritious makeover thanks to whole-grain pasta, lean chicken sausage, and the magic of cauliflower puree. (Relax, unless you have an unbelievably sophisticated palate, you won't even taste the cauliflower.)

1. Combine the cauliflower florets, water, and 1 cup of the milk in a Dutch oven or medium saucepan and bring to a boil. Lower to a simmer, cover with a lid, and cook for 20 minutes or until the cauliflower is very tender.

2. Meanwhile, bring a separate pot of salted water to a boil for the pasta. Once boiling, add the pasta and cook until a few minutes shy of al dente. (You want it undercooked and still firm, dudes—it's going to cook more in the oven.) Drain and set aside.

3. Preheat the oven to 375°F.

4. Drain the cauliflower, discarding the cooking liquid, and transfer to a blender or food processor. Puree until very smooth; you should have a little more than 1 cup of puree. Return the cauliflower puree to the Dutch oven over medium-low heat and whisk in the remaining 1 cup milk, Dijon, salt, and cayenne. Slowly add ¾ cup of the cheddar, ¾ cup of the provolone, and the Parmesan and whisk until the cheese has completely melted and the sauce is nice and smooth.

5. Heat a medium skillet over medium heat. When hot, add the diced chicken sausage and cook for 5 to 6 minutes or until lightly browned.

6. Stir the chicken sausage into the cauliflower cheese sauce. Taste and season with a little extra salt and cayenne if necessary, then stir in the pasta.

7. Transfer everything to a 9 x 9-inch baking dish or a 10- to 12-inch ovenproof skillet. (It will seem like there is too much sauce, but the

pasta will soak up a lot of it in the oven. Go with it.) Top with the remaining ¼ cup cheddar and ¼ cup provolone.

8. In a small bowl, combine the ingredients for the topping. Sprinkle on top of the mac and cheese in an even layer.

9. Transfer the casserole to the preheated oven and bake for 20 minutes or until the cheese has melted and is bubbling slightly. Serve hot, and try not to hyperventilate.

SUPER SLOPPY JOES

Mention Sloppy Joes to any dude, and you're likely to induce severe elementary school nostalgia and/or be treated to an impression of the crazy lunch lady in *Billy Madison* on the spot. Because I enjoy both reactions, I re-created this childhood classic with a grown-up spin (i.e., you don't pour it from a Manwich can) and lightened up the ingredients just a bit. These throw-back sandwiches come together in about 20 minutes with mostly pantry ingredients, so make them your go-to for instant childlike joy.

1. Heat the olive oil in a large sauté pan over medium heat. When the oil is hot and shimmering, add the ground turkey and cook for 5 to 6 minutes, stirring and breaking up the meat with a spatula or until no longer pink.

2. Add the onion, bell pepper, Worcestershire, chili powder, cumin, and salt and cook for 3 to 5 minutes or until the vegetables begin to soften. Stir in the tomato paste and cook for 1 minute, then stir in the tomato sauce, honey, and jalapeños. Simmer for 5 minutes to allow the flavors to mingle. Taste and season with a little extra salt if necessary.

3. Pile the turkey mixture onto the rolls, and grab a stack of napkins. I know how you kids like 'em extra sloppy!

YOU DO YOU: NO NEED TO LIMIT YOURSELF TO SLOPPY JOES IN SANDWICH FORM. TRY THE FILLING IN TACOS AND BURRITOS. OR USE IT AS A KILLER SAUCE FOR GRAINS AND PASTA.

---

2 tablespoons extra-virgin olive oil

1¼ pounds lean ground turkey

½ medium yellow onion, finely chopped

1 small red bell pepper, seeded and cut into small dice

1 tablespoon Worcestershire sauce

1 tablespoon chili powder

¼ teaspoon ground cumin

¼ teaspoon kosher salt, plus extra if needed

2 tablespoons tomato paste

One 15-ounce can tomato sauce (sometimes labeled "tomato puree")

½ teaspoon honey

2 tablespoons finely chopped pickled jalapeños

4 whole-grain rolls or hamburger buns

CHICKEN PARMESAN

1 cup buttermilk

4 garlic cloves, minced

1¼ teaspoons kosher salt, divided

Four 8-ounce boneless, skinless chicken breasts

2½ cups crispy brown rice cereal

¼ cup grated Parmesan cheese

1 tablespoon dried oregano

½ teaspoon freshly ground black pepper

FOR THE SAUCE
1 tablespoon extra-virgin olive oil

¼ medium yellow onion, minced

One 15-ounce can crushed tomatoes (I like San Marzano.)

¼ teaspoon pure cane sugar

Pinch of kosher salt

⅓ cup fresh basil leaves, stacked, rolled, and thinly sliced (aka chiffonade)

One 4-ounce ball fresh mozzarella cheese, grated

Back in my private chef days, one of the NFL players I was cooking for asked if I could make him Chicken Parm. The dude was newly gluten-free and doing his best to eat clean, so the traditional bread crumb–encrusted, fried recipe was obviously out, but serving him a version with grilled chicken cutlets seemed pretty bush league. Instead, I played around with different coatings and techniques until I perfected this super-tender baked Chicken Parmesan dredged in crispy brown rice cereal. It became an instant classic. Ditch the usual pasta side and responsibly round out the meal with a giant salad or your favorite green vegetable.

1. In a large shallow baking dish, whisk together the buttermilk, garlic, and 1 teaspoon of the kosher salt.

2. Place each chicken breast between two pieces of plastic wrap and, using the bottom of a skillet (or other heavy object of your choice), pound the chicken breasts to a ½-inch thickness.

3. Add the chicken breasts to the baking dish, turning them over a couple of times to ensure they're well coated in the buttermilk mixture. Cover with plastic wrap and refrigerate for at least 30 minutes. (Feel free to marinate the chicken overnight if you're a planner.)

4. Pour the crispy brown rice cereal into a shallow baking dish and lightly crush it with your hands. (You don't want to completely pulverize the cereal, but you do want to break it down into small pieces so that it will stick to the chicken more easily.) Stir in the Parmesan cheese, oregano, pepper, and the remaining ¼ teaspoon kosher salt.

5. Preheat the oven to 375°F. Line a large rimmed baking sheet with aluminum foil. Spray a wire rack with cooking spray and place it on

JUST THE TIP: CRISPY BROWN RICE CEREAL
IS JUST LIKE RICE KRISPIES. ONLY IT'S MADE WITH
BROWN RICE. I LIKE EREWHON BRAND.

top of the baking sheet. (If you don't have a wire rack, don't panic. You can bake your chicken directly on the foil-lined baking sheet.)

6. Remove the chicken breasts from the buttermilk one at a time, shaking off any excess liquid, and place each one into the crispy rice mixture. Coat each breast really well, using your hands to press the cereal onto the chicken. Transfer the coated chicken to the prepared wire rack. Bake for 20 minutes.

7. While the chicken is in the oven, whip up your simple marinara sauce. Heat the olive oil in a medium sauté pan over medium heat. When the oil is hot and shimmering, add the onion and cook for 4 to 5 minutes or until translucent and very tender. Stir in the crushed tomatoes, sugar, and salt and simmer for 5 minutes or until the sauce has thickened slightly. Remove from the heat and stir in half of the fresh basil.

8. Spoon the sauce onto each of the chicken breasts and top with the mozzarella. Bake for 5 minutes more or until the cheese has melted and is bubbling. (If you like your cheese lightly browned, you can pop the chicken under the broiler for a minute or so.)

9. Serve the chicken piping hot topped with the remaining fresh basil.

JUST THE TIP: DON'T HAVE BUTTERMILK? MIX 1 TABLESPOON LEMON JUICE OR WHITE VINEGAR WITH 1 CUP MILK. AND LET IT STAND AT ROOM TEMPERATURE FOR 10 MINUTES UNTIL SLIGHTLY THICKENED. BOOM. HOMEMADE BUTTERMILK.

EPIC MEAT LOAF

The most frequent recipe request I've received over the years has been some iteration of "dank healthy meat loaf." Ask and ye shall receive, dudes. For an old-school comfort food fix, serve thick slices over Cauliflower Puree with Parmesan and Chives (page 243).

1. Combine the quinoa and chicken broth in a small saucepan and bring to a boil. Lower to a simmer, cover the saucepan with a lid, and cook for 14 minutes or until all the liquid has been absorbed. Let the quinoa rest, covered, for 5 minutes, then fluff with a fork. Set aside to cool slightly.

2. Preheat the oven to 350°F. Line a rimmed baking sheet with aluminum foil.

3. Heat the olive oil in a medium sauté pan over medium heat. When the oil is hot and shimmering, add the onion, bell pepper, and garlic and cook for 5 to 6 minutes or until very soft but not browned. (Please be careful not to burn the garlic!) Stir in the tomato paste and cook for 1 minute, then transfer the veggie mixture to a large mixing bowl. Let cool for at least 5 minutes.

4. While the veggies are cooling, whisk together all the ingredients for the glaze. Set the glaze aside.

5. Add the beef, turkey, cooked quinoa, Worcestershire, salt, red pepper flakes, yogurt, and eggs to the mixing bowl with the veggies. Using your hands, mix everything together just until combined. (Really try not to overmix this stuff, or you'll end up with dry meat loaf. Be gentle.)

6. Dump the meat mixture onto the prepared baking sheet. (It will be very soft and pretty wet. Don't panic.) Mold the meat with your hands into a roughly 9 x 5-inch rectangular loaf. Spread half of the glaze evenly on top.

⅓ cup uncooked quinoa, rinsed and drained

½ cup low-sodium chicken broth (or water)

1 tablespoon extra-virgin olive oil

½ medium yellow onion, minced

½ red bell pepper, seeded and cut into small dice

2 garlic cloves, minced

1 tablespoon tomato paste

1 pound 90 percent lean ground beef (preferably grass-fed)

1 pound 93 percent lean ground turkey (99 percent lean will be too dry!)

2 tablespoons Worcestershire sauce

1 teaspoon kosher salt

1½ teaspoons crushed red pepper flakes

¾ cup low-fat plain Greek yogurt

2 large eggs, lightly beaten

(cont.)

¼ cup tomato paste

2 teaspoons
Worcestershire
sauce

1½ teaspoons apple
cider vinegar

1 teaspoon honey

3 tablespoons warm
water

7. Bake for 45 minutes, add the remaining glaze, and bake for 15 minutes more (1 hour total) or until the meat loaf is cooked through. Let the loaf rest for a full 10 minutes to allow the juices to redistribute. (You'll notice that the meat loaf has oozed some thick, slimy-looking juice onto the foil. Sorry, but this is unavoidable. Just use a spoon to scoop that stuff into the trash and forget about it.)

8. Slice your meat loaf into thick pieces and serve warm.

1-HOUR PULLED PORK

1 tablespoon extra-virgin olive oil

1 small yellow onion, minced

2 garlic cloves, minced

⅓ cup ketchup

12 ounces beer of your choice (I recommend a good old Coors Light, but feel free to use whatever you have on hand.)

2 tablespoons sriracha sauce

1 tablespoon apple cider vinegar

1 tablespoon honey

1 pound pork tenderloin, cut into roughly 3-inch cubes

FOR SERVING (OPTIONAL)
4 whole-grain rolls or hamburger buns

Bread and butter pickles

I have this recurring nightmare where I come home to find a cryptic, barbecue sauce–stained note on the bed that reads, "You'll find me at Hill Country." Filled with inexplicable dread, I run 15 blocks in the pouring rain to the infamous NYC barbecue joint. As soon as I push through the heavy wooden doors, I see him. Logan is sitting at his own picnic table, visibly drunk, elbows deep in a mountain of pulled pork and meat sweating through a "My Girlfriend Is Out of Town" tank top. He looks up at me and whispers, "You did this. This is what happens when I feel deprived." I usually wake up screaming.

While Logan swears he would never do such a thing (except maybe on Super Bowl Sunday), I've started making double batches of this easy, and much leaner, pulled pork tenderloin on a regular basis. Better safe than sorry.

1. Heat the olive oil in a Dutch oven or sauté pan over medium heat. When the oil is hot and shimmering, add the onion and garlic and cook for about 3 minutes or until the onion becomes translucent, and you can smell the garlicky deliciousness.

2. Stir in the ketchup, beer, sriracha sauce, vinegar, and honey and bring to a boil. Lower to a simmer and add the pork tenderloin chunks. Cover and cook for 40 minutes.

3. Remove the pork pieces from the sauce and place them on a cutting board. Continue to simmer the sauce, uncovered, for 10 minutes or until slightly thickened.

4. Shred the meat with two forks. Return the shredded pork to the sauce and cook for another 10 minutes over low heat.

5. Serve the pork on its own with your favorite sides, or pile it on whole-grain burger buns with Avocado-Dijon Coleslaw (page 234) or pickles for a bomb BBQ sandwich.

summer spaghetti

Whole wheat spaghetti generally gets a bad rap, but don't knock it till you try it, dudes. There's a strong chance you'll dig the hearty taste, especially once you get summer's sexiest produce and some crispy pancetta involved.

1. Bring a large pot of salted water to a boil.

2. Quarter the zucchini lengthwise, and then slice them crosswise into ¼-inch-thick triangles. Set aside.

3. Heat the olive oil in a large sauté pan over medium heat. When the oil is hot and shimmering, add the pancetta and cook for 6 to 7 minutes or until lightly browned. Add the garlic and red pepper flakes and cook for 30 seconds. Add the shallot and cook until soft, about 2 minutes, then add the zucchini, cherry tomatoes, and salt. Cook for 7 to 8 minutes, stirring occasionally, or until the zucchini is tender (but not mushy!) and the tomatoes have softened and released some of their juices. Stir in the vinegar and two-thirds of the basil.

4. Meanwhile, cook the pasta al dente (aka just until tender) according to the package directions and drain.

5. Add the pasta to the "summer sauce" and toss to combine. (I highly recommend using tongs for this if you have them.)

6. Divide the spaghetti among four bowls and top with shaved ricotta salata and the remaining basil. (If you can't find ricotta salata, feel free to use shaved pecorino Romano or Parmesan instead.) Serve immediately.

2 medium zucchini (7 to 8 inches long)

2 teaspoons extra-virgin olive oil

One 4-ounce chunk pancetta, cut into ¼-inch cubes

3 garlic cloves, minced

¼ teaspoon crushed red pepper flakes

1 large shallot, finely chopped

3 cups cherry tomatoes, halved

½ teaspoon kosher salt

1 teaspoon balsamic vinegar

¾ cup fresh basil leaves, stacked, rolled, and thinly sliced (aka chiffonade)

8 ounces 100 percent whole-wheat spaghetti

1 ounce shaved ricotta salata cheese

KNOWLEDGE BOMB: WHITE PASTA IS TOUGH TO DIGEST, HAS ALMOST ZERO NUTRITIONAL VALUE, AND SENDS YOUR INSULIN LEVELS THROUGH THE ROOF. WHEN POSSIBLE, PLEASE WORK WHOLE-GRAIN PASTA INTO THE ROTATION. ITS HIGHER LEVELS OF PROTEIN AND FIBER LEAVE YOU MORE SATISFIED WITH LESS FOOD, AND EACH SERVING DELIVERS A SOLID DOSE OF MUCH-NEEDED VITAMINS AND MINERALS.

LOADED CHICKEN ENCHILADAS

2 boneless, skinless chicken breasts
2 cups low-sodium chicken broth
1½ tablespoons extra-virgin olive oil
½ yellow onion, finely chopped
1 small red bell pepper, seeded and cut into small dice
1 garlic clove, minced
2 packed cups baby spinach
1 chipotle pepper canned in adobo sauce, finely chopped
1 tablespoon adobo sauce from the chipotle can
¾ cup canned black beans, drained and rinsed
¾ cup sweet corn kernels (from 1 ear of corn)
8 medium whole-grain tortillas
1 cup grated mild cheddar cheese

(cont.)

These enchiladas are delicious, nutritious, and likely to induce high-pitched squeals of delight from adult males, which is the holy trinity of Dude Diet recipe requirements. Keep a batch in the freezer for impromptu fiestas.

1. Preheat the oven to 400°F.

2. Put the chicken breasts in a Dutch oven or sauté pan, add the chicken broth, and bring to a boil. Immediately lower to a gentle simmer, cover with a lid, and cook for 20 minutes or until the chicken is cooked through. Transfer the chicken breasts to a cutting board and, using two forks (or your hands), shred the meat. Set aside.

3. Meanwhile, combine all the ingredients for the enchilada sauce in a saucepan and bring to a boil. Lower to a simmer and cook for 10 minutes. Season with salt to taste, and set the sauce aside until ready to use.

4. Heat the olive oil in a large skillet over medium heat. When the oil is hot and shimmering, add the onion and bell pepper and cook for 3 minutes or just until tender. Add the garlic and cook for 1 minute until fragrant. Stir in the spinach and cook for about 1 minute or just until wilted. Add the chopped chipotle pepper, adobo sauce, black beans, corn kernels, and shredded chicken, along with 1 cup of the reserved enchilada sauce. Cook for another 2 minutes and remove from the heat. Taste the filling and season with a little kosher salt if necessary.

5. Time to assemble the enchiladas! Pour ½ cup of the enchilada sauce into a 9 x 13-inch baking dish. Place about ½ cup of filling into the center of each tortilla. Roll the tortillas up like cigars and line them up in the baking dish, seam side down. Pour the remaining enchilada sauce over the stuffed tortillas and top with an even layer of the cheese.

FOR THE ENCHILADA SAUCE
One 15-ounce
can tomato sauce
(sometimes labeled
"tomato puree")

1½ cups low-sodium
chicken broth

1 tablespoon hot
sauce of your choice,
such as Cholula

1 tablespoon
Mexican chili
powder

½ teaspoon ground
cumin

¼ teaspoon garlic
powder

Kosher salt

FOR GARNISH (OPTIONAL)
½ cup nonfat sour
cream or plain
Greek yogurt

1 avocado, pitted,
peeled, and diced

3 scallions, thinly
sliced

¼ cup fresh cilantro
leaves, chopped

6. Cover the baking dish loosely with aluminum foil and bake for 25 minutes or until the cheese has melted and the sauce is bubbling.

7. Serve the enchiladas warm. Free to get weird with the toppings.

SOUTHWESTERN STUFFED PEPPERS

SERVES 4—5

Between their retro comfort food vibes and the melted cheese factor, these brightly colored flavor bombs are guaranteed to get you all kinds of hot and bothered. If you're lucky enough to have leftovers, they make a badass breakfast with an egg on top, and they're perfectly portioned Dude Diet snacks.

1. Combine the quinoa in a small saucepan with ½ cup of the chicken broth and bring to a boil. Lower the heat to a simmer, cover the saucepan with a lid, and cook for 14 minutes, or until all of the liquid has been absorbed. Let the quinoa rest, covered, for 5 minutes, then fluff with a fork.

2. Meanwhile, slice the bell peppers in half lengthwise and remove the seeds and any white membrane. Arrange the pepper halves in an extra-large baking dish. (If you don't have a baking dish large enough, go ahead and use two baking dishes.)

3. Preheat the oven to 375°F.

4. Heat the olive oil in a large saucepan over medium heat. When the oil is hot and shimmering, add the corn kernels, onion, and garlic and cook for 5 minutes or until the corn is tender and the onion becomes translucent. Add the ground turkey and cook for about 6 minutes, stirring and breaking up the meat with a spatula or until no longer pink. Stir in the chili powder, oregano, cumin, salt, and cayenne and cook for 1 minute to toast the spices. Add the black beans, tomatoes, and cooked quinoa and cook for 5 minutes more. Remove the mixture from the heat.

5. Spoon the filling into each of the pepper halves. Pour the remaining 1 cup chicken broth into the bottom of the baking dish(es), and cover the dish(es) tightly with aluminum foil. Bake for 30 minutes

⅓ cup uncooked quinoa, rinsed and drained

1½ cups low-sodium chicken broth, divided

5 large bell peppers (I like to use a mix of colors.)

1 tablespoon extra-virgin olive oil

¾ cup sweet corn kernels (from 1 ear of corn)

½ medium yellow onion, finely chopped

2 garlic cloves, minced

1 pound lean ground turkey

1 tablespoon chili powder

1½ teaspoons dried oregano

1 teaspoon ground cumin

1 teaspoon kosher salt

⅛ teaspoon cayenne pepper

(cont.)

One 15-ounce can
black beans, drained
and rinsed

One 15-ounce can
diced fire-roasted
tomatoes

1 cup grated sharp
cheddar cheese

½ cup fresh cilantro
leaves, finely
chopped (optional)

or until the peppers are just tender. (I prefer a tiny bit of crunch to my peppers for texture, but if you dig softer peppers, bake them for an extra 10 to 15 minutes.)

6. Remove the foil and sprinkle the peppers with the grated cheddar. Bake for 5 minutes more or until the cheese has melted and is bubbling.

7. Serve the stuffed peppers warm with a generous sprinkling of chopped cilantro.

DUDE DIET SHEPHERD'S PIE

1 large head cauliflower, cored and broken into florets

1 cup 2 percent milk

4 cups water

Kosher salt

Freshly ground black pepper

1 tablespoon extra-virgin olive oil

1 small yellow onion, minced

1 cup finely chopped carrots

2 garlic cloves, minced

½ teaspoon smoked paprika, plus extra for serving (optional)

Pinch of cayenne pepper

1 pound 93 percent lean ground turkey

1 tablespoon tomato paste

1½ tablespoons low-sodium soy sauce

1 tablespoon plus 1 teaspoon Worcestershire sauce

¾ cup low-sodium vegetable broth

1 cup frozen green peas

1 tablespoon finely chopped fresh chives (optional)

This pie was one of the very first Dude Diet recipes, and I credit its supremely comforting flavor profile for shepherding so many hesitant dudes into the fold. There's a hint of sweetness and smoke in the lean turkey and vegetable filling, and topped with a silky cauliflower puree, it's the kind of hearty, satisfying meal that warms you up from the inside out. The badass health benefits are just gravy.

1. Put the cauliflower florets, milk, and water in a Dutch oven or large saucepan and bring to a boil. Lower to a simmer, cover with a lid, and cook for 15 to 20 minutes or until the cauliflower is very tender. Using a slotted spoon, transfer the florets to a blender or food processor and puree until smooth. Season the puree generously with salt and black pepper and set it aside.

2. Meanwhile, preheat the oven to 375°F.

3. Heat the olive oil in a large skillet over medium heat. When the oil is hot and shimmering, add the onion and carrot and cook for 5 minutes or until the carrot has softened slightly and the onion is translucent. Add the garlic, paprika, and cayenne and cook for 1 minute more or until the garlic is fragrant. Add the ground turkey, and cook for about 5 minutes, breaking up the meat with a spatula, until no longer pink. Add the tomato paste and cook for 1 minute (just to mellow the acidity), then stir in the soy sauce, Worcestershire, and vegetable broth. Simmer for about 5 minutes or until most of the liquid has been absorbed, then stir in the peas.

4. Transfer the filling to a medium baking dish (a 9 x 9-inch or a 7 x 11-inch dish is ideal) and top with the cauliflower puree, spreading it out in an even layer. Add a couple of dashes of smoked paprika if you like.

5. Bake the shepherd's pie for 25 minutes or until piping hot and bubbling around the sides. Remove from the oven and let cool for 5 to 10 minutes. Serve garnished with fresh chives if you feel like it.

JUST THE TIP: IN A HURRY? SKIP THE BAKING. AND SIMPLY SPOON THE TURKEY FILLING INTO BOWLS. TOP WITH CAULIFLOWER PUREE. AND SERVE. IT WILL BE MORE STEWLIKE (AND LESS AESTHETICALLY PLEASING). BUT IT WILL TASTE JUST AS AWESOME.

CHEESEBURGER QUINOA BAKE

SERVES 4—6

1 cup quinoa, rinsed and drained

1½ cups low-sodium beef broth (Low-sodium chicken broth or water will also work.)

⅓ cup whole-wheat panko bread crumbs

2 teaspoons sesame seeds (optional)

1 teaspoon smoked paprika, divided

1 tablespoon extra-virgin olive oil

1 medium yellow onion, finely chopped

2 garlic cloves, minced

1 pound 90 percent lean ground beef (preferably grass-fed)

1¼ teaspoons kosher salt

¾ teaspoon freshly ground black pepper

3 tablespoons tomato paste

2 tablespoons Dijon mustard

2 tablespoons Worcestershire sauce

One 14.5-ounce can diced tomatoes

Since cheeseburgers are practically their own food group in most dudes' diets, instituting a ban on the artery-clogging classic would be cruel and unusual punishment. The occasional indulgence (probably) won't kill you, but please swap at least some of your regular burgers for this significantly healthier quinoa bake. Given the casserole's obscene deliciousness, I think that's a pretty reasonable ask.

1. Combine the quinoa and beef broth in a small saucepan and bring to a boil. Lower to a simmer, cover the saucepan with a lid, and cook for 14 minutes, or until all of the liquid has been absorbed. Let the quinoa rest, covered, for 5 minutes, then fluff with a fork.

2. Preheat the oven to 375°F.

3. In a small bowl, combine the panko, sesame seeds, and ½ teaspoon of the smoked paprika. Set aside.

4. Heat the olive oil in a large, 12-inch ovenproof skillet over medium heat. When the oil is hot and shimmering, add the onion and garlic, and cook for 4 to 5 minutes or until the onion is soft and translucent. Add the ground beef, salt, pepper, and remaining ½ teaspoon smoked paprika to the skillet. Cook for about 7 minutes, stirring and breaking up the meat into small pieces with a spatula, until no longer pink. Stir in the tomato paste, mustard, and Worcestershire and cook for 3 more minutes, then stir in the diced tomatoes.

5. Turn off the heat and fold in the cooked quinoa and ½ cup of the cheese. Smooth the top of the filling with a spatula. Add the remaining cheese in an even layer and sprinkle with the panko mix. Bake for 25 minutes, or until the cheese has melted and the topping is very lightly browned.

6. Let your kick-ass quinoa bake rest for 10 minutes. (Trust me, it will be crazy hot.) Serve topped with chopped lettuce and pickles.

1¼ cups grated sharp cheddar cheese, divided

1 cup chopped hearts of romaine or iceberg lettuce

½ cup finely chopped bread-and-butter pickles

KILLER CUBAN SANDWICHES

MAKES 4 SANDWICHES

Juice of 1 orange

Juice of 1 lime

1 teaspoon dried oregano

1 teaspoon ground cumin

1 teaspoon kosher salt

½ teaspoon crushed red pepper flakes

½ teaspoon freshly ground black pepper

1 pound pork tenderloin, trimmed of excess fat

1 tablespoon vegetable oil

4 soft whole-wheat sandwich rolls

½ cup coarse ground Dijon mustard

12 kosher dill pickle sandwich slices

4 ounces low-sodium ham

Four 1-ounce slices Swiss cheese

2 tablespoons extra-virgin olive oil

For years, one of Logan's favorite pastimes was tagging me in photos of Cubanos on Instagram. Terrified by the barrage of virtual gut bombs, I felt compelled to develop a lighter version of the recipe, which has changed both our lives for the better. Logan now happily indulges his cravings in a non-destructive way, and my newsfeed no longer resembles a creepy shrine to pressed pork sandwiches. Win-win.

1. In a small bowl, whisk together the orange and lime juices, oregano, cumin, kosher salt, red pepper flakes, and black pepper. Reserve 3 tablespoons of the marinade in a separate bowl.

2. Put your pork tenderloin in a large ziplock food storage bag and pour in the remaining marinade. Seal the bag, removing as much air as you possibly can, and refrigerate for 1 hour.

3. Place an ovenproof skillet in the oven, then preheat the oven to 450°F. Once pre-heated, carefully remove the skillet from the oven wearing oven mitts, and add the vegetable oil, swirling to coat the bottom of the pan. (Watch out—it may spit a little!) Add the tenderloin to the skillet and return it to the oven. Roast for 10 minutes. Turn the tenderloin over, and immediately return it to the oven. Reduce the oven temperature to 400°F and roast the pork for 10 minutes more (a total of 20 minutes).

4. Transfer the pork to a cutting board, cover loosely with aluminum foil, and let rest for a full 10 minutes to allow the juices to redistribute. Slice the tenderloin crosswise as thinly as you possibly can.

5. Now it's time to build your killer Cubans. Slice the sandwich rolls in half. To assemble each sandwich: Spread both halves of the roll with 1 tablespoon mustard. Add 3 pickle slices to the bottom half, top with sliced pork, and drizzle with about 2 teaspoons of the reserved marinade. Add a slice of ham and cheese, and close the sandwich with the top half of the roll. Brush the sandwich all over with ½ tablespoon olive oil.

6. Heat a large skillet over medium heat. When hot, add 1 or 2 sandwiches to the pan and place another heavy skillet (or any other heavy pan) on top. (It's a MacGyver panini maker!) Cook for 3 to 4 minutes per side or until the outside is golden brown and the cheese has melted. Repeat with the remaining sandwiches.

7. Slice each sandwich in half and serve immediately.

DUDE DIET
PHILLY CHEESESTEAKS

1 pound top round steak

1½ bell peppers, seeded and thinly sliced (I like to use a mix of red, green, and yellow peppers, but you do you.)

1 medium yellow onion, thinly sliced

2 large portobello mushroom caps

2½ tablespoons extra-virgin olive oil

1 garlic clove, minced

1 tablespoon plus 2 teaspoons Worcestershire sauce

1 tablespoon plus 1 teaspoon low-sodium soy sauce

Kosher salt

Freshly ground black pepper

Four 1-ounce slices provolone cheese

Four 6-inch whole-wheat sub rolls

Logan was born and raised in the cheesesteak capital of the world, and his love for Philly's greatest (and most fattening) sandwich runs deep. I'm intimately familiar with the great Pat's vs. Geno's Philly cheesesteak debate, and I've heard many a disturbing story revolve around the procurement of these epic sandos. Logan even had his parents smuggle the foil-wrapped treats in their carry-ons when they came to visit him in college. Nothing says dedication to a sandwich quite like convincing your parents to act as cross-country cheesesteak mules.

Since there's a snowball's chance in hell of Logan giving up his favorite hoagie, I created this slimmed down, veggie-heavy version that's doable in about 30 minutes. Apologies for the lack of whiz, dudes, but that shit will kill you.

1. Place your top round steak in the freezer for 20 minutes. (This will make the beef so much easier to slice.)

2. Meanwhile, prepare your vegetables. I'm sure you know how to slice bell peppers and onions, dudes, but the portobellos require a little extra attention. Remove the stems from each mushroom, and use a spoon to scrape off the brown gills on the underside. Slice the caps in half, and then thinly slice each half crosswise. Set the vegetables aside.

3. Remove the steak from the freezer and slice it across the grain as thinly as you possibly can.

4. Heat 1 tablespoon of the olive oil in a large skillet or sauté pan over medium-high heat. When the oil is hot and shimmering, add the steak to the pan and cook for about 2 minutes, stirring constantly and breaking it up into smaller pieces with a spatula or until no longer pink. Remove the steak from the pan and set aside.

5. Wipe out the skillet, return it to the heat, and add the remaining 1½ tablespoons olive oil. Add the vegetables and garlic and cook for 7 to 8 minutes or until tender (but not mushy) and lightly browned.

6. Add the steak back to the skillet and stir in the Worcestershire sauce and soy sauce. Season with kosher salt and black pepper to taste.

7. Reduce the heat to medium, place the slices of provolone on top of the steak and vegetables and allow it to melt completely. (This should only take about 2 minutes, tops!)

8. Slice your sub rolls three-quarters of the way through and hollow out their insides, leaving a ½-inch shell. (You won't miss the extra bread, I promise.)

9. Divide the cheesesteak filling among the four hollowed-out rolls. Serve warm.

YOU DO YOU: THE CHEESESTEAK FILLING IS ALSO DOPE IN WHOLE-GRAIN TORTILLAS AND PITAS. OVER BROWN RICE. OR WRAPPED IN SOME BUTTER LETTUCE LEAVES.

DUDE DIET
Lasagna

2 tablespoons extra-virgin olive oil

12 ounces (3 to 4 links) sweet Italian turkey sausage, casings removed

1 small yellow onion, minced

8 ounces baby bella mushrooms, stems removed, caps finely chopped

3 garlic cloves, minced

5 ounces baby spinach

One 28-ounce can crushed tomatoes (I strongly recommend San Marzano.)

½ teaspoon crushed red pepper flakes

½ cup fresh basil leaves, chopped

One 9-ounce box no-boil brown rice lasagna noodles (I like Jovial brand.)

8 ounces part-skim ricotta cheese

8 ounces fresh mozzarella, grated (about 2 cups)

Post-Lasagna Panic—aka the immediate and overpowering need to get horizontal after eating a traditional slab of the Italian classic—is a very real, and very scary, thing. But thanks to this layered masterpiece, which is packed with lean turkey sausage, veggies, fiber-rich brown rice noodles, and a responsible amount of cheese, you can now enjoy all of lasagna's good, without the bad and the ugly.

1. Heat the olive oil in your largest sauté pan over medium heat. When hot, add the sausage to the pan and cook, stirring and breaking up the meat with a spatula, for 7 to 8 minutes or until lightly browned. Add the onion, mushrooms, and garlic to the pan and cook for 4 minutes or until the onion is translucent and the mushrooms have softened.

2. Add the spinach to the pan. (It will seem like too much, dudes, but it will cook down very quickly.) Cook for about 2 minutes, stirring constantly or until the spinach has wilted. Stir in the crushed tomatoes, red pepper flakes, and basil and simmer for 5 minutes to allow the flavors to combine. Remove that magical sauce from the heat. Taste and season with a little salt if necessary.

3. Preheat the oven to 375°F.

4. Spread the bottom of a 9 x 13-inch baking dish with 1 cup of the sauce. (You can also use a 10 x 10-inch dish or a large cast-iron skillet in a pinch.) Arrange the lasagna noodles in an even layer, trying not to overlap the noodles too much. (It's totally cool if you have to break noodles into smaller pieces to make them fit.) Top the noodles with 1¾ cup of the sauce. Spread half of the ricotta over the sauce and sprinkle with ⅓ cup mozzarella. Repeat these layers—noodles, sauce, ricotta, mozzarella—a second time, then top with a third and final layer of

lasagna noodles. (Depending on the size of your baking dish, you may not need the entire box of noodles.) Spread the remaining sauce on top of the noodles and sprinkle evenly with the remaining mozzarella.

5. Cover the baking dish tightly with aluminum foil and bake the lasagna for 40 minutes. Remove the foil and bake for 10 minutes more or until the cheese has melted and is bubbling.

6. Let the lasagna rest for 5 to 10 minutes before cutting and serving.

JUST THE TIP: IF YOU CAN'T FIND BROWN RICE LASAGNA NOODLES, WHOLE-WHEAT NOODLES ARE THE NEXT BEST THING.

Farro RISOTTO with Corn, Bacon, and Cherry Tomatoes

In addition to its awesome nutty taste and satisfying chew, whole-grain farro adds plenty of fiber, protein, and essential vitamins to this drool-worthy summertime feast. Up your culinary street cred by serving it to guests and introducing the dish as a "seasonal farrotto." (Mic drop.)

1. Preheat the oven to 375°F.

2. Line a rimmed baking sheet with aluminum foil. Spray a wire rack with cooking spray and place it on top of the baking sheet. Arrange the bacon on the wire rack and bake for 25 to 30 minutes or until it's very brown and crispy. Remove from the oven, let cool for 5 minutes, then transfer to a paper towel–lined plate to drain. Crumble the bacon into small pieces, and set aside until ready to use.

3. Meanwhile, pour the chicken broth into a saucepan and bring to a simmer. Once simmering, turn down the heat to the lowest setting to keep the broth warm.

4. Heat 2 tablespoons of the olive oil in a medium Dutch oven or sauté pan over medium heat. When the oil is hot and shimmering, add the onion and garlic and cook for 5 to 6 minutes or until the onion is very soft and translucent. Add the farro and cook for 2 minutes, stirring constantly, to toast the grains. Add the wine and cook for 1 to 2 minutes, scraping up any brown bits from the bottom of the pot or until the liquid has been completely absorbed.

5. Add the corn kernels and 1 cup of the warm broth to the pot. Simmer, stirring occasionally, until the broth has been almost completely absorbed, about 7 minutes. Repeat this process, adding broth, ½ cup at a time, until the farro is al dente (aka just tender). This process should take about 30 minutes.

---

4 slices thick-cut bacon (preferably with no added nitrates)

4 cups low-sodium chicken broth

3 tablespoons extra-virgin olive oil, divided

1 small yellow onion, minced

1 garlic clove, minced

1¼ cups semipearled farro

½ cup dry white wine, such as Sauvignon Blanc or Pinot Grigio

¾ cup sweet corn kernels (from 1 ear of corn)

½ teaspoon kosher salt

Freshly ground black pepper

1 cup cherry tomatoes, halved from pole to pole

⅓ cup fresh basil leaves, finely chopped, plus extra for serving

¼ cup grated Parmesan cheese

6. After the last addition of broth has been mostly absorbed (you still want a little liquid hanging out in the pan), stir in the salt, a few cranks of black pepper, the cherry tomatoes, and basil. Cook for 2 minutes or until the tomatoes have softened slightly. Remove from the heat and stir in the remaining 1 tablespoon of olive oil, Parmesan cheese, and reserved crumbled bacon.

7. Ladle the risotto into bowls and serve immediately. Garnish each serving with some extra basil if you're feeling fancy.

> **JUST THE TIP:** SEMIPEARLED FARRO IS BEST FOR THIS RECIPE. BUT PEARLED WILL ALSO WORK. AVOID FARRO LABELED "WHOLE" OR "UNPEARLED"—IT TAKES A RIDICULOUSLY LONG TIME TO COOK. IF YOU DON'T HAVE ACCESS TO FARRO OR NEED A GLUTEN-FREE OPTION. FEEL FREE TO USE ARBORIO RICE.

TRASHED-UP TURKEY BURGERS

Forget the dry, tasteless turkey burgers of your past, and embrace the swoon-worthy patties of your future. Mashed avocado keeps these lean burgers extra juicy, turkey bacon adds a guilt-free savory boost, and melted pepper Jack seals the deal. Keeping things extra tight? Ditch the bun, and lettuce-wrap your burger, you sexy beast.

1. Cook the turkey bacon in a skillet over medium heat until browned and crispy, about 4 to 5 minutes per side. Transfer to a paper towel–lined plate to cool, then finely chop.

2. Place the ground turkey in a mixing bowl and add the chopped turkey bacon, avocado, garlic, paprika, pepper, cumin, and salt and mix until well combined. (I recommend using your hands for this, but a fork will do if you're squeamish.)

3. With damp hands, mold the turkey mixture into 4 patties, about 1 inch thick, and place them on a piece of parchment or wax paper.

4. Heat the olive oil in a large nonstick skillet over medium heat. When the oil is hot and shimmering, carefully add the burgers to the pan. Cook for 6 to 7 minutes, undisturbed or until lightly browned on the undersides and beginning to firm, then flip with a spatula, and cook for another 6 minutes on the opposite sides. (The uncooked burgers are very soft, so I need you to wait to flip them until they're ready, or they will fall apart. You've been warned.) During the last 2 minutes of the cooking time, top each patty with a slice of the cheese and let it melt.

5. Serve the turkey burgers on buns, piled high with lettuce, tomato, and onion.

3 slices turkey bacon

1 pound lean ground turkey

½ ripe avocado, pitted, peeled, and mashed

2 garlic cloves, minced

1 teaspoon smoked paprika

½ teaspoon freshly ground black pepper

¼ teaspoon ground cumin

¼ teaspoon kosher salt

1 tablespoon extra-virgin olive oil

Four 1-ounce slices pepper Jack cheese

FOR SERVING

4 whole-grain burger buns or English muffins

8 leaves Boston lettuce (Bibb lettuce or romaine are also great.)

1 beefsteak tomato, sliced

1 small red onion, thinly sliced

YOU DO YOU: WANT TO TURN UP THE HEAT? TRY SMOTHERING THESE BURGERS IN SRIRACHUP (SEE SIDEBAR PAGE 144).

ITALIAN HERB MEATBALLS
WITH SPICY MARINARA

1 cup cauliflower florets

1 pound 85 percent lean ground beef (preferably grass-fed)

½ cup grated Parmesan cheese

⅓ cup basil leaves, finely chopped

⅓ cup fresh flat-leaf parsley leaves, finely chopped

1 teaspoon dried oregano

1 teaspoon kosher salt

½ teaspoon freshly ground black pepper

2 garlic cloves, minced

1 large egg

FOR THE SPICY MARINARA

1½ tablespoons extra-virgin olive oil

½ medium yellow onion, minced

2 garlic cloves, minced

¼ teaspoon kosher salt

One 28-ounce can crushed tomatoes (I recommend San Marzano.)

I don't want to get ahead of myself here, but I really think these grain-free meatballs may be the wave of the future. They're tender, juicy, and bursting with fresh herb goodness. And replacing the typical bread crumbs with cauliflower "rice" trims empty calories while adding a welcome nutrition boost. You can eat these balls on their own, but I recommend serving them over zucchini noodles, quinoa, or whole-grain pasta.

1. Preheat the oven to 400°F. Line a large baking sheet with aluminum foil. Spray a wire rack with cooking spray and place it on top of the prepared baking sheet.

2. Put the cauliflower florets in a food processor or blender and pulse several times until the florets become small granules. (The cauliflower should look sort of like couscous here.) Transfer to a large mixing bowl.

3. Add the remaining ingredients for the meatballs to the bowl with the cauliflower. Using your hands (this is nonnegotiable), mix gently just until all the ingredients are combined. Try not overmix, dudes, or you'll end up with dry, dense meatballs.

4. With lightly oiled hands, *gently* roll the meat mixture into 16 balls (roughly 2 inches in diameter), and place them an inch or so apart on the wire rack. Bake for 20 minutes or until cooked through.

5. Meanwhile, get going on the marinara. Heat the olive oil in a medium Dutch oven or sauté pan over medium heat. When the oil is hot and shimmering, add the onion, garlic, and salt and cook for 5 to 6 minutes or until the onion is very soft and the garlic is fragrant. Add the crushed tomatoes, red pepper flakes, and sugar. Reduce the heat to low and simmer the sauce for 15 minutes until slightly thickened.

6. Add the meatballs to the sauce. Simmer for 5 minutes more, then stir in the basil. Serve warm.

½ teaspoon crushed red pepper flakes

¼ teaspoon pure cane sugar

5 fresh basil leaves, chopped

YOU DO YOU: THERE ARE INFINITE SERVING POSSIBILITIES FOR THIS BEAUTIFUL BIRD. TRY IT WITH YOUR FAVORITE SEXY SIDES. TOSS IT IN SALADS. OR WRAP IT UP IN WHOLE-GRAIN TORTILLAS OR LETTUCE LEAVES. (NO JUDGMENT IF YOU WANT TO JUST GET AFTER IT WITH YOUR HANDS.)

Magic FauX-Tisserie Chicken

This chicken. This chicken is the most perfect, insanely tender, unapologetically *moist* chicken you will ever make. Slow-roasting the bird at a low temperature yields the same fall-off-the-bone meat as a rotisserie, and the spice-rubbed skin is a dreamy combination of crisp and sticky. I know the 3-hour time commitment seems intense, but you're gonna have to sack up, dudes. There's only about 15 minutes of hands-on prep, and then all you have to do is sit back and let the magic happen.

1. Preheat the oven to 300°F

2. Remove any giblets and other nasty stuff from the cavity of your chicken, then rinse the chicken thoroughly with cold water, and dry it well with paper towels. Stuff the cavity with the garlic and lemon quarters.

3. In a small bowl, combine the paprika, salt, brown sugar, chili powder, black pepper, garlic powder, and cumin.

4. Carefully run your fingers under the skin on the breasts of your bird. Rub the breasts underneath the skin with 1 tablespoon of the olive oil and 1 teaspoon of the spice mixture. (This is less scary and gross than it sounds, I promise.) Rub the remaining 2 tablespoons olive oil on the chicken's skin, and season the bird all over with the remaining spice mixture. When you're finished with the spicing, tie the legs together with kitchen twine and place the bird breast side up in an ovenproof skillet or roasting pan (your choice!).

5. Roast the chicken for 2 hours 45 minutes to 3 hours (depending on whether the bird is closer to 3½ or 4 pounds), basting at the 1½- and 2½-hour marks (no need for a baster—just spoon any juices in the pan over the bird) or until the meat is very tender and the skin is dark brown. (Don't panic if the skin has blackened in some spots. That's a good thing.)

6. Let the chicken rest for 10 minutes before carving and serving.

One 3½- to 4-pound whole chicken

5 garlic cloves, smashed

½ lemon, quartered

2½ teaspoons smoked paprika

2 teaspoons kosher salt

2 packed teaspoons light brown sugar

1½ teaspoons chili powder

1 teaspoon freshly ground black pepper

½ teaspoon garlic powder

¼ teaspoon ground cumin

3 tablespoons extra-virgin olive oil

Kitchen twine

GAME DAY EATS

As a Dude Dieter, you will undoubtedly face many challenges in achieving and maintaining your wonderland body, but there is no threat more dangerous or persistent than football season. Emotions run high, and between the viewing parties, the tailgates, and the abundance of booze and finger food at your disposal, it can be difficult to stay the course.

Trust me, I get it.

To describe Logan's game-day eating habits as "disturbing" would be a gross understatement. The dude is physically incapable of watching football without getting dirty on the food front, and he's known to mindlessly push things into his mouth (he literally pushes bigger bites into his mouth with his fingers if they don't fit) during the game with no regard for serving sizes or Dude Diet decorum. Just as a point of reference, I once witnessed Logan inhale a pile of Buffalo chicken tenders, break out in a pretty severe cayenne-induced rash, and then casually pop a Benadryl with his beer and continue eating. As you can imagine, such reckless behavior has upsetting consequences, including meat sweat–soaked sheets, teary pleas for Zantac, and prolonged periods of "alone time" in the bathroom. Shit gets weird.

Clearly, game-day feasting is an integral part of the dude lifestyle, and I'm certainly not going to suggest that you limit yourself to the celery sticks on snack platters this football season. All I ask is that you rein it in a little bit when it comes to your deep-fried, cheese-laden indulgences and party with some healthier, yet equally exciting, fan food. Whether you're a chili connoisseur or a nacho enthusiast, this chapter covers all your bases, and I promise these idiotproof recipes will excite even the harshest of couch-based critics.

WARNING: You will obviously frequent bars and social events that do not serve Dude Diet–friendly fare. In these scenarios, portion control is key. If at any point you experience one or more of the following symptoms, put down whatever greasy thing is in your hand and call it quits for the day: excessive sweating, nausea, heartburn, headache, indigestion, severe gas, or diarrhea. Do NOT, under any circumstances, take an over-the-counter digestive aid and continue to eat.

BUFFALO CHICKEN TENDERS WITH YOGURT RANCH

1 pound boneless, skinless chicken tenders (sometimes labeled "tenderloins")

1 cup whole-wheat panko bread crumbs

1 cup Frank's RedHot Buffalo Wing Sauce (This is NOT the same thing as traditional Frank's RedHot Sauce.)

FOR THE YOGURT RANCH
1½ cups nonfat plain Greek yogurt

1 teaspoon dried parsley, crushed (Just use your fingers to crush the flakes.)

½ teaspoon dried dill weed

½ teaspoon kosher salt

¼ teaspoon garlic powder

¼ teaspoon freshly ground black pepper

⅛ teaspoon smoked paprika

I once asked Logan whether he liked Buffalo tenders more than Buffalo wings. His response? "FUCK YES! Cleaner, juicier, and more meat. And they don't require as much work for Daddy!" The last reason is actually quite dangerous, as the boneless aspect of chicken tenders means that Logan is able to ingest them more quickly, and with less chewing, than a standard wing. This exponentially increases both his calorie intake and choking risk, and I worry about him eating them unsupervised. Death by Buffalo "fingie" is a very real risk for the dude.

With that said, if Logan is going to die at the hands of Buffalo chicken, these amazing baked tenders would be an epic (and health conscious!) way to go out. The chicken is marinated in ranch dressing before it's breaded in crispy whole-wheat panko, so each fiery bite has a layer of tangy ranch *baked in*...

1. Start by making the yogurt ranch. In a medium bowl, mix together all the ingredients for the dressing until well combined.

2. Place the chicken tenders in a large ziplock food storage bag and add ¾ cup of the yogurt ranch. Seal the bag, removing as much air as possible. Gently squish the chicken around, making sure that each tender gets coated in dressing. Refrigerate for 30 minutes. Go ahead and pop that extra ranch in the fridge, too.

3. Preheat the oven to 350°F. Spray a wire rack with cooking spray and place it on top of a baking sheet. Set aside. (If you don't have a wire rack, you can cook your tenders directly on a baking sheet lined with parchment paper or aluminum foil. They won't be quite as crispy, but it's not a big deal.)

4. Pour the panko into a shallow bowl and mix with a good pinch of kosher salt. Place this bowl next to the prepared baking sheet and get your marinated chicken from the fridge. (You're setting up a little assembly line to make your life easier.) One at a time, remove

the chicken tenderloins from the bag and dredge them in the bowl of panko. Use your fingers to gently press the panko onto the chicken tenders; you want each tender to be really well coated. Transfer the breaded tenders to the prepared wire rack, leaving a little bit of space between each one.

5. Bake for 25 minutes or until the tenders are cooked through.

6. Heat the wing sauce in a medium sauté pan. When hot, remove from the heat and add a few chicken tenders at a time. Use tongs to make sure they get completely coated in sauce. (Just a heads up, the sauce is HOT, so if you're sensitive to spice, you may only want to coat one side of the tenders.)

7. Transfer the Buffalo "fingies" to a plate and serve immediately with the reserved ranch for shameless dipping.

KNOWLEDGE BOMB: THREE STANDARD DEEP-FRIED BUFFALO CHICKEN FINGERS CLOCK IN AT AROUND 510 CALORIES AND 33 GRAMS OF FAT (AND THAT'S BEFORE YOU DUNK THEM IN COPIOUS AMOUNTS OF THE CREAMY FATNESS THAT IS RANCH OR BLUE CHEESE DRESSING). WHILE THREE OF THESE DUDE DIET TENDERS WILL RUN YOU LESS THAN 300 CALORIES AND 1.5 GRAMS OF FAT. CHEST BUMP.

CHIPOTLE GUACAMOLE

Of all the game day staples, guacamole is one of the most nutritionally sound. Avocados are loaded with fiber, healthy fats, and more than 20 vitamins and minerals, and since they're known to boost metabolism and lower cholesterol, a healthy guac habit can actually be a good thing. A chopped chipotle pepper and a little adobo sauce take this classic dip to the next level, giving it a mild kick and an underlying smokiness that can't be beat.

Keep your football season physique in check by serving the guacamole with baked whole-grain chips or crackers and crunchy raw vegetables.

1. Slice the avocados in half lengthwise and remove the pits. Scoop the flesh into a large bowl. Immediately add the kosher salt and lime juice and mash with a fork. (Don't worry about getting things completely smooth, dudes. A little texture is a good thing.)

2. Stir in the minced red onion, chipotle pepper, adobo sauce, and cilantro. Taste and season with a little extra salt if necessary.

3 ripe Haas avocados

½ teaspoon kosher salt, plus extra if needed

Juice of 1 large lime

¼ cup minced red onion

1 chipotle pepper canned in adobo sauce, minced (Seed the chipotle if you fear spice.)

2 teaspoons adobo sauce from the chipotle can

¼ packed cup fresh cilantro leaves, finely chopped

JUST THE TIP: IF YOU PLAN TO MAKE THIS RECIPE IN ADVANCE AND WANT TO PREVENT IT FROM BROWNING. PLACE THE GUACAMOLE IN AN AIRTIGHT CONTAINER OR A BOWL AND SMOOTH THE TOP. ADD A THIN LAYER OF WATER. AND SEAL THE CONTAINER OR COVER IT TIGHTLY WITH PLASTIC WRAP. WHEN YOU'RE READY TO DIG IN. JUST POUR OFF THE WATER AND GIVE THE GUACAMOLE A GOOD STIR.

Green CHILI with Pork and WHITE Beans

1 pound tomatillos, rinsed well and roughly chopped (about 3 cups chopped tomatillos)

3 small jalapeños, seeds removed, roughly chopped

½ cup fresh cilantro leaves

1 tablespoon extra-virgin olive oil

1 medium yellow onion, diced

3 garlic cloves, minced

¾ teaspoon kosher salt, plus extra if needed

1 tablespoon dried oregano

2 teaspoons ground cumin

⅛ teaspoon cayenne pepper (optional)

1¾ cups low-sodium chicken broth

1 pound pork tenderloin, cut into roughly 2½-inch cubes

One 15-ounce can Great Northern beans, drained and rinsed

Chili is basically the food equivalent of your favorite sweat suit—it's warm and comforting, and while it may not be the sexiest thing to look at, it's guaranteed to make you feel all kinds of cozy. Since you can't possibly get through football season without either one, you may as well adopt a recipe that will keep what's under your "Sunday tuxedo" as tight as possible. This insanely tasty tomatillo-based chili is just the thing. Using lean pork tenderloin trims calories and fat (and cooking time) without sacrificing flavor, so you can pig out without porking up.

1. Combine the tomatillos, jalapeños, and cilantro in a blender (or food processor), and blend until relatively smooth. Set aside.

2. Heat the olive oil in a medium Dutch oven or soup pot over medium heat. When the oil is hot and shimmering, add the onion, garlic, and salt and cook for 4 minutes or until the onion is soft and translucent. (Be careful not to burn the garlic!) Add the oregano, cumin, and cayenne (if using), and cook for 1 minute or until the spices are toasted and fragrant. Stir in the tomatillo puree and chicken broth and bring to a boil. Lower to a simmer and add the pork. Simmer, uncovered, for 40 minutes.

3. Meanwhile, place half of the beans in a small bowl and mash with a fork.

4. Using tongs or a slotted spoon, transfer the pork to a cutting board and shred using two forks. Return the shredded pork to the pot, add the beans (whole and mashed), and simmer for another 15 minutes. Taste and season with a little extra salt and extra cayenne if you like.

5. Ladle the chili into bowls and garnish with toppings of your choice.

TOPPINGS (OPTIONAL)
½ cup grated
Monterey Jack
cheese

½ cup nonfat plain
Greek yogurt

½ red onion, finely
minced

½ cup fresh cilantro
leaves, finely
chopped

JUST THE TIP: TOMATILLOS. ALSO KNOWN AS MEXICAN HUSK TOMATOES. ARE SMALL GREEN
FRUITS WITH A DISTINCTIVE TANGY FLAVOR. LOOK FOR TOMATILLOS THAT ARE BRIGHT GREEN AND FIRM.
AND TAKE A PEEK UNDER THE HUSK TO MAKE SURE THE FRUIT ISN'T SHRIVELED OR BRUISED. IF YOU
CAN'T GET YOUR PAWS ON FRESH. YOU CAN USE CANNED TOMATILLOS. WHICH ARE STOCKED IN THE
ETHNIC SECTION OF MOST LARGE MARKETS. USUALLY NEXT TO THE SALSAS AND CANNED PEPPERS.

SRIRACHA HUMMUS

One 15-ounce can chickpeas, drained and rinsed

2 tablespoons tahini

2 to 2½ tablespoons sriracha sauce (depending on how much heat you can handle)

1 large garlic clove

2 tablespoons fresh lime juice

¼ teaspoon kosher salt

2 tablespoons extra-virgin olive oil

1–2 tablespoons water (optional)

FOR SERVING (OPTIONAL)
Extra-virgin olive oil

Smoked paprika

Chopped fresh cilantro

Sliced scallions

Amped up with everyone's favorite rooster sauce, this super-smooth and fluffy hummus is primed to become a game-day staple. Well-seasoned whole-wheat pita chips are the perfect vehicles for transporting the addictively spicy dip to your face.

1. First, remove the skins on the chickpeas. Place the chickpeas between two sets of paper towels and gently rub to loosen their skins. Peel off and discard the skins. (You can skip this step if you're short on time, but naked chickpeas make for an awesomely silky hummus.)

2. Place the chickpeas in the bowl of a food processor with the tahini, sriracha sauce, garlic, lime juice, and salt. Process for a minute or so until very smooth, scraping down the sides of the bowl a few times if necessary. With the processor running, drizzle in the olive oil and continue processing for 1 minute more until the mixture is silky smooth and fluffy. Taste and add a little extra sriracha if it needs more heat. If you prefer a thinner hummus, add the water 1 teaspoon at a time, with the processor running until you reach your desired consistency.

3. Transfer the hummus to a bowl. Garnish with a drizzle of olive oil, a pinch of smoked paprika, and some chopped cilantro and scallions if you like.

Chili-Lime Pita Chips | SERVES 4–6

3 tablespoons extra-virgin olive oil

1 teaspoon finely grated lime zest

2 teaspoons fresh lime juice

1 teaspoon chili powder

½ teaspoon smoked paprika

Pinch of cayenne pepper

½ teaspoon kosher salt

Four 6-inch whole-wheat pitas

1. Preheat the oven to 400°F. Line two large baking sheets with parchment paper and set aside. (If you only have one baking sheet, you'll have to bake your chips in two batches.)

2. In a small bowl, combine the olive oil, lime zest, lime juice, chili powder, paprika, and cayenne.

3. Brush both sides of each pita with the olive oil mix, and sprinkle with the salt. Slice each pita into 8 triangles. (FYI, a pizza cutter is quite handy here.)

4. Arrange the pita chips in an even layer on the prepared baking sheets.

5. Bake for 8 to 10 minutes or until the chips are browned and crispy. (Keep a close eye on them—they burn quickly!) Remove from the oven and let cool before serving.

Brown Rice Jambalaya with Shrimp and Chicken Sausage

2 tablespoons extra-virgin olive oil

3 links andouille chicken sausage, diced

½ large yellow onion, diced

1½ bell peppers, seeded and diced (I like a mix of colors.)

2 garlic cloves, minced

1 tablespoon plus 1 teaspoon smoked paprika

1 teaspoon dried oregano

¾ teaspoons ground cumin

½ teaspoon kosher salt, plus extra if needed

¼ teaspoon cayenne pepper, plus extra if needed

One 14.5-ounce can diced fire-roasted tomatoes

1¼ cups short-grain brown rice

3½ cups low-sodium chicken broth

1 pound large shrimp, peeled and deveined

This jambalaya is the ultimate one-pot wonder. It's hearty, but not overly heavy, and packed to the gills with Creole flavor. The brown rice takes on a creamy, risotto-like texture as it soaks up the broth and toasted spices, acting as the perfect base for lightly browned andouille sausage and tender shrimp. Don't be intimidated by its fancy appearance or use of shellfish, dudes. The recipe isn't remotely difficult or labor-intensive, and you can always prep the jambalaya in advance, reheat it, and add the shrimp just before serving.

1. Heat the olive oil in a medium Dutch oven or soup pot over medium heat. When hot, add the diced chicken sausage and cook for 5 to 6 minutes or until lightly browned. Add the onion, bell peppers, and garlic, and cook for 3 minutes or until the vegetables are just tender. Add the paprika, oregano, cumin, salt, and cayenne and cook for 1 minute until toasted and fragrant. Stir in the tomatoes, and bring the mixture to a simmer.

2. Once at a simmer, stir in the brown rice and cook for 1 minute, and then add the chicken broth. (It will look very soupy. Don't panic, you're doing things right.) Bring to a boil, then immediately lower to a simmer. Cover with a lid and cook for 50 to 55 minutes or until the rice is tender and most of the liquid has been absorbed. Taste your jambalaya and season with a little extra salt and cayenne if necessary.

3. Mix the shrimp into the jambalaya, cover and cook for 5 minutes or until the shrimp are bright pink and opaque.

4. Ladle the jambalaya into bowls and serve with your finest hot sauce.

YOU DO YOU: INTO TOPPINGS? GARNISH YOUR JAMBALAYA WITH SLICED SCALLIONS AND CHOPPED CILANTRO LEAVES FOR ADDED FLAIR.

STOVETOP Parmesan-RANCH POPCORN

1½ teaspoons dried parsley

1 teaspoon onion powder

¾ teaspoon garlic powder

¾ teaspoon smoked paprika

½ teaspoon fine-grain sea salt

¼ teaspoon freshly ground black pepper

Pinch of cayenne pepper (optional)

4 tablespoons extra-virgin olive oil, divided

½ cup popcorn kernels

⅓ cup grated Parmesan cheese

If your oral fixation acts up while watching sports and you feel the need to continuously put things in your mouth, try reaching for this simple and deceptively healthy snack. Stovetop popcorn happens to be loaded with anti-oxidants and fiber, which will fill you up while improving digestion, lowering cholesterol, and reducing your risk of heart disease. Plus, the spice mix tastes like an upgraded version of the stuff on Cooler Ranch Doritos. I imagine you're into that?

1. Place the dried parsley in a small bowl and rub between your fingers until it becomes a coarse powder. Add the remaining spices to the bowl and stir to combine.

2. Pour 2 tablespoons of the olive oil into a large, deep pot and swirl to coat the bottom. Place the pot over medium heat, add 3 popcorn kernels, and cover with a lid. When all 3 kernels pop, remove the lid and add the rest of the kernels. Cover the pot, and give it a few shakes. (Please hold the lid down tightly while you shake—I don't want you to injure yourself.) Cook the popcorn, shaking the pot occasionally, until the popping sound stops, 4 to 5 minutes.

3. Immediately pour the popcorn into a very large bowl. Drizzle with the remaining 2 tablespoons olive oil and toss with you hands. Add the Parmesan and toss again. Finally, add the spice mixture, and keep tossing until the popcorn is well coated. Get your snack on.

> KNOWLEDGE BOMB: WHEN I SAID POPCORN WAS GOOD FOR YOU. I WAS ONLY REFERRING TO THE STOVETOP AND AIR-POPPED STUFF. BEWARE OF MOVIE THEATER AND MICROWAVE POPCORN. WHICH IS PACKED WITH FAT. CALORIES. ARTIFICIAL FLAVORS. AND KNOWN CARCINOGENS.

CRISPY FISH TACOS
WITH MANGO-AVOCADO SALSA
AND CHIPOTLE CREMA

MAKES 8 tacos

Take a deep breath. The ingredient list is long and there are a decent amount of steps involved in bringing these tacos to life, but you can totally do this. In fact, you probably already have a lot of the building blocks in your fridge and pantry, and with a little bit of planning, pulling off this mind-blowing flavor fiesta is surprisingly easy. I swear on Logan's life.

1. Start by making the salsa. Place all the ingredients in a medium bowl and gently mix to combine, being careful not to smash the avocado. Cover and refrigerate until ready to use.

2. Preheat the oven to 375°F. Line a baking sheet with parchment paper.

3. Now you're going to prep the crispy coating for the fish. In a small bowl, combine the panko, chili powder, paprika, and cayenne. Heat the olive oil in a large nonstick skillet over medium heat. When the oil is hot and shimmering, add the panko mixture and stir to coat with the oil. Toast for 2 to 3 minutes, stirring regularly or until the panko darkens slightly and smells toasty. Transfer to a shallow bowl or small baking dish and let cool to room temperature.

4. Pat the halibut dry and season both sides of the fillet with salt and black pepper. Slice the fish across the grain into approximately 1-inch-thick "fingers."

5. Time to bread the fish! I recommend setting up a little assembly line, with the fish, egg whites, and panko each in a separate shallow bowl, and the prepared baking sheet. Dip each piece of fish in the egg whites, shake off any excess, and coat it in the seasoned panko bread crumbs, pressing gently with your fingers to help them adhere. Place

1¼ cups whole-wheat panko bread crumbs

1 teaspoon chili powder

1 teaspoon smoked paprika

Pinch of cayenne pepper

2 tablespoons extra-virgin olive oil

1 pound halibut fillet, skin removed (You could also substitute tilapia or cod.)

Kosher salt

Freshly ground black pepper

2 large egg whites, lightly beaten

Eight 5-inch flour tortillas

FOR THE SALSA

1 ripe mango, seeded, peeled, and diced

1 ripe avocado, pitted, peeled, and diced

½ small red onion, finely chopped

(cont.)

¼ cup fresh cilantro leaves, finely chopped

Juice of 1 lime

Kosher salt

FOR THE CREMA

1 cup nonfat plain yogurt

1½ teaspoons fresh lime juice

½ chipotle pepper canned in adobo sauce, minced

¾ teaspoon adobo sauce from the chipotle can

¼ teaspoon honey

Kosher salt

the breaded fish fingers on the baking sheet about an inch apart. Transfer to the preheated oven and bake for 10 minutes.

6. Meanwhile, stir together all the ingredients for the crema in a small bowl, and warm the tortillas. You can either wrap 4 tortillas at a time in a damp paper towel and microwave in 30-second increments until warmed through, or heat each tortilla right on your stovetop burner for 5 to 10 seconds per side.

7. Assemble your tacos! Each tortilla gets a piece of fish, a heaping spoonful of salsa, and a generous dollop of crema.

JUST THE TIP: ASK THE NICE DUDE AT THE FISH COUNTER TO REMOVE THE SKIN ON YOUR HALIBUT FOR YOU.

THAI CHICKEN MEATBALLS

SERVES 3—4 AS PART OF A MAIN COURSE / 6 AS AN APPETIZER

Superfood chia seeds replace the traditional bread crumbs in these savory bite-size chicken meatballs, holding them together without dulling the kick-ass Thai flavors. Based on their simple, crowd-pleasing nature, I like to skewer the balls with toothpicks and serve them as game-day finger food, but they're equally bomb as a weeknight meal. Try them over stir-fried vegetables, Vegetable Soba Noodles (page 238), or lettuce wrapped with some quinoa and raw vegetables for crunch.

1. Put all the ingredients for the meatballs in a medium bowl. Using your hands, mix all the ingredients until well combined. (This is a little gross, but also kinda fun.) Cover and refrigerate the meatball mixture for 30 minutes to allow the chia seeds to work their gelling magic.

2. Preheat the oven to 400°F. Line a large baking sheet with parchment paper and set aside.

3. With damp hands, very gently roll heaping tablespoons of the chicken mixture into balls. (Try not to squeeze the meat too much, dudes. It will make the meatballs tough.) Arrange them on the prepared baking sheet, leaving a little bit of space between each one. You should have approximately 18 balls.

4. Transfer the meatballs to the preheated oven and bake for 20 minutes or until lightly browned and cooked through.

5. In a large skillet, whisk together the ingredients for the glaze. Bring it to a boil over medium-high heat and cook for about 1 minute or until it thickens slightly. Add the meatballs to the skillet and shake gently to coat them with the glaze. Serve warm.

1 pound ground chicken breast (If you can't find ground chicken, use 93 percent lean ground turkey.)

3 garlic cloves, grated or finely minced

1½ teaspoons peeled and grated fresh ginger

3 scallions, whites and light green parts only, finely chopped

¼ cup fresh cilantro leaves, finely chopped

1½ teaspoons low-sodium soy sauce

2 teaspoons dark sesame oil

2 tablespoons chia seeds

FOR THE GLAZE
3 tablespoons low-sodium soy sauce

Juice of ½ lime

1 tablespoon honey

1 tablespoon sriracha sauce (Spice babies may wish to only use ½ tablespoon.)

JUST THE TIP: CHIA SEEDS CAN BE USED AS A NUTRITIOUS BINDER IN ALMOST ANY RECIPE FOR MEATBALLS. JUST ADD 2 TABLESPOONS PER POUND OF MEAT.

cheesy Jalapeño Poppers

5 slices turkey bacon

12 large jalapeño peppers

½ cup cream cheese, softened

1¼ cups grated Monterey Jack cheese

⅓ cup minced yellow onion

¼ cup nonfat plain Greek yogurt

¼ cup fresh cilantro leaves, finely chopped

⅓ cup whole-wheat panko bread crumbs

¾ teaspoon smoked paprika

¼ teaspoon kosher salt

Traditional jalapeño poppers are a hot mess of saturated fat and calories, and crushing them at your game-day extravaganzas will most likely lead to you popping other things. Like buttons. And Zantac. Not so with these magical little nuggets, which serve up all the creamy, cheesy, "bacon-y" deliciousness you love without any of the gut-expanding consequences.

1. Cook the turkey bacon in a large skillet over medium heat until browned and crispy, about 4 to 5 minutes per side. Transfer to a paper towel–lined plate to cool, then finely chop into very small pieces.

2. Preheat the oven to 375°F. Line a large baking sheet with parchment paper.

3. Slice the jalapeños in half lengthwise. Using a small spoon, remove the seeds and membranes from each pepper. Place the cleaned peppers on the prepared baking sheet, leaving a little bit of space between each one.

4. WASH YOUR HANDS! I don't want you touching your eyes or any other body part after handling jalapeño seeds, dudes. Very risky.

5. In a medium bowl, combine the softened cream cheese, Monterey Jack, onion, yogurt, cilantro, and chopped, cooked turkey bacon. (If you like a spicy popper, feel free to stir some of your favorite hot sauce into the filling.)

6. In a small bowl, combine the panko, paprika, and salt.

7. Spoon about a tablespoon of filling into each jalapeño half, then sprinkle the panko mixture over your poppers.

8. Bake for 25 minutes or until the poppers are lightly browned and the cheese is bubbling. Serve immediately.

JUST THE TIP: TO SOFTEN CREAM CHEESE. LET IT SIT ON THE COUNTER FOR 20 TO 30 MINUTES. OR POP IT IN THE MICROWAVE FOR 10 TO 15 SECONDS.

BISON AND SWEET POTATO WAFFLE FRY SLIDERS WITH SPECIAL SAUCE

MAKES 22 sliders / SERVES 6

Bison meat is naturally leaner, cleaner, and more nutrient-dense than beef, making it a smart and delicious alternative for those who crave red meat on the reg. If you've never tried bison, these juicy sliders, sandwiched between crispy sweet potato "buns" and slathered in your new favorite special sauce, make quite the first impression. This shareable recipe was created with a party in mind (it yields 22 sliders), but feel free to halve it for more intimate game-day soirées.

1. Preheat the oven to 425°F.

2. Form the bison into 22 little patties, about 2 inches in diameter. Make a small indentation with your thumb in the center of each one. (This will keep the patties from puffing up into mini bison footballs as they cook.) Season generously on both sides with salt and pepper. Set aside.

3. Arrange your sweet potato fries on two large baking sheets in an even layer. Cook for 25 to 30 minutes, turning the fries over once halfway through the cooking time or until they're good and crispy.

4. Meanwhile, preheat a grill pan or large skillet over medium-high heat. (Please wait for it to get really hot, or your sliders won't cook properly!)

5. While the pan is warming up, place all the ingredients for the special sauce in a medium bowl and stir to combine. Briefly set that dankness aside.

6. Place your sliders on the hot pan, thumbprint side down, and cook for 2 to 3 minutes per side for medium. Transfer the burgers to a plate.

2 pounds ground bison

Kosher salt

Freshly ground black pepper

2 bags Alexia Waffle Cut Sweet Potato Seasoned Fries (You'll have a few extra fries leftover for snacking. I assume that's cool.)

FOR THE SPECIAL SAUCE
¼ cup nonfat plain Greek yogurt

2 tablespoons canola mayonnaise

3 tablespoons ketchup

1 tablespoon sriracha sauce

¼ teaspoon smoked paprika

5 tablespoons minced bread and butter pickles

1 garlic clove, grated or finely minced

7. Get ready to assemble your sliders! As soon as the waffle fries are done, set up an assembly line: waffle fries, burgers, special sauce. Place each burger on top of a waffle fry, add a dollop of special sauce, and top with a second fry. Feel free to use toothpicks to secure your sliders if you like. (Just a heads-up, waffle fries are like snowflakes, so your sliders won't all be uniform.) Serve warm.

JUST THE TIP: WHEN YOU DON'T FEEL LIKE SHELLING OUT FOR BISON. OR CAN'T FIND IT AT YOUR LOCAL MARKET. TRY MAKING THESE SLIDERS WITH LEAN GROUND BEEF. TURKEY. OR CHICKEN.

Boss Bean Dip

2 teaspoons extra-virgin olive oil

1 medium red onion, finely chopped

3 garlic cloves, minced

2 teaspoons smoked paprika

1 teaspoon ground cumin

¾ teaspoon kosher salt

2 medium tomatoes, chopped (or one 14.5 ounce can diced tomatoes, drained)

⅓ cup finely chopped pickled jalapeños

Two 16-ounce cans fat-free refried beans

⅓ cup nonfat plain Greek yogurt

1½ cups grated sharp cheddar cheese, divided

Juice of ½ lime

4 scallions, thinly sliced

FOR SERVING
Baked tortilla chips, brown rice crackers, or Chili-Lime Pita Chips (page 114)

Logan begged me to make a seven-layer bean dip for years, and before our first Thanksgiving together, he stooped so low as to claim that it was a family tradition to eat the dip while watching football (along with pigs in a blanket *and* dumplings). Wanting to respect the dude's holiday rituals, I called his mother for the recipe, only to discover that she had never made a seven-layer bean dip in her life. Shocker.

I refused to give in to Logan's request for obvious reasons, specifically the disturbing fat and calorie content of the multilayer monstrosity, but I did eventually come around to the idea of a more nutritionally balanced bean dip. This lightened up version incorporates all the best flavors of its layered inspiration (plus a blanket of bubbling cheese), but with far fewer scary ingredients. Touchdown, Dude Diet.

1. Heat the olive oil in a 12-inch ovenproof skillet over medium heat. When the oil is hot and shimmering, add the onion and garlic and cook for about 4 minutes or until the onion is soft and translucent. Stir in the paprika, cumin, and salt and cook for 1 minute to toast the spices, then add the tomatoes and pickled jalapenos. Cook for 2 minutes or until the tomatoes have softened slightly, then add the refried beans, yogurt, and ½ cup of the cheddar. Stir until everything is well combined. Turn off the heat and stir in the lime juice.

2. Preheat the broiler on high.

3. Sprinkle the remaining 1 cup cheddar on top of the bean dip in an even layer. Broil until the cheese is bubbling and lightly browned, 3 to 4 minutes.

4. Serve your bean dip warm topped with scallions. Like a boss.

JUST THE TIP: IF YOU DON'T HAVE AN OVENPROOF SKILLET, TRANSFER THE DIP TO A BAKING DISH BEFORE BROILING. YOU CAN ALSO DIVIDE THE DIP INTO TWO OR THREE SMALLER SKILLETS OR BAKING DISHES AND WARM THEM AS NEEDED. (IT'S ALWAYS A GOOD IDEA TO BRING OUT SOMETHING HOT DURING THE SECOND HALF.)

CHIPOTLE CHICKEN TAQUITOS

2 tablespoons extra-virgin olive oil, divided

½ medium yellow onion, finely chopped

1 garlic clove, minced

1 teaspoon ground cumin

One 8-ounce can tomato sauce (also labeled "tomato puree")

⅓ cup low-sodium chicken broth

1 chipotle pepper canned in adobo sauce, finely chopped

½ teaspoon honey

1 pound boneless, skinless chicken breasts

⅓ cup grated Monterey Jack cheese

¼ cup nonfat plain Greek yogurt

Fourteen 6-inch flour tortillas

FOR SERVING (OPTIONAL)
Hot sauce, such as Cholula

2 tablespoons chopped fresh cilantro leaves

Please be very careful when emerging from the kitchen with a plate of piping hot chicken taquitos. Overly excited dudes have a tendency to pounce on these things, and they rarely know their own strength.

1. Heat 1 tablespoon of the olive oil in a medium Dutch oven or sauté pan. When the oil is hot and shimmering, add the onion and garlic and cook for 4 to 5 minutes or until the onion is soft and translucent. Stir in the cumin and cook for 1 minute to toast the spice. Stir in the tomato sauce, chicken broth, chipotle pepper, and honey and bring to a boil. Lower the heat to a gentle simmer and add the chicken breasts. Turn the chicken breasts over in the sauce, so that all sides are coated, then cover with a lid and cook for 20 minutes.

2. Preheat the oven to 425°F. Line a large baking sheet with aluminum foil and coat with cooking spray. Set aside.

3. Remove the chicken from the sauce and place it on a cutting board. Shred the meat into small pieces with two forks, then return it to the Dutch oven. Cook for 2 to 3 minutes, stirring a few times or until most of the sauce has been absorbed. Turn off the heat and stir in the cheese and yogurt. (Flavor bomb filling complete!)

4. Lightly brush one side of each tortilla with the remaining 1 tablespoon olive oil. Spoon 2 tablespoons of the filling onto the bottom third of the un-oiled side of each tortilla. Roll up the taquitos tightly like cigars, and place them, seam side down, on the prepared baking sheet about an inch apart. Bake for 15 to 17 minutes or until the edges are nicely browned and crispy.

5. Pile the taquitos on a large serving plate. Drizzle with hot sauce and sprinkle generously with cilantro if you're feeling fancy.

> YOU DO YOU: I LIKE TO SERVE THESE WITH CHIPOTLE GUACAMOLE (PAGE 111) FOR DIPPING. BUT THEY'RE ALSO BOMB WITH AVOCADO SALSA VERDE (PAGE 157). CHIPOTLE CREMA (PAGE 121). AND PLAIN OLD GREEK YOGURT.

MAPLE-BOURBON ROASTED ALMONDS

SERVES 4—6

Generally speaking, nuts are an excellent snack. They're high in protein and good fats, and most are rich in disease-fighting antioxidants. However, nuts are also calorie-dense, especially the ones coated in crazy amounts of oil, salt, and sugar (i.e., "bar nuts"). Please stop eating them by the fistful and congratulating yourself on making healthy choices.

Since raw nuts are about as thrilling to many of you as diced tofu, I'm offering these roasted almonds as a sweet, bourbon-laced alternative. I recommend keeping a jar on hand at all times.

2 cups raw almonds

1½ teaspoons liquid extra-virgin coconut oil

3 tablespoons pure maple syrup

1 tablespoon bourbon

¾ teaspoon flaky sea salt, such as Maldon (Kosher salt will also work.)

1. Preheat the oven to 350°F. Line a large baking sheet with parchment paper.

2. Arrange the almonds in an even layer on the prepared baking sheet and roast for 6 to 7 minutes or until they're lightly toasted and fragrant.

3. In a medium bowl, whisk the coconut oil, maple syrup, and bourbon until well combined. Stir in the toasted almonds, making sure they're well coated.

4. Pour the almonds back onto the parchment-lined baking sheet, along with any extra syrup mixture, and spread them out in an even layer. Sprinkle with the salt. Roast for 13 to 15 minutes, stirring once halfway through the cooking time or until the nuts are a deep shade of brown, but not burnt. (Keep a close eye on them!)

5. Transfer the almonds to a clean baking sheet. Spread them in an even layer to keep them from clumping and let cool to room temperature. Be patient—they won't reach their maximum crunch potential until fully cooled.

6. Break up any rogue nuts that have stuck together and serve immediately, or store in an airtight container for future snack attacks.

> **YOU DO YOU:** WANT TO SPICE THINGS UP? ADD A DASH OF CAYENNE, FRESHLY GROUND BLACK PEPPER, OR CINNAMON TO THE MAPLE MIXTURE BEFORE COATING THE NUTS.

FIERY GINGER WINGS

3 pounds chicken wings

1 tablespoon light sesame oil

¾ teaspoon kosher salt

¼ teaspoon freshly ground black pepper

2 scallions, finely chopped

FOR THE SAUCE

½ cup nonalcoholic ginger beer

3 tablespoons honey

2 tablespoons low-sodium soy sauce

1 tablespoon plus 1 teaspoon sriracha sauce

2 garlic cloves, grated or finely minced

1 teaspoon cornstarch

Baked, not fried, and tossed in a sweet gingery sauce with a serious kick, these are The Dude Diet's answer to your chicken wing prayers. (Can I get an amen?) If you decide to double (or triple) the recipe for a large crew, consider separating the flats and drumettes and making the fiery ginger sauce up to a day in advance. Then all you'll have to do come party time is pop the wings in the oven, reheat the sauce, and field endless compliments on your finger food domination.

1. Preheat the oven to 400°F. Line two large baking sheets with aluminum foil. Spray 2 wire racks with cooking spray and place them on top of the prepared baking sheets. (Don't have wire racks? Don't panic. You can also cook your wings directly on the baking sheets. Just make sure to flip them over halfway through the cooking time.)

2. Start by prepping the chicken wings. Remove and discard the wing tips (just cut them off at the joint), then separate the wings into flats and drumettes. Don't be scared—it's actually pretty simple. Just bend each wing backwards at the joint until the bones separate, and then use your sharpest knife to cut between them.

3. Place the wings into a large bowl. Drizzle with sesame oil and sprinkle with salt and pepper. Toss to coat. Arrange the wings on the sprayed wire racks, leaving a little bit of space between each one. Bake for 45 minutes or until crispy and golden brown.

4. About 10 minutes before your wings are done, whisk together all the ingredients for the sauce in a medium bowl. Heat your largest skillet over medium-high heat. When hot, pour in the sauce and bring it to a boil. Lower to a simmer and cook for 4 to 5 minutes or until syrupy. Remove the skillet from the heat.

5. Transfer the cooked wings to the skillet with the sauce and toss to coat. Depending on the size of your pan, you may need to do this in two batches. (Tongs are very helpful here, dudes.)

6. Pile your wings on a large plate or platter. Drizzle with any extra sauce from the pan, sprinkle with chopped scallions, and serve warm.

YOU DO YOU: MORE OF A CHICKEN WING TRADITIONALIST? TOSS YOUR BAKED WINGS IN FRANK'S REDHOT BUFFALO WING SAUCE. IT PACKS A TON OF BUFFALO FLAVOR WITHOUT ANY ADDED BUTTER OR OIL. (FRANK IS A MAGICIAN.)

FIESTA BBQ CHICKEN NACHOS

Ever wondered what it's like to jog out onto a stadium field and be greeted by the deafening roar of your adoring fans? Try unveiling a tray of these nachos midway through a Super Bowl party. Same difference.

1. Start by cooking your chicken breasts. Dice those babies into small cubes and set aside.

2. Preheat the oven to 400°F. Line two large baking sheets with aluminum foil or parchment paper. (If you only have one baking sheet, cook your chips in two batches.)

3. Brush both sides of the tortillas with 1 tablespoon of the olive oil. Using a sharp knife or pizza cutter, slice the tortillas into three roughly equal strips, then slice each strip into 4 to 6 triangles. (You can also make rectangular chips if you like.) Arrange the tortilla pieces on the prepared baking sheets, making sure to leave a little bit of space between each one, and sprinkle with a little salt. Bake for 6 minutes or until lightly browned, then remove the chips from the oven, turn them over, and bake for another 2 to 3 minutes or until crispy. (Keep an eye on them, dudes, they burn quickly!) Set your chips aside.

4. Heat the remaining 1 teaspoon olive oil in a small sauté pan over medium-high heat. When the oil is hot and shimmering, add the corn kernels and a pinch of salt and pepper. Cook for 5 to 6 minutes or until tender and lightly browned.

5. Place the chicken and barbecue sauce in a bowl and toss to combine. (If your chicken is cold, microwave it for about 30 seconds to warm it up.)

6. Preheat the broiler on high.

1 recipe Idiotproof Chicken Breasts (page 257), diced

4 brown rice tortillas (I like Food for Life brand.)

1 tablespoon plus 1 teaspoon extra-virgin olive oil, divided

Kosher salt

¾ cup sweet corn kernels (from 1 ear of corn)

Freshly ground black pepper

½ cup barbecue sauce of your choice

6 ounces (about 1½ cups) grated Monterey Jack cheese

1 cup cherry tomatoes, quartered

¼ cup pickled jalapeños, chopped

½ cup minced red onion

3 scallions, thinly sliced

½ cup fresh cilantro leaves, finely chopped

Hot sauce of your choice

7. Spread the tortilla chips on a large rimmed baking sheet (or in a large oven-proof baking dish). Sprinkle with half the cheese, then add the corn, barbecue chicken, cherry tomatoes, and pickled jalapeños. Top with the remaining cheese and broil until the cheese has melted and is bubbling, 2 to 3 minutes.

8. Top your 'chos with minced red onion, scallions, and cilantro. Serve piping hot with your favorite hot sauce.

DUDE DIET PARTY MIX

Back in The Dude Diet's early days, I once caught Logan giddily wrapping up a combo of pretzels and bar nuts in slices of ham and eating them as a light snack. He claimed that he was making an "epic party mix in his mouth," before wondering aloud why no one had ever thought to put meat in traditional Chex mix. I couldn't get behind Logan's version of cold cut party mix from a nutritional (or practical) standpoint, but it did inspire the addition of diced beef jerky to this healthier version of the game-day classic.

1. Preheat the oven to 250°F. Line a large baking sheet with parchment paper. Set aside.

2. In a large bowl, combine the Rice Chex, Wheat Chex, pretzels, cashews, and almonds.

3. In a separate bowl, whisk the olive oil, Worcestershire sauce, hot sauce, paprika, onion powder, garlic powder, chili powder, salt, and sesame seeds.

4. Drizzle the spice mixture over the Chex mixture, and stir gently with a spatula until everything is evenly coated.

5. Spread out the snack mix on the prepared baking sheet in an even layer. Bake for 1 hour, stirring every 15 minutes, until the mix is dry and lightly browned. Remove from the oven and let cool completely. The snack mix will continue to crisp up as it cools. (Patience is a virtue, dudes.)

6. Toss the cooled snack mix with the jerky and serve.

JUST THE TIP: IF YOU PLAN TO STORE YOUR SNACK MIX, WAIT TO ADD THE JERKY UNTIL JUST BEFORE SERVING TO PREVENT SOGGINESS.

2 cups Rice Chex cereal

1 cup Wheat Chex cereal

2 cups spelt pretzels (Yes, you can use regular pretzels if you want.)

¾ cup raw cashews

¾ cup raw almonds

2 tablespoons extra-virgin olive oil

2 tablespoons Worcestershire sauce

1 teaspoon hot sauce of your choice

1½ teaspoons smoked paprika

½ teaspoon onion powder

½ teaspoon garlic powder

½ teaspoon chili powder

½ teaspoon fine-grain sea salt

1 tablespoon sesame seeds

2 ½ ounces (about ½ cup) chicken or turkey jerky, diced (I recommend barbecue- or teriyaki-flavored jerky, but you do you.)

SKIRT STEAK AND AVOCADO QUESADILLAS

SERVES 4

¾ pound skirt steak

1½ teaspoons smoked paprika

Kosher salt

Freshly ground black pepper

1 tablespoon extra-virgin olive oil

1 small red bell pepper, seeded and thinly sliced

1 small red onion, thinly sliced

½ teaspoon ground cumin

Juice of 1 lime, divided

1 ripe avocado

¼ cup fresh cilantro leaves, finely chopped

4 large (10- to 12-inch) whole-wheat tortillas

2 cups grated pepper Jack cheese

FOR SERVING (OPTIONAL)
Salsa of your choice

You can never go wrong with a 'dilla on game day, and this one's a show-stopper. Juicy grilled flank steak, zesty peppers and onions, and fiery pepper Jack are a winning team, but avocado is the all-star, adding an unexpected creamy element to each crispy, cheesy bite.

1. Preheat a lightly oiled grill or grill pan over medium-high heat.

2. Pat your steak dry and season it all over with the paprika, salt, and black pepper. Place the steak on the hot grill and cook for about 3 minutes per side for medium-rare. Transfer the steak to a cutting board and let it rest for a full 10 minutes before slicing it very thinly against the grain.

3. While the steak is resting, get going on the veggies. Heat the olive oil in a large sauté pan over medium heat. When hot, add the bell pepper, onion, cumin, a good pinch of salt, and a few cranks of black pepper. Cook for 10 minutes or until softened and lightly browned. Add half of the lime juice and cook for 30 seconds more. Remove the mixture from the heat.

4. Slice the avocado in half lengthwise, remove the pit, and scoop the flesh into a small bowl. Add a pinch of salt, the remaining lime juice, and the cilantro. Mash with a fork until relatively smooth.

5. Time to cook your quesadillas! Heat a large skillet over medium heat. When hot, add a tortilla to the pan and sprinkle the entire surface with ½ cup of the cheese. Add a quarter of the sliced steak and a quarter of the vegetable mixture to the bottom half of the tortilla and cook for 2 to 3 minutes or until the cheese has melted and the bottom of the tortilla is lightly browned. Spread a quarter of the avocado mash on top of the steak and veggies and fold the top half of the tortilla over to close the quesadilla. Cook for 30 more seconds, and then transfer to a cutting board. Repeat this process with the remaining quesadillas.

6. Slice each quesadilla into four triangles and serve with your favorite salsa.

chronic CHILI-CHEESE DOGS

Most dudes experience a range of emotions when eating a standard chili-cheese dog. There's giddy anticipation during the dog's construction, sheer bliss while demolishing it, and ultimately, extreme regret (and digestive issues) afterward. I'm pleased to report that these dogs, made with leaner, less-processed ingredients, deliver the thrill of their namesake without the unfortunate aftermath. That said, please exercise portion control—they're still chili-cheese dogs, people.

1. Start by making the chili. Heat the olive oil in a medium Dutch oven or sauté pan over medium heat. When the oil is hot and shimmering, add the onion and garlic and cook for about 4 minutes or until the onion is soft and translucent. Stir in the chili powder, paprika, cumin, salt, and cayenne and cook for 1 minute or until toasted and fragrant. Add the bison and cook for 5 minutes, stirring and breaking up the meat into very small pieces with a spatula or until no longer pink. Stir in the diced tomatoes, tomato puree, and Worcestershire sauce. Bring the chili to a boil, then lower to a gentle simmer and cook for 15 minutes or until thickened.

2. While the chili is simmering, heat a large skillet or grill pan over medium heat. Cut an x into the ends of each hot dog. (This will keep the casings from bursting and help the dogs crisp up.) Place the hot dogs in the hot pan and cook for 5 to 6 minutes, turning regularly or until they're heated through and lightly browned. (You can cook them a little longer if you dig a more charred dog.)

3. Nestle the hot dogs in the buns and smother with chili. Sprinkle each with cheddar cheese, and top with red onion and pickled jalapeños if you're feeling extra festive.

> YOU DO YOU: FEEL FREE TO SUB LEAN GROUND BEEF (PREFERABLY GRASS-FED) OR TURKEY FOR BISON IN YOUR CHILI.

2 teaspoons extra-virgin olive oil

1 small yellow onion, minced

1 large garlic clove, minced

1 tablespoon chili powder

2 teaspoons smoked paprika

½ teaspoon ground cumin

½ teaspoon kosher salt

¼ teaspoon cayenne pepper

12 ounces ground bison

One 14.5-ounce can diced fire-roasted tomatoes

1 cup tomato sauce

1 teaspoon Worcestershire sauce

Eight 100 percent beef or bison hot dogs

8 whole-grain hot dog buns

¾ cup grated sharp cheddar cheese

FOR SERVING (OPTIONAL)
½ small red onion, minced

½ cup chopped pickled jalapeños

CRISPY SPICED OVEN FRIES WITH SRIRACHUP

Swapping your greasy take-out fries for these spice-rubbed baked beauties is the easiest way to keep your Dude Dieting efforts on track this football season. Serve them with homemade spicy ketchup (aka Srirachup) for a truly transcendent dipping experience.

1. Preheat the oven to 425°F. Line two large baking sheets with parchment paper. Spray the parchment paper with cooking spray. (Do NOT skip this step, or your fries may stick to the paper.)

2. Slice the potatoes lengthwise into ¼-inch planks. Pat the planks dry with paper towels, then slice the planks lengthwise into ¼-inch-wide fries. (Just as a point of reference, you're aiming for McDonald's-size fries here, dudes.) Pat the fries dry a second time and place them in a large bowl.

3. Combine the salt and spices in a small bowl. Drizzle the fries with the olive oil and sprinkle with half of the spice mixture. Toss to coat.

4. Arrange the fries on the baking sheets in an even layer, making sure there's a little bit of space between each fry. (If you crowd them, they'll steam instead of getting nice and crisp.) Bake for 15 minutes. Remove the fries from the oven, and carefully flip them over with a spatula. Return to the oven and bake for 10 to 15 minutes more or until browned and crisp. (Keep a close eye on them during the last few minutes of the cooking time; they go from brown to burnt very quickly.)

5. Sprinkle the fries with the remaining spice mixture and toss to coat. Serve with Srirachup for dipping.

3 medium russet potatoes, scrubbed well

1 teaspoon kosher salt

1½ teaspoons smoked paprika

½ teaspoon freshly ground black pepper

¼ teaspoon ground cumin

Pinch of cayenne pepper (optional)

2 tablespoons extra-virgin olive oil

Srirachup (page 144)

Srirachup | MAKES 1½ CUPS

One 6-ounce can tomato paste
½ cup water
2 tablespoons sriracha sauce
2 tablespoons honey

1 tablespoon plus 1 teaspoon apple cider vinegar
¼ teaspoon kosher salt

1. Place all the ingredients in a small saucepan and whisk until smooth. Bring to a boil, then lower to a very gentle simmer and cook for 10 minutes, stirring periodically.

2. Let your Srirachup cool to room temperature. Transfer to an airtight container and refrigerate until ready to use.

CHAPTER 6

ON THE GRILL

Grilling is a simple and generally healthy way to prepare a wide variety of foods, and I'm a die-hard fan of cooking over an open flame. Because food cooks quickly on the high heat of the grill, it retains much of its natural moisture, which means that you don't need excess butter and oil to keep your proteins, vegetables, and fruits super juicy and flavorful. Grill grates also allow *some* of the existing fat in meat to drip away as it cooks—versus pooling in a pan or baking dish—decreasing the overall fat and calorie content of the cut(s) in question. Better still, grilling gives your favorite eats an amazing smoky flavor (not to mention sexy grill marks) and seriously cuts down on kitchen cleanup.

Based on these exciting facts, you'd think grilling season would be The Dude Diet's strongest quarter, right? Sadly, that is not the case.

I first realized the dangers of grilling season several years ago while grocery shopping with Logan for a midsummer barbecue we were hosting. He practically skipped through the aisles, filling our cart with kielbasa and other sausages, giant steaks, and pounds upon pounds of ground beef. After casually high-fiving random dudes at the checkout, all of whom had similarly meaty hauls, he loaded a second cart with Coors Light, squishy white buns, and family-size bags of potato chips. Not a lean protein, whole grain, or vegetable in sight. When we returned home, Logan removed his shirt, tied on an apron, and spent the next several hours lovingly tending to the aforementioned meats, occasionally (and unironically) asking if anyone wanted to taste his sausage.

This grilling scene has been replayed many times, and honestly, it poses some pretty serious health and safety hazards. Not only does eating red meat in excess raise cholesterol and contribute to heart disease, cancer, and diabetes, but Logan's proximity to an open flame also puts him at risk of singeing his plentiful chest hair. Worse, the meat sweats and a few six-packs on top of his naturally high summer perspiration levels make sudden death by dehydration a legitimate concern.

I wish I could write off Logan's grilling behavior as a unique case, but sadly he is not alone. Whether or not they share Logan's affinity for grilling shirtless, most dudes tend to prepare red meat–heavy feasts when exercising their grill master skills. This stops now.

First of all, dudes, a grill does not magically transform fatty cuts of beef and pork into slimming health food. As tempting as it may be to shotgun beers on the beach all day and then eat your weight in burgers and sausages, try to remember your long-term Dude Dieting goals. In order to keep your health and beach bod under control, you need to expand your grilling repertoire beyond the usual suspects and experiment with poultry, lean pork, fish, and vegetables. As you'll discover in this chapter, these awesome foods were practically made for the grill, and they'll do you a world of good on the nutrition front. And, should you decide to cook for guests, I guarantee they'll be blown away by your culinary creativity and dedication to clean eating. Plus, they won't leave with stomachaches.

P.S. When you do grill "man meats," portion control is crucial. Unless you are participating in a meat-eating competition, there is never an acceptable reason to crush a burger, steak, sausage, and ribs at the same time.

GRILLED MAHI MAHI WITH CITRUS-JALAPEÑO SALSA

SERVES 4

2 tablespoons tequila

Juice of 1 lime

1 tablespoon extra-virgin olive oil

2 garlic cloves, minced

½ teaspoon kosher salt

½ teaspoon freshly ground black pepper

Four 8-ounce mahi mahi fillets, skin removed

FOR THE SALSA
2 pink grapefruits

2 oranges

Juice of 1 lime

½ small red onion, minced

1 small jalapeño pepper, sliced very thinly into rings (If you're not a spice fan, seed the jalapeño or only use half.)

½ cup fresh cilantro leaves, finely chopped

Pinch of kosher salt

Pay attention, dudes! Fish is good for you, and you should be eating more of it. Not only is fish a low-fat, high-quality protein, it's also chock-full of omega-3 fatty acids, which are essential for a healthy brain and heart. According to the Mayo Clinic, eating 1 to 2 servings of fish a week could reduce your risk of dying from a heart attack by *more than a third*. FISH COULD SAVE YOUR LIFE.

Luckily, this grilled mahi mahi will get you all fired up about working more fish into your diet. Mahi mahi is a firm fish with a very mild (read: not "fishy") flavor, making it a great starter fish for seafood skeptics, and the bright, spicy citrus salsa is guaranteed to keep you coming back for more.

1. In a small bowl, combine the tequila, lime juice, olive oil, garlic, salt, and black pepper. Pat the mahi mahi fillets dry and place them in a large ziplock food storage bag. Pour in the marinade and seal the bag, removing as much air as possible. Gently squish the fillets around in the bag, making sure each one gets some of the marinade action. Let the fish marinate at room temperature for 20 minutes, turning the bag over once halfway through.

2. Meanwhile, whip up the salsa. First, you're going to need to segment the citrus. Using a sharp knife, carefully slice the top and bottom from the grapefruits. Slice the peel and white pith from all around the grapefruits. (Don't worry if it's not perfect, dudes.) Working over a medium bowl, cut between the membranes to release the grapefruit segments into the bowl. Repeat the peeling and segmenting process with the oranges. Remove the grapefruit and orange segments from the bowl and slice them crosswise into ½-inch pieces. Return all the citrus to the bowl and add the lime juice, red onion, jalapeño, cilantro, and salt. Gently stir to combine. Refrigerate the salsa until ready to use.

3. Preheat a grill (or grill pan) over medium-high heat. When hot, carefully remove the fillets from the bag and place each one on the

150 THE DUDE DIET

YOU DO YOU: IF YOU OR ONE OF YOUR DINING
PARTNERS IS FISH PHOBIC. I RECOMMEND GETTING
SOME GRILLED CORN TORTILLAS INVOLVED. EVERY-
THING GOES DOWN BETTER AS A TACO.

grill with the more rounded side facing up. Cook for 5 minutes, undisturbed. (If you try to move the fish too early, it will stick to the grill, dudes!) Gently turn them over and cook them for 4 to 5 minutes on the opposite sides or until firm to the touch.

4. Serve each fillet topped with a generous amount of salsa.

KNOWLEDGE BOMB: CHICKEN AND TURKEY SAUSAGES HAVE A FRACTION OF THE CALORIES AND FAT OF THEIR PORK AND BEEF COUNTERPARTS. AND THANKS TO THE MANY AVAILABLE VARIETIES, YOU DON'T HAVE TO COMPROMISE ON FLAVOR. PLEASE CHOOSE A MINIMALLY PROCESSED BRAND (I.E., MAKE SURE YOU CAN PRONOUNCE MOST OF THE INGREDIENTS ON THE PACKAGE) FOR ALL FUTURE SAUSAGE FESTS.

GRILLED CHICKEN SAUSAGE WITH SUMMER SUCCOTASH

Every June, Logan and I attend The Big Apple Barbecue Block Party in our 'hood. The dude looks forward to this meaty extravaganza with the type of extreme enthusiasm most people reserve for puppies, Christmas, or the birth of their first child, and when it finally rolls around, he goes hog wild. Literally. Every type of BBQ pork and beef is consumed, but he gets particularly high on sausages, feeling a "moral obligation" to try as many varieties as humanly possible. It's all saucy fun and boozy games until things inevitably take a dark turn around 4:00 P.M., when Logan starts making dying animal sounds, begging for a belly rub, and swearing off sausage for life.

The ban only lasts a few weeks before his sausage cravings return, but the memory of post–Block Party pain is usually fresh enough for Logan to embrace the lean chicken variety. This swap is hardly a sacrifice, since chicken sausage is bomb—especially when it's butterflied, lightly charred, and served with a mountain of smoky summer succotash.

1. Heat the olive oil in a large skillet over medium-high heat. When the oil is hot and shimmering, add the onion, corn kernels, zucchini, bell pepper, garlic, and salt. Cook for 8 to 9 minutes or until the vegetables are tender (but not mushy!) and lightly browned in spots. Stir in the paprika and black pepper and cook for 1 minute more to bring out the paprika's flavor. Add the edamame, cherry tomatoes, and hot sauce and cook for 2 to 3 minutes or until the edamame has thawed completely and the tomatoes have slightly softened. Keep warm over very low heat until ready to serve.

2. Heat a grill (or grill pan) over medium heat. Butterfly your sausages by slicing them almost in half lengthwise, leaving one side intact. (You want them to be able to lie flat, dudes.) Cook the sausages for 4 to 5 minutes on each side or until heated through with some sexy grill marks.

3. Transfer the sausages to plates or a platter and smother with warm succotash.

6 links chicken sausage (I like Aidells Chorizo Smoked Chicken Sausage for this.)

FOR THE SUCCOTASH

2 tablespoons extra-virgin olive oil

½ medium Vidalia onion, finely chopped

1½ cups sweet corn kernels (from 2 ears of corn)

1 medium zucchini, diced

1 red bell pepper, seeded and diced

2 garlic cloves, minced

1 teaspoon kosher salt

1 teaspoon smoked paprika

¼ teaspoon freshly ground black pepper

1 cup frozen shelled edamame

8 ounces cherry tomatoes, halved

1 teaspoon hot sauce of your choice

GRILLED TUNA SANDWICHES WITH HERBED AVOCADO SAUCE AND HOISIN

SERVES 4

Four 6-ounce tuna steaks, about 1 inch thick

Juice of 1 lemon

Juice of 1 lime

3 garlic cloves, minced

2 scallions, thinly sliced

½ jalapeño pepper, thinly sliced into rounds

¼ cup low-sodium soy sauce

Freshly ground black pepper

1 red onion, sliced into ¼-inch-thick rounds

1 teaspoon extra-virgin olive oil

4 whole-grain buns

⅓ English cucumber (aka seedless cucumber), thinly sliced into rounds

1⅓ cups alfalfa sprouts

¼ cup hoisin sauce

The crazy amount of flavor and texture in these powerhouse sandwiches is tough to describe, but one taste-testing dude summed it up quite nicely when he said, "Sweet baby Jesus! It's like a million tiny angel kisses on my tongue!" Don't let the number of ingredients scare you—a lot of them should already be kicking around in your kitchen, and hoisin is readily available in the Asian section of your local market.

1. Pat the tuna steaks dry and place them in a large ziplock food storage bag. In a small bowl, whisk together the lemon juice, lime juice, garlic, scallions, jalapeño, and soy sauce. Pour the marinade over the fish and seal the bag, removing as much air as possible. Marinate at room temperature for 30 minutes, turning the bag over once halfway through.

2. Meanwhile, get going on the herbed avocado sauce. Place the avocado in a food processor (or high-speed blender) and pulse a few times until it's relatively smooth. Add the cilantro, scallions, garlic, yogurt, lemon juice, salt, and black pepper. Process until completely smooth. With the motor running, drizzle in the olive oil and process for 15 to 20 seconds or until well incorporated. Transfer the dressing to a bowl, cover tightly with plastic wrap, and refrigerate until ready to use.

3. Preheat a lightly oiled grill (or grill pan) over high heat.

4. Remove your tuna steaks from the marinade and pat them dry, making sure to remove any rogue pieces of garlic or scallions from the fish. (Discard the marinade.) Season both sides of each steak with a little black pepper. Grill the tuna for 2 minutes on each side. Transfer to a plate and let rest for 5 to 10 minutes. (Be careful not to overcook your tuna, dudes! You want to keep the fish tender with a raw, pink center.)

1 medium-size ripe
avocado, pitted,
peeled, and diced

⅓ packed cup fresh
cilantro leaves

2 scallions, roughly
chopped

1 garlic clove,
chopped

2 tablespoons nonfat
plain yogurt

2 tablespoons fresh
lemon juice

½ teaspoon kosher
salt

¼ teaspoon freshly
ground black pepper

1 tablespoon extra-
virgin olive oil

5. Brush your onion rounds with the olive oil. Grill for 2 to 3 minutes per side until soft and lightly charred. Toss the buns on the grill, cut side down, for about 1 minute until grill marks appear.

6. Assembly time! Spread both halves of each bun with a generous amount of the herbed avocado sauce. Place a tuna steak on the bottom bun, and top with a few cucumber slices, a grilled onion round, and a pile of sprouts. Drizzle with a tablespoon of hoisin sauce, then sandwich everything together.

JUST THE TIP: THIS RECIPE MAKES ABOUT 2 CUPS OF SALSA VERDE. WHICH IS MORE THAN ENOUGH FOR THE STEAK. DRIZZLE ANY LEFTOVER SAUCE ON CHIPOTLE CHICKEN BURRITO BOWLS (PAGE 211). OR USE IT AS A SALAD DRESSING. SANDWICH SPREAD. OR DIP.

GRILLED FLANK STEAK WITH AVOCADO SALSA VERDE

SERVES 4

On days when nothing but a beefy grill sesh will do, throw this marinated flank steak on the grates. Flank steak is a super-flavorful and relatively lean cut of meat that's amazingly tender when thinly sliced across the grain. Topped with antioxidant-rich salsa verde and served with the sexy side of your choice (I recommend the Southwestern Sweet Potato Salad on page 230), it's a smarter steak dinner that makes it easy to stay on the Dude Diet path.

1. In a small bowl, combine the lime juice, olive oil, garlic, and cumin. Place the flank steak in a large ziplock food storage bag, and pour in the marinade. Seal the bag, removing as much air as possible, and gently squish the steak around in the bag to make sure it's nicely coated. Marinate for 20 minutes at room temperature.

2. Meanwhile, get to work on the salsa. Preheat your broiler on high. Remove the husks from your tomatillos and rinse them well under warm water until their skins are no longer sticky. Cut each tomatillo in half crosswise, and place them on an aluminum foil–lined baking sheet. Broil for 4 to 5 minutes, flip them over, and broil for another 4 minutes until softened and charred in spots. Transfer the tomatillos to a food processor or high-speed blender, and add the remaining ingredients for the salsa verde. Process until nice and smooth. Transfer the salsa verde to a bowl and refrigerate until ready to use.

3. Preheat a grill (or grill pan) over medium-high heat. Pat the steak dry and season both sides generously with salt and black pepper.

4. Grill the steak for 5 to 6 minutes per side for medium-rare. Transfer to a cutting board and let the steak rest for a full 10 minutes to allow the juices to redistribute.

5. Using a sharp knife, thinly slice the steak across the grain. Serve with the chilled avocado salsa verde.

Juice of 2 limes

2 tablespoons extra-virgin olive oil

3 garlic cloves, peeled and smashed

½ teaspoon ground cumin

One 1½-pound flank steak

Kosher salt

Freshly ground black pepper

FOR THE AVOCADO SALSA VERDE

3 medium tomatillos (For tips on picking tomatillos, see sidebar on page 113.)

½ small jalapeño, chopped

2 garlic cloves

½ ripe avocado, pitted and peeled

¼ packed cup fresh cilantro leaves

1 tablespoon fresh lime juice

¼ teaspoon kosher salt

LAMB AND FETA BURGERS WITH MINT TAHINI SAUCE

1½ pounds 85 percent lean ground lamb (preferably grass-fed)

⅔ cup finely crumbled feta cheese

¼ cup minced shallot

¼ cup finely chopped fresh flat-leaf parsley

¾ teaspoon kosher salt

¾ teaspoon crushed red pepper flakes

1 large tomato, sliced into rounds

2 large whole-wheat pitas with pockets

2 cups arugula

FOR THE SAUCE
3 tablespoons tahini

2 tablespoons water

2 tablespoons nonfat plain Greek yogurt

2 tablespoons fresh lemon juice

2 tablespoons finely chopped fresh mint leaves

¼ teaspoon kosher salt

Grilled to juicy perfection, studded with creamy feta, and nestled in a warm pita with tomatoes, arugula, and refreshing tahini sauce, this burger will slap you in the face with its layers of epic deliciousness. The recipe scales easily for a crowd, so keep it in mind for warm weather entertaining. You can prep the patties and sauce in advance, leaving you free to practice your pool tricks and compete in boozy lawn games with your guests (or whatever sophisticated activities you happen to enjoy at your summer get-togethers).

1. Start by making the sauce. In a small bowl, whisk the tahini and water until it's completely smooth. Add the remaining ingredients, and whisk to combine. Cover and refrigerate the sauce until ready to use.

2. Preheat a grill (or grill pan) over medium-high heat.

3. Place the lamb, feta, shallot, parsley, salt, and red pepper flakes in a medium bowl. Using your hands, mix the ingredients together until everything is well incorporated. (Be gentle, dudes! Squeezing the meat too hard or overmixing will lead to dense burgers.) Mold the meat into four 1-inch-thick oval patties. (The oval shape will help them fit better in the pita pockets.) Make a small indent with your thumb in the center of each burger to keep it from puffing up on the grill.

4. Place the burgers on the grill, thumbprint side down, and cook for about 4 minutes per side for a medium burger. Remove the burgers from the grill and let them rest for 5 minutes.

5. Meanwhile, toss the pitas on the grill for a minute or two until they're nice and warm.

6. Slice the pitas in half. Nestle each burger inside a pita half. Top each with a slice (or two) of tomato, and add ½ cup of the arugula. Drizzle generously with Mint Tahini Sauce and serve immediately.

YOU DO YOU: IF YOU'RE NOT INTO THE IDEA OF A GIANT LAMB BURGER. FORM SMALLER PATTIES AND SERVE THEM AS SLIDERS. OR ADD THEM TO SALADS. GRAIN BOWLS. AND LETTUCE WRAPS.

KNOWLEDGE BOMB: OUNCE FOR OUNCE. PORK LOIN HAS LESS FAT THAN CHICKEN BREAST. PORK ALSO CONTAINS MORE B VITAMINS. WHICH HELP IMPROVE METABOLISM AND INCREASE ENERGY PRODUCTION. THAN MOST OTHER TYPES OF MEAT.

Fiery Pork AND Pineapple Skewers

MAKES **6 skewers**

If you're into sweet and savory flavor combos, the awesomeness of spicy citrus-spiked pork tenderloin nestled between chunks of juicy, caramelized pineapple and red onion is guaranteed to rock your world. Serve the skewers with a side of Vegetable Soba Noodles with Peanut Sauce (see page 238) when you're looking to turn the party on a stick into a full-blown rager.

1. If you're using bamboo skewers, soak them in a baking dish filled with water for at least 30 minutes. (If you skip this step, the skewers will catch fire on the grill, and that will suck.)

2. In a small bowl, combine the lime zest, lime juice, soy sauce, sriracha sauce, sesame oil, ginger, and garlic.

3. Place the cubed pork tenderloin in a large ziplock food storage bag and pour in the marinade. Seal the bag, removing as much air as possible, and gently squish the pork so that every piece gets coated in marinade. Refrigerate for at least 45 minutes and up to overnight. Preheat a lightly oiled grill over medium heat.

4. Thread each skewer with a cube of marinated pork. Add a square of onion (2 to 3 layers thick), and a cube of pineapple. Add a second cube of pork, a second square of onion, a second cube of pineapple, and a third cube of pork. (That's 7 items per skewer, dudes.)

5. Place the skewers on the grill and cook for 9 to 10 minutes, turning once or twice during the cooking time or until the pork is cooked through (aim for a very light pink center) and the pineapple is soft and caramelized. If things start to burn, don't panic. Just move the skewers to a slightly cooler part of the grill.

6. Transfer the skewers to a serving plate. Drizzle with extra sriracha (for a more serious kick) and sprinkle with scallions. Serve warm.

12 to 14 metal or bamboo skewers (If using bamboo skewers, you may want to use 2 skewers per kebab for stability.)

Finely grated zest and juice of 2 limes

¼ cup low-sodium soy sauce

2½ tablespoons sriracha sauce

2 teaspoons dark sesame oil

2 teaspoons peeled and grated fresh ginger

4 garlic cloves, peeled and smashed

2 pounds pork tenderloin, cut into 1½-inch cubes

1 medium red onion, diced into roughly 1½-inch pieces

1 pineapple, peeled, cored, and chopped into 1½-inch cubes (about 4 cups cubed pineapple)

FOR SERVING (OPTIONAL)
Sriracha sauce

4 scallions, thinly sliced

GRILLED CHICKEN PAILLARD
WITH AVOCADO, CORN, AND CHERRY TOMATO RELISH

Juice of 2 lemons

¼ cup extra-virgin olive oil

1 shallot, minced

4 garlic cloves, sliced

2 teaspoons crushed red pepper flakes

Four 8-ounce boneless, skinless chicken breasts

Kosher salt

FOR THE RELISH

2 teaspoons extra-virgin olive oil

¾ cup sweet corn kernels (from 1 ear of corn)

1 cup cherry tomatoes, halved from pole to pole (or quartered if your tomatoes are on the large side)

1 ripe avocado, pitted, peeled, and diced

8 fresh basil leaves, chopped

Juice of ½ lemon

¼ teaspoon freshly ground black pepper

Kosher salt

*P*aillard is the fancy French term for a piece of meat that's been pounded thin, and it's high up on the list of idiotproof cooking techniques. Not only is pounding a chicken breast surprisingly fun, it also tenderizes the meat and thins it to a point that it cooks quickly on the grill without drying out. A short soak in a spicy, lemon-based marinade gives this particular paillard a major boost, but it's the cooling, summery relish that really knocks it out of the park.

1. In a small bowl, whisk together the lemon juice, olive oil, shallot, garlic, and red pepper flakes in a small bowl. Set aside.

2. One at a time, place each chicken breast between two pieces of plastic wrap. Using the bottom of a skillet, pound the chicken to a ¼-inch thickness. (Don't get too crazy, dudes. You don't want to tear the meat.)

3. Place the pounded chicken breasts in a large ziplock food storage bag, and add the marinade. Seal the bag, removing as much air as possible, and gently squish the chicken around so each breast gets coated in the marinade. Refrigerate for 20 to 25 minutes.

4. Meanwhile, get going on the relish. Heat the olive oil in a small skillet over medium heat. When hot, add the corn kernels and cook for about 5 minutes, stirring periodically or until tender and lightly browned. Transfer the corn to a medium bowl and let cool to room temperature.

5. Once the corn has cooled, add the cherry tomatoes, avocado, basil, lemon juice, and pepper to the bowl and gently mix to combine. Season with salt to taste. (Resist the urge to eat all of the relish with a spoon.) Cover and refrigerate while you grill the chicken.

6. Preheat a grill (or grill pan) over medium-high heat. Remove the chicken from the marinade, shaking off any excess, and season the breasts on both sides with kosher salt. Place the chicken on the hot grill and cook for 3 to 4 minutes per side or until cooked through.

7. Serve the chicken warm or at room temperature topped with relish.

YOU DO YOU: IF YOU HAVE A SHELL-FISH ALLERGY OR SIMPLY DON'T DO SHRIMP. TRY THIS RECIPE WITH SALMON OR FIRM WHITE FISH CUT INTO ROUGHLY 1½-INCH CUBES. JUST INCREASE THE COOKING TIME BY A MINUTE OR TWO PER SIDE.

LEMON-HERB SHRIMP

Despite their tiny size, shrimp boast plenty of brain-enhancing omega-3s, as well as high levels of the powerful antioxidant astaxanthin, which promotes healthy, glowing skin; and copper, which helps prevent hair loss and thickens your existing hair. In layman's terms, getting down with these tasty (and shockingly low-cal) marinated shrimp skewers will make you smarter and better-looking. Fact.

1. If you're using bamboo skewers, make sure to soak them in a shallow baking dish filled with water for at least 30 minutes to prevent them from catching fire on the grill. Do NOT skip this step.

2. In a medium bowl, whisk together the garlic, lemon juice, olive oil, salt, and red pepper flakes. Stir in two-thirds of the chopped basil and cilantro. Transfer the remaining herbs to a small bowl, cover them with a damp paper towel, and refrigerate until ready to use.

3. Place the shrimp in a large ziplock food storage bag and pour in the marinade. Seal the bag, removing as much air as humanly possible, and gently squish the shrimp around to make sure they all get coated in herby goodness. Refrigerate for 30 minutes.

4. Preheat a grill (or grill pan) over medium-high heat.

5. Remove the shrimp from the marinade, and thread 4 shrimp onto each skewer. (You want the skewer to pierce each shrimp twice, once just above the tail shell and once near the head, to form a tight C-shape.)

6. Place the skewers on the hot grill and cook for 1½ to 2 minutes per side until the shrimp are pink and opaque throughout. Be very careful not to overcook them!

7. Transfer the skewers to a large serving plate and sprinkle with the reserved herbs. Serve warm or at room temperature.

12 metal or bamboo skewers

4 garlic cloves, minced

Juice of 2 lemons

3 tablespoons extra-virgin olive oil

1¼ teaspoons kosher salt

¼ teaspoon crushed red pepper flakes

⅔ cup fresh basil leaves, finely chopped

⅔ cup fresh cilantro leaves, finely chopped

2 pounds large shrimp, peeled and deveined with the tail shells still on (You can find them at pretty much any supermarket fish counter.)

ON THE GRILL **165**

GRILLED VEGETABLES WITH GOAT CHEESE AND BALSAMIC

4 tablespoons extra-virgin olive oil, divided

1 tablespoon balsamic vinegar

1 garlic clove, grated or finely minced

Kosher salt

2 large zucchini, halved crosswise, then sliced lengthwise into ¼-inch planks

2 yellow squash, sliced lengthwise into ¼-inch planks

2 red bell peppers, seeded and quartered

½ bunch asparagus, woody ends removed

Freshly ground black pepper

½ cup fresh flat-leaf parsley leaves, finely chopped

3 ounces goat cheese, crumbled

If you thought you'd never lose your cool over a vegetable platter, think again, dudes. This multicolored stunner absolutely slays on the flavor and nutrition fronts—I'm talking vitamins, minerals, and disease-fighting antioxidants out the wazoo—and it's so simple that even grilling noobs will be able to nail it. Serve it with your favorite meat or fish, and try not to let all the compliments go to your head.

1. Preheat a lightly oiled grill (or grill pan) over medium-high heat. (If you have a grill basket, feel free to use it.)

2. In a small bowl whisk together 2 tablespoons of olive oil, the balsamic vinegar, garlic, and a pinch of kosher salt. Set the vinaigrette aside until ready to use.

3. Brush the vegetables all over with the remaining 2 tablespoons olive oil, and season them with plenty of kosher salt and black pepper.

4. Place the vegetables on the hot grill and let them cook until they're tender (but not mushy!) and have developed sexy grill marks. The veggies will have slightly different cooking times, so pay attention: 5 minutes for the asparagus (turn them every 1 to 2 minutes); 7 to 8 minutes for the zucchini and squash (3 to 4 minutes per side); and 8 to 10 minutes for the bell peppers (4 to 5 minutes per side). Please use tongs to avoid unnecessary grilling accidents.

5. Transfer the grilled vegetables to a large plate or serving platter. Drizzle with the vinaigrette, and top with parsley and crumbled goat cheese. Serve warm or at room temperature.

YOU DO YOU: THESE VEGGIES ARE GREAT AS A SIDE DISH. BUT YOU CAN ALSO SANDWICH THEM BETWEEN SLICES OF WHOLE-GRAIN BREAD. OR DOUBLE THE BALSAMIC VINAIGRETTE AND SERVE THEM OVER SALAD.

GRILLED PORK CHOPS WITH ASIAN CUCUMBER SALAD

SERVES 4

Fall off the Dude Diet wagon? It happens. A juicy grilled pork chop with crunchy, tangy cucumber salad is just the thing to help you climb right back on. You'll love the explosion of Asian flavors, and the clean, protein-packed nature of this meal will leave you feeling instantly lighter and tighter. Serve it over chilled quinoa or brown rice for a whole-grain boost.

1. Place the salt, sugar, red pepper flakes, garlic, and ginger in a small saucepan with 1 cup of the water and bring to a boil. Lower to a simmer and cook for 5 minutes, swirling the saucepan occasionally or until the salt and sugar have dissolved completely. Pour the mixture into a small baking dish and stir in the remaining 2 cups cold water and ice. At this point it should be room temperature or cool. (Congratulations, dudes, you just made a brine!)

2. Poke the chops all over with a fork to help them absorb the brine. (No need to go crazy, 4 to 5 pokes per chop should do it.) Submerge the chops in the brine and cover the dish with plastic wrap. Refrigerate for 30 minutes.

3. While your chops are brining, get going on the salad. In a medium bowl, whisk together the rice vinegar, soy sauce, honey, sesame oil, red pepper, and garlic. Set aside.

4. Peel your cucumbers and slice them in half lengthwise. Using a teaspoon, scoop out the seeds from each half and discard. Thinly slice the seeded cucumbers crosswise into half-moons. Place them between two layers of paper towels and pat them dry.

5. Add the cucumbers, carrot, red onion, and cilantro to the bowl with the dressing. Toss to coat. Cover and refrigerate for at least 15 minutes to let those kick-ass flavors mingle.

6. Preheat a grill (or grill pan) over medium-high heat.

3 tablespoons kosher salt

2 tablespoons pure cane sugar

2 teaspoons crushed red pepper flakes

4 garlic cloves, peeled and smashed

One 1-inch piece fresh ginger, peeled and thinly sliced

3 cups cold water, divided

1 cup ice

Four 8-ounce boneless pork loin chops, about 1 inch thick

FOR THE SALAD
¼ cup unseasoned rice vinegar

1 tablespoon low-sodium soy sauce

1 tablespoon honey

2 teaspoons toasted sesame oil

1 teaspoon crushed red pepper flakes

1 garlic clove, grated or finely minced

2 medium English cucumbers (aka seedless cucumbers)

(cont.)

1 medium carrot, shaved into ribbons with a vegetable peeler

½ small red onion, very thinly sliced

2 tablespoons finely chopped cilantro leaves

7. Remove the pork chops from the brine and pat them dry. (Do NOT season them with extra salt—they're already salty from the brine.) Place the chops on the hot grill and cook for about 5 minutes on each side, or until they reach an internal temperature of 140°F. (If you don't have a thermometer, don't panic. The chops are done when they feel firm to the touch, but not rock hard.) Transfer the chops to a cutting board. Let them rest for 5 minutes to allow the juices to redistribute.

8. Thinly slice the chops and serve over the Asian Cucumber Salad. Make sure to drizzle any remaining dressing from the salad bowl on top of the meat.

> JUST THE TIP: BRINING IS THE PROCESS OF SUBMERGING A CUT OF MEAT IN A SALTED WATER MIXTURE TO GIVE IT FLAVOR AND HELP KEEP IT JUICY AS IT COOKS. IT'S MOST EFFECTIVE ON LEAN CUTS OF MEAT THAT TEND TO DRY OUT QUICKLY.

CHIPOTLE STREET CORN

Logan is non-discriminatory in his love of street food, but he does have a special soft spot for Mexican, particularly when it comes to Mexican grilled corn, which he considers a healthy snack. (You know, because "corn is a vegetable.") Since corn is actually a grain, and traditional *elote* is smothered in mayonnaise or sour cream (or both) and then rolled in cheese, Logan's nutritional assessment of the street food favorite is slightly flawed. This version, brushed with a smoky, yogurt-based sauce and sprinkled with a responsible amount of Cotija, is a slimmed-down re-creation of the original. Think of it as the ultimate summer snack or side for all your shirtless grilling adventures. *De nada.*

1. Preheat a lightly oiled grill (or grill pan) over medium-high heat.

2. In a small bowl, combine the yogurt, mayonnaise, garlic, chipotle pepper, adobo sauce, and salt. Set aside.

3. Place the ears of corn directly on the hot grill. Cook for 8 to 10 minutes, rotating the corn every 2 to 3 minutes or until tender and lightly charred in spots.

4. Brush each ear of corn all over with the chipotle sauce and sprinkle with cheese and cilantro. Serve with lime wedges for a little extra zip.

Ingredients

⅓ cup nonfat plain yogurt

3 tablespoons canola mayonnaise

1 garlic clove, grated or finely minced

1 chipotle pepper canned in adobo sauce, minced

½ teaspoon adobo sauce from the chipotle can

¼ teaspoon kosher salt

6 ears sweet corn, shucked

⅓ cup finely crumbled Cotija cheese (Feta also works.)

2 tablespoons finely chopped fresh cilantro

1 lime, cut into wedges

> **KNOWLEDGE BOMB:** WHEN IT COMES TO CONDIMENTS. MAYONNAISE IS BY FAR THE MOST DANGEROUS. AND A SINGLE TABLESPOON WILL SET YOU BACK OVER 100 CALORIES AND 12 GRAMS OF FAT. PLEASE BE MINDFUL OF YOUR CONSUMPTION. AND WHEN POSSIBLE SWITCH TO A CANOLA- OR OLIVE OIL-BASED VARIETY. THE FAT AND CALORIE CONTENTS ARE THE SAME. BUT THESE OILS ARE AT LEAST HEALTHIER FOR YOUR HEART THAN THE SOYBEAN OIL USED IN REGULAR MAYO.

CHAPTER

SERIOUS SALADS

There are two things to keep in mind when it comes to building a Dude Diet–friendly relationship with salad. First and foremost, salads are the easiest way to knock out several servings of fruits and vegetables, and you should be eating more of them. Eating a side salad with your pizza once or twice a month isn't going to cut it. (And, no, the lettuce, tomato, and onion on your burgers do not count.) Second, you need to ensure that the salads you do eat are in fact nutritious. To be clear, the terms "salad" and "health food" are not synonymous, especially when the former contains various fried foods, candied nuts, and obscene amounts of cheese and dressing. To avoid any confusion, please internalize the following Dude Diet salad rules.

The Dude Diet Salad Guidelines

- **A SALAD SHOULD NOT CONTAIN ANYTHING FRIED.** Chicken fingers, onion rings, tortilla chips, and other deep-fried items do not become healthy simply because they are briefly in contact with lettuce.

- **ICEBERG LETTUCE IS THE SADDEST OF SALAD BASES.** The purpose of eating a salad is to consume as many nutrients as possible in a single sitting, and iceberg contains only a fraction of the vitamins and minerals found in other leafy greens. There's a world of lettuce options out there, dudes. Find a new favorite.

- **COOL IT ON THE CHEESE.** A sprinkling is fine, a block of cheddar is not.

- **DITCH THE CROUTONS.** You are literally putting buttered bread in your salad. Stop it.

- **LIMIT NUTS AND DRIED FRUIT.** Raw nuts are good for you, but they are also calorie-dense, so don't go dumping them on your salad with reckless abandon. Ditto when it comes to dried fruit, which is also loaded with sugar.

- **DIAL BACK THE DRESSING.** The purpose of dressing is to add moisture to your salad and highlight the already delicious flavors of the fresh ingredients—there's no need to use a gallon of the stuff. Creamy dressings like ranch and blue cheese are especially high in fat and calories, and they should be limited to special occasions and No-Calorie Sunday.

Devastated by these rules? Keep your (increasingly chiseled) chin up. Salads can be delicious without any of the gut-busting additions, and there are some seriously chronic combinations to be made. I know the odds are stacked against me when it comes to getting the dude community psyched about eating more greens, but the recipes in this chapter may just achieve the impossible. After all, Logan loved each and every one of the following creations. Coming from a dude who once claimed he'd "rather light his hair on fire and run around than eat a stupid salad," that's saying a lot . . .

BUFFALO CHICKEN salad

1 recipe Idiotproof
Chicken Breasts
(page 257), diced

⅓ cup Frank's
RedHot Buffalo
Wing Sauce

6 cups chopped
romaine hearts

2 ribs celery, thinly
sliced into half-
moons

1 cup shredded
carrots

¼ medium red
onion, thinly sliced

2 ounces crumbled
blue cheese

FOR THE DRESSING
½ cup nonfat plain
Greek yogurt

2 tablespoons extra-
virgin olive oil

½ teaspoon onion
powder

¼ teaspoon garlic
powder

¼ teaspoon kosher
salt

¼ teaspoon honey

⅛ teaspoon ground
cumin

If you've ever wondered why your Buffalo chicken salad habit has yet to reveal a set of washboard abs, the answer is simple. Your "salad" is actually an order of fried chicken fingers tossed with multiple servings of cheese and a vat of fatty dressing. (The handful of lettuce involved doesn't come close to redeeming the nutritional shitshow.) Clean up your act with this lighter spin on the dude community's go-to "greens." The streamlined recipe delivers the fiery blast of flavors you love along with an impressive list of nutrition benefits, and it won't set you back more than 25 minutes, tops. So grab your Frank's and get busy.

1. Place the diced chicken breasts in a bowl and add the wing sauce. Toss to coat. Cover and keep warm until ready to use.

2. In a small bowl, whisk together all the ingredients for the dressing. (The dressing can be made up to 2 days in advance and stored in an airtight container in the refrigerator.)

3. In a large bowl, combine the romaine, celery, carrots, and red onion. Add the dressing and toss to coat. (If you like a more lightly dressed salad, add the dressing little by little, tossing between each addition, until you reach your personal sweet spot. Save any leftovers for another salad, or use it as a dip for vegetables.)

4. Divide the salad between two large bowls or plates. Top each salad with half of the buffalo chicken and sprinkle with crumbled blue cheese. Go to town.

JUST THE TIP: FRANK'S REDHOT BUFFALO WING SAUCE IS THICKER AND LESS SPICY THAN THE ORIGINAL FRANK'S REDHOT CAYENNE PEPPER SAUCE. IF YOU CAN'T FIND THE WING SAUCE, YOU MAY USE THE ORIGINAL, BUT START WITH A MUCH SMALLER QUANTITY AND BUILD TO YOUR DESIRED LEVEL OF HEAT.

ASIAN KALE SALAD WITH CHIA-CRUSTED TUNA

SERVES 2

1 bunch lacinato kale, center ribs removed, leaves finely chopped

1 tablespoon extra-virgin olive oil

Kosher salt

1 medium carrot, shaved into ribbons with a vegetable peeler (or ½ cup shredded carrots)

½ red bell pepper, seeded and very thinly sliced

½ cup frozen shelled edamame, thawed

3 scallions, whites and light green parts only, thinly sliced

FOR THE DRESSING
Juice of 1 lime

2 garlic cloves, grated or finely minced

1½ tablespoons low-sodium soy sauce

2 teaspoons sriracha sauce

2 teaspoons honey

1 teaspoon peeled and grated fresh ginger

Kale is a nutritional powerhouse. It's packed with calcium, fiber, and mass quantities of vitamins A, C, and K, as well as a host of essential minerals. It also amps up your body's natural detoxifying power with phytonutrients like kaempferol, which has been shown to activate the genes associated with longevity. Kale fights cancer. It helps to prevent heart disease. It promotes brain health and clear skin. Plus, the leafy green clocks in at a mere 33 calories per cup, so eating it will definitely help you drop a few. In short, kale is leafy green MAGIC.

If your response to the above is "Yeah, but kale sucks!" this superfood salad may just change your tune. Massaging the kale—which is far less creepy than it sounds—leaves the greens incredibly tender, and once you toss them with an addictive Asian-inspired dressing and get some seared chia-crusted tuna involved, you've got quite the man-friendly meal. Trust.

1. First you're going to massage the kale. Place the chopped kale in a medium bowl, drizzle it with the olive oil, and add a pinch of kosher salt. Massage the kale in handfuls—literally rub the leaves between your fingers—for a minute or two, until the leaves soften and darken in color. (Yes, I know getting handsy with your salad is kind of weird, but it will be worth it. DO NOT SKIP THIS STEP.)

2. Add the carrot, bell pepper, edamame, and scallions to the massaged kale and toss to combine.

3. In a small bowl, whisk together the ingredients for the dressing. Drizzle about two-thirds of the dressing over the salad and toss to coat. Set the salad and remaining dressing aside while you prepare your tuna.

4. Pour the chia seeds onto a plate. Pat the tuna steaks dry and season both sides with kosher salt and black pepper. Dredge the tuna in the chia seeds, using your hands to help press the seeds onto the fish.

FOR THE TUNA

2 tablespoons chia seeds

Two 6-ounce tuna steaks, about 1-inch thick

Kosher salt

Freshly ground black pepper

2 tablespoons extra-virgin coconut oil (Light sesame oil also works well.)

5. Heat the coconut oil in a large nonstick skillet over medium-high heat. When the oil is hot and shimmering (but not smoking!), add the tuna steaks. Cook for 1½ minutes per side for rare. Transfer the steaks to a cutting board and thinly slice across the grain.

6. Divide the salad between two plates or bowls. Fan a sliced tuna steak over each salad, and drizzle with the remaining dressing. Serve immediately.

YOU DO YOU: NOT INTO RARE TUNA? COOK YOUR FISH FOR 2 TO 2½ MINUTES PER SIDE FOR MEDIUM-RARE. OR 3 MINUTES PER SIDE FOR MEDIUM.

STEAK SALAD WITH ROASTED SWEET POTATOES AND GOAT CHEESE

The first time Logan tried this salad, he hoovered the entire thing in three minutes flat. When he finally came up for air, he simply said, "That was a total man salad." I'm inclined to agree.

1. Preheat the oven to 375°F. Line a baking sheet with parchment paper.

2. Take your steak out of the fridge, and let it hang out on the counter. You want the meat to come up to room temperature before you cook it, which will take about 25 minutes. (This is optional, but it will yield a much more tender steak, dudes.)

3. Arrange the sweet potatoes in an even layer on the prepared baking sheet. Drizzle with 2 teaspoons of the olive oil and sprinkle with the cinnamon and a pinch of kosher salt. Toss to coat. Roast the sweet potatoes for 25 minutes, turning them once with a spatula halfway through the cooking time, until tender. Remove from the oven and let cool slightly.

4. Meanwhile, whisk together all the ingredients for the dressing in a large bowl. Set aside.

5. Preheat a medium skillet (preferably cast iron) over medium heat until it's very hot. Rub both sides of your steak with the remaining 1 teaspoon olive oil, and season it generously with salt and black pepper. Place the steak in the hot pan and cook for 5 to 6 minutes on each side for medium-rare. (If you're more into medium or medium-well meat, let it cook for an extra couple of minutes per side.) Transfer to a cutting board. Let the steak rest for 10 minutes to allow the juices to redistribute, then slice it very thinly against the grain.

6. Add the spring mix, roasted sweet potatoes, red onion, and pepitas to the bowl with the dressing and toss to coat.

7. Divide the salad between two plates. Fan half of the sliced steak over each salad and sprinkle with goat cheese. Serve immediately.

One 8-ounce eye round steak

1 medium sweet potato, peeled and cut into ¾-inch cubes

3 teaspoons extra-virgin olive oil, divided

¼ teaspoon ground cinnamon

Kosher salt

Freshly ground black pepper

4 ounces baby spring mix

½ small red onion, thinly sliced

¼ cup pepitas (aka shelled pumpkin seeds)

2 ounces goat cheese, crumbled

FOR THE DRESSING

4 tablespoons extra-virgin olive oil

3 tablespoons balsamic vinegar

2 garlic cloves, grated or finely minced

¼ teaspoon kosher salt

"SUMMER ROLL" SALAD
WITH SHRIMP AND MANGO

½ pound (10 to 12) medium shrimp, peeled and deveined

Kosher salt

Freshly ground black pepper

1 tablespoon extra-virgin olive oil

4 cups shredded cabbage (I like to use a mix of green and purple cabbages.)

½ cup shredded carrots

½ English cucumber, peeled, seeds removed, sliced into thin matchsticks

½ mango, peeled and diced

½ cup fresh basil leaves, stacked, rolled, and thinly sliced (aka chiffonade)

½ cup fresh cilantro leaves

½ ripe avocado, pitted, peeled, and diced

¼ cup chopped peanuts

Bright and citrusy with a mild kick and an out-of-this-world crunch factor, this salad delivers all the badass fresh flavors of a Thai summer roll. No rice paper or mini burrito rolling skills required.

1. Starting with the shrimp! Pat them dry and season all over with salt and pepper. Heat the olive oil in a large nonstick skillet over medium-high heat. When the oil is shimmering, add the shrimp and cook for 3 to 4 minutes, shaking the pan periodically to make sure they cook evenly, until bright pink and opaque. Transfer the shrimp to a plate and let cool to room temperature.

2. Meanwhile, whisk together all the ingredients for the dressing in a medium bowl. Set aside

3. Add the cabbage, carrot, cucumber, mango, basil, and cilantro to a large bowl. Drizzle the salad with about three-quarters of the dressing and toss to coat.

4. Divide the salad between two bowls (or among four if you're planning to serve it as an appetizer), and top with the avocado and shrimp. Drizzle with the remaining dressing and sprinkle with the peanuts. Serve immediately.

FOR THE DRESSING

Juice of 1 lime

1 tablespoon extra-virgin olive oil

1 garlic clove, grated or finely minced

1½ tablespoons low-sodium soy sauce

1 teaspoon honey

1 to 2 Thai red "bird's-eye" chiles, thinly sliced (You can also use ½ to 1 teaspoon sriracha sauce or chili paste. Add this gradually until you reach your desired level of heat.)

Arugula Salad with Crispy Prosciutto, Parmesan, and Fried Eggs

SERVES 2

2 ounces sliced prosciutto

5 ounces baby arugula

¼ cup shaved Parmesan cheese

1 teaspoon extra-virgin olive oil

2 large eggs

Freshly ground black pepper

FOR THE DRESSING
3 tablespoons minced shallots

3 tablespoons extra-virgin olive oil

1 tablespoon sherry vinegar

2 teaspoons Dijon mustard

¼ teaspoon honey

This is essentially a fancy breakfast sandwich in salad form. You've got the requisite pork product in the form of oven-crisped prosciutto, plus shaved Parmesan and lots of peppery arugula, all tossed with sherry-shallot vinaigrette. That's a rock solid combo, but the fried egg is the real money-maker. When you break the yolk and bathe everything in warm eggy goodness, you'll be transported to a place you may not recognize . . .

Welcome to Salad Nirvana, dudes. Invite your friends.

1. Preheat the oven to 375°F. Line a large baking sheet with parchment paper.

2. Arrange the prosciutto in an even layer on the prepared baking sheet and bake for 15 minutes or until lightly browned and crisp. Crumble into large pieces.

3. While the prosciutto is crisping, whisk together all the ingredients for the dressing in a large bowl. Add the arugula to the bowl (it will seem like too much, but it's going to wilt in the dressing). Add the Parmesan and crumbled prosciutto and toss to coat. Taste and season with a tiny bit of salt if necessary. Divide the salad between two plates or bowls.

4. Time to fry those eggs! Heat the olive oil in a nonstick skillet over medium heat. When the oil is hot and shimmering (but not smoking!), carefully crack the eggs into the pan, leaving a little bit of space between them. Cook for 3 to 4 minutes or until the whites are just set, but the yolks are still runny. (If the whites aren't setting, put a lid on the pan for a minute or so to help them along.)

5. Top each salad with a fried egg and serve with plenty of freshly ground black pepper.

YOU DO YOU: THIS LIGHTER SALAD IS IDEAL FOR BRUNCHING/LUNCHING. BUT IF YOU WANT A HEARTIER MEAL, ADD SOME ROASTED POTATOES OR BUTTERNUT SQUASH INTO THE MIX. A SIDE OF TOASTED WHOLE-GRAIN BREAD OR PITA IS ALSO ALLOWED.

CHOPPED CHICKEN CLUB SALAD
WITH HONEY-MUSTARD DRESSING

The great thing about a chopped salad is that you never get a mouthful of just lettuce, which is many dudes' worst nightmare. Each bite is a smorgasbord of flavors unleashed on your taste buds simultaneously—in this case, all the crunchy, creamy, "bacon-y" awesomeness of a club sandwich (minus the bread). Do the chopping and whisk the dressing while the chicken and bacon cook, and you'll have lunch or dinner on the table in 20 minutes flat.

1. Heat a large skillet over medium heat. When hot, add the turkey bacon and cook for about 4 to 5 minutes per side or until browned and crisp. Transfer the bacon to a paper towel–lined plate and let cool to room temperature. Chop into small pieces.

2. In a large bowl, whisk together all the ingredients for the dressing.

3. Add the chicken, romaine, basil, tomatoes, and avocado to the bowl with the dressing, and toss gently to combine.

4. Divide the salad between two plates or bowls, top each with half of the chopped turkey bacon and serve.

1 recipe Idiotproof Chicken Breasts (page 257), cooled to room temperature and diced small

3 slices turkey bacon

4 cups finely chopped romaine hearts

6 fresh basil leaves, chopped

¾ cup grape or cherry tomatoes, quartered

½ ripe avocado, pitted, peeled, and cut into small dice

FOR THE DRESSING

Juice of ½ lemon

2 tablespoons extra-virgin olive oil

2 tablespoons Dijon mustard

2 teaspoons honey

¼ teaspoon kosher salt

Pinch of cayenne pepper

summer salad with Pan-seared salmon

Two 6-ounce center-cut salmon fillets, about 1¼ inches thick, skin removed

3 teaspoons extra-virgin olive oil, divided

¾ cup sweet corn kernels (from 1 ear of corn)

Kosher salt

Freshly ground black pepper

5 ounces mixed baby lettuces

1 cup cherry or grape tomatoes, halved from pole to pole

1 yellow peach, pitted and diced (A nectarine or plum will also be awesome.)

¼ small red onion, very thinly sliced

½ ripe avocado, pitted, peeled, and sliced

2 ounces feta cheese, crumbled (optional)

Tom Brady reportedly eats a lot of salmon and salads. Tom Brady is also ripped and married to Gisele. That's not a coincidence, dudes. Am I saying eating this outrageously delicious salmon salad will snag you the body of your dreams and a supermodel spouse? Of course not. But it might . . .

If you're vehemently anti-salmon, this salad is equally boss with grilled chicken breasts or steak. You could also get really crazy and try eating a vegetarian meal. Just throwing that out there.

FOR THE DRESSING

3 tablespoons extra-virgin olive oil

2 tablespoons fresh lemon juice

2 tablespoons finely chopped fresh basil

1 teaspoon Dijon mustard

¾ teaspoon honey

Kosher salt

Freshly ground black pepper

1. Take your salmon out of the fridge and let it come to room temperature. (This should take about 15 minutes.)

2. Heat 1 teaspoon of the olive oil in a medium skillet over medium heat. When the oil is hot and shimmering, add the corn kernels along with a pinch of salt and pepper, and cook for 4 to 5 minutes until tender and lightly browned in spots. Transfer to a bowl and let cool to room temperature.

3. In a large bowl, whisk together all the ingredients for the dressing. Season with salt and pepper to taste. Set aside.

4. Pat your salmon dry and season generously on both sides with salt and pepper. Heat a large skillet over medium-high heat. When the pan is hot, add the remaining 2 teaspoons olive oil and swirl to coat the bottom of the pan. Add the salmon to the pan, skinned side up, and cook for 4 minutes, undisturbed. (Seriously, don't touch the

salmon, dudes! You want the fish to develop a nice golden-brown crust.) Carefully flip the fillets over, reduce the heat to medium, and cook for 3 to 4 minutes more or until the salmon is just cooked through. Transfer to a plate, while you finish up the salad.

5. Add the cooled corn kernels, lettuce, tomatoes, peach, and red onion to the bowl with the dressing. Toss to coat.

6. Divide the salad between two plates. Top each with sliced avocado, feta (if using), and a salmon fillet. Serve immediately.

KNOWLEDGE BOMB: WHEN IT COMES TO BUYING SALMON. IT'S BEST TO OPT FOR WILD-CAUGHT OVER FARMED FILLETS WHENEVER POSSIBLE. YES. WILD FISH IS PRICIER. BUT IT'S WORTH SHELLING OUT TO AVOID THE HIGHER LEVELS OF CONTAMINANTS (INCLUDING ANTI-BIOTICS AND DISEASE-CAUSING CHEMICALS) FOUND IN FARMED VARIETIES. WILD SALMON ALSO CONTAINS SIGNIFICANTLY FEWER CALORIES AND FAT PER OUNCE THAN FARMED.

DIJON CHICKEN SALAD

A serious departure from traditional chicken salad—which should be filed under "things mixed with mayo" and restricted to No-Calorie Sunday—this mustard-based version is light and fresh with epic pops of crunch and sweetness. It's surprisingly satisfying wrapped in a few crisp lettuce leaves or served over mixed greens, but you can also use it as a sandwich filling, or crush it straight up as a protein-packed snack.

1. In a large bowl, whisk together the yogurt, mustards, lemon juice, and honey.

2. Add the diced chicken, apple, celery, walnuts, cranberries, and shallot to the bowl with the dressing. Toss to coat.

3. Serve immediately or store in an airtight container in the refrigerator for up to 3 days.

1 recipe Idiotproof Chicken Breasts (page 257), cooled to room temperature and diced

¼ cup nonfat plain Greek yogurt

2 tablespoons Dijon mustard

2 tablespoons whole-grain Dijon mustard

1 tablespoon fresh lemon juice

¾ teaspoon honey

½ small Granny Smith apple, finely chopped

¼ cup finely chopped celery

¼ cup chopped walnuts

3 tablespoons dried cranberries

2 tablespoons minced shallot

FOR SERVING (OPTIONAL)
Bibb or Romaine lettuce leaves

Whole-grain crackers, crisps, or bread

Vegetable Fajita Salad
with Chipotle Vinaigrette

SERVES 2 — 3 AS A MEAL / 4—6 AS A SIDE

2½ tablespoons extra-virgin olive oil, divided

¾ cup sweet corn kernels (from 1 ear of corn)

1 small zucchini, diced

Kosher salt

1 red bell pepper, seeded and thinly sliced

1 yellow bell pepper, seeded and thinly sliced

1 small red onion, halved and thinly sliced

½ teaspoon ground cumin

¼ teaspoon chili powder

Juice of ½ lime

2 romaine hearts, chopped (about 5 cups)

2 scallions, whites and light green parts only, thinly sliced

¼ packed cup fresh cilantro leaves

¾ cup canned black beans (about half of a 15-ounce can), drained and rinsed

Cómo se dice "DANK" en español? This party-ready salad is layer upon layer of chipotle-laced fiesta flavor that will have guests tipping their sombreros to your impressive culinary skills. Chilled beergaritas (see page 287) optional, but recommended.

1. In a small bowl, whisk together all of the ingredients for the chipotle vinaigrette. Set aside.

2. Heat a tablespoon of the olive oil in a large skillet over medium heat. When hot, add the corn kernels, zucchini, and a pinch of salt. Cook until tender and lightly browned, about 7 minutes. Transfer the corn and zucchini to a bowl and let cool to room temperature.

3. In the same skillet, heat the remaining 1½ tablespoons olive oil. When hot, add the bell peppers, onion, and a pinch of salt. Cook for about 10 minutes or until the vegetables have softened and lightly browned. Stir in the cumin and chili powder and cook for another 2 minutes to toast the spices. Stir in the lime juice. Remove from the heat and set aside.

4. Place the chopped romaine, scallions, and cilantro in a large bowl or serving dish. Add the corn, zucchini, and black beans to the greens. Drizzle with the chipotle vinaigrette and toss gently to coat. Top with the bell pepper mixture, diced avocado, and queso fresco, and serve immediately.

> YOU DO YOU: IF YOU MUST HAVE MEAT. BOTH GRILLED FLANK STEAK (PAGE 157) AND IDIOTPROOF CHICKEN BREASTS (PAGE 257) ARE EXCELLENT SALAD TOPPERS.

1 ripe avocado, pitted, peeled, and diced

¼ cup crumbled queso fresco (or mild feta cheese)

FOR THE CHIPOTLE VINAIGRETTE
Juice of 1 lime

2 garlic cloves, grated or finely minced

1 chipotle pepper canned in adobo sauce, minced (If you're sensitive to spice, seed the chipotle first.)

2 teaspoons adobo sauce from the chipotle can

1½ teaspoons honey

⅒ teaspoon ground cumin

1 tablespoon plus 1 teaspoon extra-virgin olive oil

Kosher salt

CHAPTER

8

TAKE-OUT FAVORITES

Logan's delivery behavior is batshit crazy, yet strangely endearing at the same time. The dude practically vibrates with anticipatory excitement from the time he places his order until the apartment's buzzer sounds, at which point he sprints to open the door and has the type of intimate interaction with the delivery person that's usually reserved for finger-food servers at cocktail parties. There are often high fives and fist bumps involved.

When Logan and I first became roommates, I had the pleasure of witnessing this scene play out several times per week. And while I appreciated the entertainment, his delivery habit quickly began to weigh on me. Delivery itself wasn't the problem—I'm all for convenience—it was the type of food being ordered. Outsourcing kale salads and grilled chicken dinners is one thing, but like most dudes, Logan's go-tos were more of the Italian, Mexican, and Chinese variety, and slowly but surely, these greasy, artery-clogging feasts were taking a serious toll on both his body and his wallet. As much as the thought of breaking up Logan's close relationships with local deliverymen pained me, something had to be done.

So, in an effort to help Logan and the dude community at large ease up on Domino's and white-carton Chinese, I made it my personal mission to re-create the most beloved take-out meals in a Dude Diet–friendly fashion. This chapter contains my greatest successes. From Sesame-Orange Chicken (page 204) to Smarter Sausage Pizza (page 220), the following recipes will satisfy your more exotic cravings without compromising your health or bank account, and most are doable in the time it would take to have the fattier version delivered. Even better, whipping up these delicious feasts in your own kitchen means never having to deal with lukewarm soggy food, extended delivery times, or "rookies" screwing up your order. Hell hath no fury like Logan with a botched burrito . . .

CHICKEN SHAWARMA
WITH GARLICKY YOGURT SAUCE

Juice of 1 lemon

¼ cup extra-virgin olive oil

1½ tablespoons curry powder

1 tablespoon smoked paprika

1½ teaspoons kosher salt

½ teaspoon freshly ground black pepper

½ teaspoon garlic powder

¼ teaspoon cayenne pepper

2 pounds boneless, skinless chicken tenders (They're sometimes labeled "tenderloins.")

FOR THE TOPPINGS
1 large beefsteak tomato, diced

1 romaine heart, finely chopped

½ medium red onion, very thinly sliced

½ English cucumber (aka seedless cucumber), diced

4 to 6 whole-wheat pitas OR whole-grain lavash

This "shawarma" may not be spit-roasted with layers of excess fat, but all the smoky, curry-laced flavors of your favorite street meat are present and accounted for in these juicy grilled chicken tenders. Piled on warm pita or lavash with lots of crunchy veggies and a tangy, dill-spiked yogurt sauce, it's food cart–worthy fare with a hefty side of health benefits.

1. In a shallow baking dish, whisk together the lemon juice, olive oil, curry powder, paprika, salt, black pepper, garlic powder, and cayenne. Add the chicken tenders to the baking dish and, using your hands, make sure each one gets coated in this magical marinade. Let the chicken marinate for 20 minutes at room temperature.

2. In the meantime, prep your toppings and yogurt sauce. Arrange the diced tomatoes, romaine, red onion, and cucumber on a large plate. Cover with plastic wrap and refrigerate until ready to use. In a medium bowl, combine all the ingredients for the yogurt sauce. Taste and season with a little extra salt if necessary. Pop that deliciousness in the fridge as well.

3. Time to cook the chicken, dudes. Heat a lightly oiled grill (or grill pan) over medium-high heat. When hot, remove the chicken tenderloins from the marinade and place them on the grill. (If you're using a grill pan, you'll need to do this in 3 or 4 batches.) Cook the tenderloins for about 4 minutes per side or until lightly charred on the outside and cooked through.

4. Last but not least, warm those pitas or lavash. I recommend placing them directly on a grill or gas burner, but you can also use the microwave if you prefer.

5. To serve your "shawarma," pile each pita or lavash with plenty of chicken. Add toppings of your choice and finish with a generous amount of yogurt sauce. Eat it as you would a taco. A giant, dank, Mediterranean-themed taco.

FOR THE GARLICKY YOGURT SAUCE

1 cup nonfat plain yogurt

1 large garlic clove, grated or finely minced

1 teaspoon fresh lemon juice

1 teaspoon finely chopped fresh dill

¼ teaspoon kosher salt, plus extra if needed

YOU DO YOU: IF YOU ABSOLUTELY CAN'T STOMACH THE THOUGHT OF TOFU, YOU MAY USE GROUND CHICKEN OR TURKEY IN YOUR WRAPS.

Basil Tofu Lettuce Wraps

Don't turn the page!!! I know tofu is a deal breaker for most people, but I beg you to give it a shot just this once. These wraps are good. Really good. So good that when I made them for Logan and his notoriously picky best friend, Henry, for dinner one night—saying nothing about the tofu factor (for obvious reasons)—they crushed these sassy little Asian numbers like they were going out of style and showered me with the type of praise usually limited to creations involving meat, cheese, or chocolate.

Feeling cocky, I proudly informed them that they had just happily eaten a bunch of bean curd. Big mistake. They went into meltdown mode instantly, backpedaling on their enthusiastic compliments and claiming that they "knew it the whole time!!!" But the truth is, they didn't. (They thought it was chicken.) And no matter what those two say, I know in my heart of hearts that they loved everything about these tofu wraps. There's a strong chance you will, too.

1. Start by draining the tofu. Remove the tofu from its packaging and pat it dry. Place the block between two layers of paper towels, and put a heavy skillet on top. (A thick book or a couple of plates will also do the trick.) Let the tofu drain for at least 20 minutes, changing the paper towels halfway through. You want to get as much moisture out of the stuff as humanly possible.

2. Heat the sesame oil in a large nonstick skillet over medium-high heat. (The nonstick element is crucial here, dudes.) When the oil is hot, crumble the tofu into the pan and cook for 5 to 6 minutes, stirring and breaking up the tofu into very small pieces or until it's dry and very lightly browned.

3. Add the bell pepper, onion, carrots, and garlic to the tofu and cook for 3 minutes or until the veggies are just tender. Add the soy sauce, sriracha sauce, and rice vinegar and cook for 1 minute more. Turn off the heat and stir in the chopped basil.

4. Spoon the filling onto lettuce leaves and sprinkle with the scallions and chopped peanuts.

One 14-ounce package extra-firm tofu

2 tablespoons dark sesame oil (Light sesame oil and coconut oil also work well.)

1 small red bell pepper, seeded and finely chopped

1 small red onion, finely chopped

1 cup grated carrots (about 2 medium carrots)

3 garlic cloves, minced

¼ cup low-sodium soy sauce

2 tablespoons sriracha sauce

1 tablespoon unseasoned rice vinegar

¾ cup fresh basil leaves, finely chopped

16 leaves Bibb or iceberg lettuce

4 scallions, thinly sliced

⅓ cup chopped peanuts or cashews

DUDE DIET SUSHI BOWLS

¾ cup uncooked short-grain brown rice

¼ cup plus 1 tablespoon finely chopped scallions (white and light green parts only)

¼ cup low-sodium soy sauce

2 teaspoons dark sesame oil

1 teaspoon unseasoned rice vinegar

1 teaspoon peeled and grated fresh ginger

1 teaspoon sriracha sauce

12 ounces sushi-grade ahi tuna, sliced into ½-inch cubes

FOR SERVING
1 cup shredded carrots

¾ cup thinly sliced English cucumber (aka seedless cucumber)

½ ripe avocado, pitted, peeled, and sliced or cubed

2 tablespoons fresh lime juice

2 teaspoons toasted sesame seeds

Let's be real, rolling sushi is a bitch, and as much as I love to imagine a bunch of dudes excitedly whipping out their sushi mats and sprinting to the kitchen, I'm pretty sure most of you have neither the patience nor the aforementioned mats for such meticulous work. *Enter*: sushi bowls. Despite their impressive appearance, assembly is a total breeze. All you have to do is cook some rice, slice a few veggies, toss the tuna with dressing, and pile everything into bowls. Done and done.

If tuna isn't your thing, feel free to sub fresh salmon in its place. And for those that don't do raw, you can always sear the fish first, or try tossing some steamed shrimp or firm tofu with the dressing.

1. Cook your brown rice according to the package directions. Once cooked, let it cool to room temperature. (Keep in mind this will take about 50 minutes, dudes. Plan accordingly.)

2. Meanwhile, prepare the dressing. In a medium bowl, combine the scallions, soy sauce, sesame oil, rice vinegar, ginger, and sriracha sauce. Add the cubed tuna to the bowl and toss gently to coat. Cover with plastic wrap and refrigerate for at least 10 minutes (or up to 2 hours).

3. Assemble your sushi bowls! Divide the brown rice between two bowls. Top with the carrots, cucumbers, and avocado. (You can obviously just pile things in the bowl, but it will take less than 30 seconds to make it look attractive. Please consider it.)

4. Remove your tuna from the fridge. Add the lime juice, and toss gently to combine.

5. Top each bowl with half of the tuna mixture. Sprinkle with toasted sesame seeds and serve immediately. Nice work, my little Morimotos.

KNOWLEDGE BOMB: WHEN IT COMES TO SUSHI. THE WORDS "SPICY." "CRUNCHY." AND "TEMPURA" ROUGHLY TRANSLATE TO "FAT." "FATTER." AND "FATTEST." SPICY MAYONNAISE AND FRIED FOOD ARE NOT DUDE DIET-FRIENDLY CHOICES. AND THE AVERAGE SHRIMP TEMPURA ROLL CLOCKS IN AT ABOUT 550 CALORIES AND 21 GRAMS OF FAT (ON PAR WITH A MCDONALD'S QUARTER POUNDER WITH CHEESE). STICK WITH STRAIGHT UP FISH AND VEGGIE ROLLS WHEN DINING OUT. AND ALWAYS OPT FOR LOW-SODIUM SOY SAUCE.

sesame-orange CHICKEN

⅓ cup water

1 tablespoon plus 1½ teaspoons cornstarch

¼ cup distilled white vinegar

Finely grated zest of 1 orange

3 tablespoons low-sodium soy sauce

3 tablespoons honey

2 garlic cloves, grated or finely minced

2 tablespoons finely chopped scallions

1 tablespoon sesame seeds

¼ teaspoon crushed red pepper flakes

1½ pounds boneless, skinless chicken breasts, cut into 1-inch cubes

¼ teaspoon kosher salt

2 tablespoons extra-virgin coconut oil, divided

3 cups broccoli florets

1 small red bell pepper, seeded and diced

1 small green bell pepper, seeded and diced

Ask any dude to name his favorite Chinese food and the likely response is either orange chicken or sesame chicken. This epic hybrid recipe combines the zing and sticky sweetness of both dishes, minus the unnecessary deep-frying and common chemical additives. And while it may seem strange that there's no orange juice in a recipe for orange chicken, I promise the zest alone packs a serious citrus punch.

1. In a medium bowl, whisk together the water and cornstarch until smooth. Add the vinegar, orange zest, soy sauce, honey, garlic, scallions, sesame seeds, and red pepper flakes and whisk until well combined. Set the sauce aside.

2. Season the chicken cubes with kosher salt.

3. Heat 1 tablespoon of the coconut oil in a large nonstick skillet over medium-high heat. When the oil is hot and shimmering, add the chicken in an even layer. Cook for 2 minutes, undisturbed, to let the chicken brown slightly. Cook for another 3 to 4 minutes, tossing occasionally or until opaque throughout. Using a slotted spoon or tongs, transfer the chicken to a bowl.

4. Pour out any excess liquid in the skillet and return it to medium-high heat. Add the remaining 1 tablespoon coconut oil. When the oil is hot and shimmering, add the broccoli and bell peppers and cook for 2 to 3 minutes or until the broccoli is bright green and crisp-tender.

5. Give the sauce another whisk to smooth out any cornstarch clumps. Return the chicken to the pan and pour in the sauce. Cook for about 1 minute, tossing the chicken and vegetables together or until the sauce has thickened. (If the sauce starts to thicken too quickly, don't panic—just reduce the heat to medium and keep stirring.)

6. Serve warm over brown rice or quinoa if you like.

YOU DO YOU: YOU CAN DEFINITELY DEVOUR THIS CHICKEN ON ITS OWN. BUT I RECOMMEND SERVING IT OVER BROWN RICE OR QUINOA.

Beef and Broccoli

⅓ cup low-sodium soy sauce

3 garlic cloves, grated or finely minced

2 packed tablespoons light brown sugar

1 tablespoon peeled and grated fresh ginger

1 tablespoon unseasoned rice vinegar

½ teaspoon crushed red pepper flakes

1 teaspoon plus 1 tablespoon cornstarch, divided

1 pound skirt steak

1½ cups water

1 pound broccoli florets (about 4 cups)

¼ cup low-sodium beef broth

1½ tablespoons dark sesame oil

2 scallions, thinly sliced

2 teaspoons sesame seeds (optional)

FOR SERVING (OPTIONAL)
2 to 3 cups cooked brown rice or quinoa

Logan once told me about a friend who eats Chinese food in bed naked every Sunday. When I asked why the nudity was necessary, he immediately answered, "Why wouldn't it be?! He needs to be comfortable when his stomach expands!" To be honest, I'm not sure if this person is actually a friend, or if it was Logan before we became roommates, but either way, it's aggressive and avoidable—especially when a dude has this recipe for quick-and-easy beef and broccoli on hand. Given the wholesome ingredients and lack of deep-frying, I'm hoping you'll be able to enjoy this feast fully clothed.

1. In a small bowl, whisk together the soy sauce, garlic, sugar, ginger, rice vinegar, and red pepper flakes.

2. Transfer 2 tablespoons of sauce to a medium bowl and whisk in 1 teaspoon of cornstarch. Slice your steak very thinly across the grain (I'm talking ⅛-inch pieces if you can manage it) and add it to the bowl. Using your hands, toss the steak with the sauce, making sure each piece is lightly coated. Set aside to marinate at room temperature for 15 minutes.

3. Meanwhile, bring the water to a boil in your largest nonstick pan. Once boiling, add the broccoli, cover with a lid, and cook for 2 minutes or until the florets are bright green and crisp-tender. Drain immediately and set aside.

4. Whisk the remaining 1 tablespoon cornstarch and the beef broth into the reserved sauce.

5. Preheat the same pan you used for the broccoli over high heat. When it's screaming hot, pour in the sesame oil and quickly swirl to coat the bottom of the pan. (Careful, the oil may spit a little!) Add the marinated steak in an even layer and cook for 2 to 3 minutes, tossing occasionally with tongs or until lightly browned and cooked through.

6. Pour the sauce over the steak and cook for 30 seconds or until it thickens slightly. (It's going to bubble really vigorously. That's a good thing!) Add the broccoli and scallions to the pan, and cook for 30 to 60 seconds, using your tongs to toss everything together, until the broccoli is heated through. Immediately transfer to a large serving bowl or platter and sprinkle with sesame seeds (if using). Serve with brown rice or quinoa if you like.

JUST THE TIP: BE PROACTIVE AND COOK A LARGE BATCH OF BROWN RICE. QUINOA. OR YOUR FAVORITE WHOLE GRAIN WHENEVER YOU HAVE SOME FREE TIME. KEEP IT IN AN AIRTIGHT CONTAINER IN THE FRIDGE TO ADD TO MEALS LIKE THIS ONE THROUGHOUT THE WEEK.

SHRIMP PAD THAI

Even the shortest stint in a plastic container is enough to dry out Pad Thai and dull its signature brightness, so skip the sad delivery noodle brick in favor of this simple homemade version. All you need is 30 minutes and a Thai-ny bit of motivation . . .

1. Fill a sauté pan or baking dish with hot water. Soak the noodles according to the package directions just until tender, usually between 8 and 10 minutes. Drain, rinse with cold water (this is essential to keep the noodles from sticking), and set aside.

2. In a small bowl, whisk together the soy sauce, lime juice, honey, sriracha sauce, and fish sauce (if using). Set aside.

3. Place the shrimp, beaten eggs, prepped vegetables, noodles, and sauce by the stove along with an empty mixing bowl. Things are going to happen fast once you start cooking, dudes—you want to have all the goods handy.

4. Heat 1 tablespoon of the coconut oil in your largest nonstick pan over medium-high heat. When hot, add the shrimp and cook for about 90 seconds, shaking the pan a few times or until the shrimp are bright pink and just opaque. Transfer the shrimp to the empty mixing bowl.

5. Return the pan to the heat and pour in the beaten eggs. Scramble the eggs with a spatula, breaking them up into small curds, just until set, 30 to 45 seconds. Add them to the bowl with the shrimp.

6. Add the remaining 1 tablespoon of coconut oil to the pan. When the oil is hot and shimmering, add the shallot, garlic, carrots, and snow peas and cook for 2 minutes, just until tender. Add the noodles and half of the sauce to the pan and cook for 2 minutes, tossing with

8 ounces brown rice pad Thai noodles (sometimes labeled "stir-fry noodles")

¼ cup low-sodium soy sauce

¼ cup fresh lime juice

2 tablespoons plus 2 teaspoons honey

1 tablespoon sriracha sauce

1 tablespoon Thai fish sauce (optional)

1 pound medium shrimp, peeled and deveined with the tail shells removed

2 large eggs, lightly beaten

1 large shallot, finely chopped

3 garlic cloves, minced

1 cup shredded carrots

1 cup snow peas, ends trimmed and tough strings removed

2 tablespoons extra-virgin coconut oil, divided

(cont.)

1 cup bean sprouts

½ cup fresh cilantro leaves, chopped

⅓ cup crushed peanuts

Lime wedges

tongs or until the noodles have softened and the liquid has been absorbed. Add the shrimp and eggs back to the pan along with the remaining sauce and cook for 1 minute until heated through.

7. Immediately transfer your pad Thai to a large serving dish. Serve garnished with bean sprouts, cilantro, peanuts, and lime wedges.

CHIPOTLE CHICKEN BURRITO BOWLS

Witnessing Logan order a burrito from a take-out Mexican joint is truly a unique experience. Bending over the counter to watch the masterpiece materialize, he'll attempt to strike up a rapport with his burrito-builder while filling his tortilla with every possible ingredient: multiple meats, pinto *and* black beans, lettuce, corn salsa, regular salsa, double cheese, sour cream, and extra guacamole.

When it comes to assessing the nutritional value of these ~~meat footballs~~ burritos, though, he's a lot less methodical. He once told me that burritos are "health food," especially since he switched to brown rice and he puts some lettuce in those bad boys. I'm well aware that this is a common delusion, as most dudes I know mindlessly inhale burritos on the reg. But the basic nutrition facts for one of Logan's burritos—a pretty standard order—are terrifying. I'm talking 1300+ calories and 50+ grams of fat.

So, in the hope of promoting smarter burrito-eating ways, I created this Dude Diet–friendly burrito bowl. Packed with chipotle marinated chicken, fresh vegetables, black beans, and cilantro-lime brown rice, it's built to hit the spot without wreaking havoc on your waistline.

1. Put all the ingredients for the marinade in a blender or food processor and puree until smooth. Reserve ½ cup of the marinade (you'll use it for the vegetables and chicken later).

2. Place the chicken breasts in a large ziplock food storage bag and pour in the remaining marinade. Seal the bag, removing as much air as possible, and squish the chicken around slightly to make sure each breast is well coated. Allow the chicken to marinate in the fridge for at least 1 hour or up to 24 hours.

3. Cook the brown rice according to the package directions. Stir in the lime juice and cilantro. Season with salt to taste and keep warm until ready to use.

1 pound thinly sliced chicken breasts (aka "chicken cutlets")

FOR THE MARINADE
½ medium red onion, roughly chopped

3 garlic cloves

2 chipotle peppers canned in adobo sauce, seeded and roughly chopped

1½ tablespoons adobo sauce from the chipotle can

Juice of 1 lime

1 tablespoon dried oregano

2¼ teaspoons ground cumin

1¼ teaspoons kosher salt

1 cup low-sodium chicken broth

FOR THE RICE
1 cup uncooked brown rice (I recommend short-grain brown rice.)

Juice of ½ lime

2 tablespoons finely chopped fresh cilantro leaves

Kosher salt

(cont.)

FOR THE VEGETABLES

1 tablespoon extra-virgin olive oil

¾ cup sweet corn kernels (from 1 ear of corn)

1 red bell pepper, seeded and cut into small dice

1 green bell pepper, seeded and cut into small dice

½ medium red onion, finely chopped

1 cup canned black beans, drained and rinsed

FOR SERVING (OPTIONAL)

1 romaine heart, finely chopped

½ cup grated Monterey Jack or sharp cheddar cheese

Salsa of your choice

Guacamole

4. Meanwhile, cook the vegetables. Heat the olive oil in a large skillet or sauté pan over medium-high heat or until shimmering. Add the corn kernels and sauté until lightly browned, about 5 minutes. Add the bell peppers, onion, and black beans, and cook for 4 to 5 minutes until the vegetables are just tender. Stir in ¼ cup of the reserved marinade, and cook for 1 minute more. Cover and set aside while you cook your chicken. (You can reheat the veggies quickly before serving if necessary.)

5. Preheat a grill (or grill pan) over medium-high heat. Remove the chicken from the marinade, shaking off any excess, and cook for 4 to 5 minutes per side or until cooked through. Let the chicken rest for 5 minutes, then chop into small cubes and transfer to a mixing bowl. Add the remaining ¼ cup reserved marinade and toss to coat.

6. Time to assemble your burrito bowls! If you like romaine, go ahead and add a handful to the bottom of your bowl. Divide the rice, vegetables, and chicken among four bowls. Garnish with the cheese, salsa, and a responsible amount of guacamole. Serve with lime wedges. Chipotle ain't got nothin' on you.

"TACO BELL" BEEF TACOS

MAKES 12 tacos / SERVES 4—6

1½ teaspoons chili powder

¾ teaspoon onion powder

½ teaspoon ground cumin

½ teaspoon garlic powder

½ teaspoon smoked paprika

¼ teaspoon crushed red pepper flakes

¼ teaspoon dried oregano

1 teaspoon kosher salt

1½ pounds 90 percent lean ground beef

One 8-ounce can tomato sauce (sometimes labeled "tomato puree")

1 cup water

12 whole-grain corn taco shells (I like Bearitos and Garden of Eatin' brands.)

FOR SERVING

1 cup grated sharp cheddar cheese

2 cups thinly sliced iceberg lettuce

2 tomatoes, diced

½ cup sour cream or plain Greek yogurt

Salsa of your choice (optional)

On my first day private chef-ing for one of my NFL players, I sat down to chat with him about his diet and food preferences. Having already spoken to the team's nutritionist, I kicked off the conversation with, "So, I hear you're on a pretty strict diet." "WHAT?!" He responded in panic. "I'm not on a diet!! I'm just trying to eat less Taco Bell!" I blinked several times to make sure that Logan had not miraculously teleported into a stranger's apartment, before assuring my client that I could make that happen. I fed him all manner of Dude Diet–friendly meals during our time together, but I made sure to work this simple copycat taco recipe into the mix every once in a while so he'd never miss the Bell too much.

1. Combine all the spices and salt in a small bowl. Place this bomb seasoning mix by the stove for easy access.

2. Heat a large skillet or sauté pan over medium-high heat. When hot, add the ground beef to the pan. Cook for about 7 to 8 minutes, stirring and breaking up the meat into very small pieces with a spatula or wooden spoon, until completely browned. Drain the meat in a mesh colander (just like pasta, dudes) to get rid of excess grease. Wipe out your pan and return it to the heat.

3. Return the beef to the pan and stir in the spice mix. Cook for 1 minute to toast the spices. Stir in the tomato sauce and water and bring the liquid to a boil, then lower to a simmer, and cook for 10 to 12 minutes or until most of the liquid has been absorbed.

4. Spoon the meat into taco shells and garnish with cheese, lettuce, tomatoes, sour cream, and salsa (if using). Live Más.

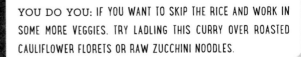

YOU DO YOU: IF YOU WANT TO SKIP THE RICE AND WORK IN SOME MORE VEGGIES. TRY LADLING THIS CURRY OVER ROASTED CAULIFLOWER FLORETS OR RAW ZUCCHINI NOODLES.

COCONUT GREEN CURRY CHICKEN

Coconut milk contains a host of beneficial vitamins and minerals as well as lauric acid, a rare medium-chain fatty acid that boosts immunity and fights heart disease. Combined with the lean chicken breast, vegetables, and fiber-rich brown rice in this curry, it creates a meal that covers all your nutritional bases, while blowing your mind with a heady mix of sweet and spicy flavors. No need to fear the exotic nature of this recipe, dudes. If you can stir things in a pot, you can make curry. I really hope that applies to everyone reading this book . . .

1. Cook your rice according to the package directions. (Unless you're using quick-cooking rice, this will take 40 to 50 minutes. Plan accordingly.)

2. Meanwhile, heat the coconut oil in a medium Dutch oven or sauté pan over medium heat until shimmering. Add the curry paste, garlic, and ginger and cook for 3 minutes to unlock all the curry's glorious flavors. Add the onion, bell pepper, red pepper flakes, and water. Stir to coat the vegetables with the curry mixture, and cook for 3 minutes or until slightly softened.

3. Add the sugar, soy sauce, fish sauce, coconut milk, chicken, and lime zest to the pan. (Don't panic if the coconut milk has separated in the can, dudes, it's totally normal. Just go ahead and scrape everything into the pan.) Bring the mixture to a boil, then lower to a simmer, cover, and cook for 10 minutes or until the chicken is opaque and cooked through. Turn off the heat and stir in the lime juice.

4. Divide the brown rice among four bowls. Ladle the curry over the rice and top with plenty of chopped cilantro.

1 cup uncooked brown rice

1 tablespoon extra-virgin coconut oil

3 tablespoons Thai green curry paste

3 garlic cloves, minced

1 tablespoon peeled and grated fresh ginger

1 small white onion, thinly sliced

1 red bell pepper, seeded and thinly sliced

½ teaspoon crushed red pepper flakes

2 tablespoons water

2 packed teaspoons light brown sugar

2 teaspoons low-sodium soy sauce

2 teaspoons Thai fish sauce

One 13.5-ounce can full-fat coconut milk

1½ pounds boneless, skinless chicken breasts, sliced into roughly 1-inch cubes

Finely grated zest of 1 lime

Juice of ½ lime

½ bunch fresh cilantro leaves, finely chopped

pork un-fried rice

1 pound pork tenderloin, trimmed of excess fat

1 teaspoon smoked paprika

½ teaspoon kosher salt

2 tablespoons light sesame oil, divided (Coconut oil will also work.)

¼ cup low-sodium soy sauce

1 tablespoon fresh lime juice

1 tablespoon sriracha sauce, plus extra for serving

2 garlic cloves, grated or finely minced

1 teaspoon peeled and grated fresh ginger

1 small red bell pepper, seeded and cut into small dice

1 medium carrot, cut into small dice

½ medium yellow onion, minced

½ cup frozen peas

2 large eggs

3 cups cooked brown rice (1 cup uncooked)

The fried rice from your favorite Chinese spot most likely contains a significant amount of a flavor-enhancing additive called monosodium glutamate (MSG). There's a lot of controversy regarding the long-term health impact of MSG (some believe excess consumption may cause nervous disorders and hormone fluctuations), but many people experience the following short-term symptoms after eating it: headache, flushing, sweating, facial pressure or tightness, heart palpitations, chest pain, nausea, and weakness. TRANSLATION: MSG GIVES YOU THE MEAT SWEATS. Keep this in mind the next time you're jonesing for a white-carton fix, and ditch delivery in favor of this nutrient-rich "un-fried" rice with lean pork tenderloin.

1. Place a large ovenproof skillet in the oven. Preheat the oven to 450°F.

2. Pat the pork tenderloin dry with paper towels and rub it all over with the paprika and salt.

3. Using oven mitts—it's going to be scary hot!—remove the skillet from the oven, and add 1 tablespoon of the sesame oil. Swirl to coat the bottom of the skillet. (Careful, the oil will spit a little.) Add the pork tenderloin to the pan and roast in the preheated oven for 10 minutes. Turn the tenderloin over, and immediately return it to the oven. Reduce the oven temperature to 400°F, and roast for another 10 minutes (20 minutes total). Transfer the tenderloin to a cutting board and cover it loosely with aluminum foil. Let it rest for 10 minutes to allow the juices to redistribute, then slice the tenderloin into ½-inch cubes.

4. In a medium bowl, combine the soy sauce, lime juice, sriracha sauce, garlic, and ginger. Set aside.

5. Heat the remaining 1 tablespoon sesame oil in a large wok or nonstick skillet over medium heat until shimmering. Add the bell pepper, carrot, and onion and cook for 4 to 5 minutes just until tender. Add the peas and cook for about 1 minute just until thawed.

6. Push the veggies to one half of the pan. Crack the eggs into the empty half of the pan and scramble with a spatula until set. (This should take less than 1 minute.) Mix the eggs into the vegetables.

7. Add the cooked brown rice, cubed pork tenderloin, and soy sauce mixture to the pan, folding everything together with a spatula. Cook for 1 to 2 minutes until piping hot.

8. Divide the rice among four bowls and serve with extra sriracha.

JUST THE TIP: IF YOU'RE STARTING WITH UNCOOKED BROWN RICE, IT WILL TAKE ABOUT 50 MINUTES TO COOK. MAKE SURE TO FACTOR THAT INTO YOUR PLANS.

smarter sausage pizza

1 pound whole-wheat pizza dough (Whole Foods and Trader Joe's both make a good whole-wheat dough.)

2 links sweet Italian turkey sausage, casings removed

½ small red onion, very thinly sliced

¼ teaspoon crushed red pepper flakes (optional)

Flour for rolling the dough

1½ teaspoons extra-virgin olive oil, divided

4 ounces fresh mozzarella, grated (about 1 cup)

2 cups baby arugula

½ cup cherry tomatoes, quartered

Pinch of kosher salt

Freshly ground black pepper

FOR THE SAUCE
One 14.5-ounce can whole peeled tomatoes (I highly recommend San Marzano), drained well

(cont.)

I want to be very clear on one thing: Pizza is a wonderland body's worst enemy, especially when you order it from large chains that favor highly processed ingredients and scary additives. (Cheese should not have 15 un-recognizable ingredients, dudes!) You can obviously get dirty with delivery on occasion, but when it comes to everyday pizza parties, please try this home-made pie. It's not the most slimming option in this book, but at least the whole-grain crust and minimally processed toppings will prevent you from feeling shitty and swelling up like an Oompa-Loompa immediately afterward—small victories.

Completely baking the pizza crust and then broiling the toppings is a little unconventional, but unless you have a pizza oven, it's the only way to avoid a doughy, uncooked center without skimping on sauce and sausage. Trust me.

1. Take your dough out of the refrigerator and let it come to room temperature. (This will take about 30 minutes, but it will make the dough so much easier to roll out.)

2. Place a pizza stone (if you have one) or an overturned baking sheet in bottom third of your oven and preheat the oven to 450°F. You want your stone/baking sheet to be ridiculously hot before you put your pizza in, so if you've got the time, let it heat up in the oven for at least 30 minutes.

3. Meanwhile, make the tomato sauce. Place all the ingredients in a blender or food processor and blend until relatively smooth. Set the sauce aside.

4. Heat a medium nonstick skillet over medium heat. When hot, crumble the sausage into the pan and cook for about 5 minutes, stirring and breaking up the meat with a spatula, until no longer pink. Add the onion and red pepper flakes (if using) and cook for 2 minutes just until softened. Remove the skillet from the heat and set aside.

KNOWLEDGE BOMB: SOME WELL-KNOWN PIZZA GIANTS REFUSE TO DISCLOSE THEIR INGREDIENT LISTS. GOD KNOWS WHAT THEY'RE PUTTING IN THEIR 'ZA. BUT IT'S SAFE TO ASSUME THAT WHATEVER THEY'RE HIDING ISN'T GOOD. CONSIDER YOURSELF WARNED.

2 garlic cloves,
roughly chopped

½ teaspoon dried
oregano

½ teaspoon balsamic
vinegar

¼ teaspoon pure
cane sugar

¼ teaspoon kosher
salt

Freshly ground
black pepper

5. Place a large piece of parchment paper (at least 16 x 15 inches) over your biggest cutting board and sprinkle it with flour. Place the dough in the center of the paper and sprinkle with more flour. Roll the dough out until it has a uniform thickness of ⅛ inch. (If you don't have a rolling pin, a wine bottle works well.) You can make any shape pizza you like—circle, rectangle, oval—just make sure it's very thinly and evenly rolled out. Brush the dough with 1 teaspoon of the olive oil.

6. Carefully slide the pizza (still on the parchment paper) onto the hot pizza stone or baking sheet. (The parchment paper will brown, but it won't burn, I promise.) Bake for 10 minutes or until the crust is cooked through. It will bubble up in spots, but that's cool. If you don't like bubbles, simply pierce them with a knife after removing the crust from the oven.

7. Slide the crust onto a clean baking sheet and place it on the stovetop. Loosen the crust with a spatula and remove the parchment paper. (You should be able to slide it right out from under the cooked crust.)

8. Preheat the broiler on high.

9. Spread the crust with the tomato sauce, leaving a ¼- to ½-inch border. (You don't have to use all of the sauce if you don't want to— you can serve any leftover sauce with the pizza. Some dudes may want to dip their crusts in it.) Add the mozzarella in an even layer, and top with the cooked sausage and onion.

10. Place the pizza under the broiler until the cheese has melted and is bubbling and the crust has browned, 3 to 4 minutes. (Keep a close eye on it!)

11. Place the arugula and cherry tomatoes in a mixing bowl. Drizzle with the remaining ½ teaspoon olive oil and season with salt and some freshly ground black pepper. Toss to combine.

12. Top your pizza with the arugula mix. Slice into 8 pieces and serve immediately.

CHAPTER 9

SEXY SIDES

Side dishes are a major nutritional stumbling block for a lot of the dudes I know. And it's not because these guys fear vegetables, aren't sure how to pronounce "quinoa," or always choose the fries option (although such factors occasionally come into play)—it's mostly due to the fact that they don't consider sides "real food." Side dishes are so often overshadowed by the size and flavor of the main attraction (i.e., a steak, chili, sandwich, etc.) that their nutrition facts tend to fall by the wayside.

For example, Logan regularly attends work dinners at fancy steak houses. When I asked him what he ate, he used to simply respond, "Steak!" or on the days when he'd felt particularly virtuous, "Fish!" Only when pressed did he recall the mountains of mashed potatoes, creamed spinach, and onion rings consumed alongside his protein of choice, and even then, the fact that he'd racked up half a day's worth of calories in sides alone didn't seem to register. He'd breezily write off that portion of his feast, arguing that potatoes, spinach, and onions are vegetables, and vegetables "don't count."

Listen up, dudes. As I explained to Logan, the "invisible sides" mentality is both ridiculous and dangerous. Side dishes make up more than 50 percent of your meals, and if you have any hope of turning your body into a wonderland, you need to take stock of *everything* on your plate and recognize the additions that are bringing you down. The following guidelines should help.

The Dude Diet Side Dish Guidelines

- **EAT MORE VEGETABLES.** When there's a vegetable option, take it. Bonus points if it's green.

- **THE WORDS** *STEAMED*, *GRILLED*, *ROASTED*, **AND** *BAKED* **ARE YOUR FRIENDS.** These cooking methods tend to involve the least amounts of added butter and oil.

- **PASS ON ALL THINGS FRIED.** (That includes vegetables.) While you're at it, avoid dishes with the words "creamed" or "gratin" in their name. They're just fancy euphemisms for "fat bomb."

- **A SIDE DISH SHOULD NOT CREATE A POOL OF BUTTER, OIL, OR CREAM ON YOUR PLATE.** But if it does, do NOT use a spoon or worse, bread, to transfer the extra fat to your mouth.

- **ALWAYS REMIND YOURSELF OF DUDE DIET COMMANDMENT #4, "IF IT'S WHITE I SHALL ALWAYS THINK TWICE."** White rice? White pasta? Dinner rolls? Just say no. When it comes to carb-heavy sides, choose whole-grain options and limit yourself to a single serving. (Reminder: A serving is ¾ cup cooked grains or a single roll/slice of bread.)

In short, ditch the creamy, cheesy, deep-fried extras and responsibly round out your meals with fresh vegetables, legumes, whole grains, and heart-healthy oils. As you'll soon discover, these sides are far sexier than you may think . . .

ROASTED CAULIFLOWER WITH CHIMICHURRI

If you turn your nose up at cauliflower, there's a pretty solid chance you've never tried it roasted. Just 20 minutes in the oven transforms boring florets into epic bite-size treats—lightly caramelized and crispy on the outside, tender and buttery on the inside. I've used this recipe to convert many a cauliflower skeptic over the years. The roasted cauliflower is shockingly delicious on its own, but the fresh chimichurri sauce really puts it over the edge. It's 100 percent worth the extra (but still minimal) legwork.

1. Preheat the oven to 425°F. Line a large baking sheet with parchment paper.

2. Place the cauliflower florets on the prepared baking sheet. Drizzle with the olive oil, season generously with salt and black pepper, and toss to coat. Arrange the cauliflower in an even layer, leaving a little bit of space between each floret.

3. Transfer the baking sheet to the preheated oven and roast for 20 to 25 minutes, stirring once halfway through the roasting time or until the cauliflower is tender and nicely browned.

4. Meanwhile, combine all the ingredients for the chimichurri in a small bowl. Set aside for 10 minutes to let the badass flavors mingle.

5. Transfer the roasted cauliflower to a large bowl or plate and spoon the chimichurri over top. Serve warm or at room temperature.

1 large head cauliflower, cored and broken into florets

1 tablespoon extra-virgin olive oil

Kosher salt

Freshly ground black pepper

FOR THE CHIMICHURRI
¼ cup fresh flat-leaf parsley leaves, finely chopped

¼ cup fresh cilantro leaves, finely chopped

3 garlic cloves, minced

½ small shallot, minced

3 tablespoons extra-virgin olive oil

2 teaspoons fresh lemon juice

¼ teaspoon crushed red pepper flakes

JUST THE TIP: SAVE TIME BY PULSING ALL THE INGREDIENTS FOR THE CHIMICHURRI IN A FOOD PROCESSOR OR BLENDER UNTIL RELATIVELY SMOOTH. THE RESULTING SAUCE IS A LITTLE LESS RUSTIC. BUT THE FLAVORS WILL BE THE SAME. (SOME PEEPS MAY ACTUALLY PREFER THE SMOOTHER VERSION.)

SOUTHWESTERN SWEET POTATO SALAD

SERVES 4—6

2 medium sweet potatoes, peeled and cut into ¾-inch cubes

2 tablespoons extra-virgin olive oil, divided

Kosher salt

1½ cups sweet corn kernels (from 2 ears of corn)

One 15-ounce can black beans, drained and rinsed

1 large red bell pepper, seeded and diced

½ small red onion, finely chopped

¼ cup fresh cilantro leaves, finely chopped

FOR THE DRESSING
Juice of 1 lime

1 tablespoon extra-virgin olive oil

1½ teaspoons honey or agave syrup

1½ teaspoons hot sauce, such as Cholula, or more if you're feeling wild

Kosher salt

Let's talk about the boss nutritional benefits of sweet potatoes for a hot sec. Prized for their anti-inflammatory properties, the orange spuds are an excellent source of fiber, vitamin C, and a laundry list of disease-fighting antioxidants. They're particularly high in beta-carotene, which boosts your immune system, keeps your eyesight on point, and defends your skin against sun damage—great news for all you rugged outdoorsy types!

On top of all that, sweet potatoes are fucking delicious, and you should work more of them into your diet ASAP. (Sweet potato fries don't count.) This roasted sweet potato salad loaded with corn, black beans, bell peppers, and a sprinkling of fresh cilantro is the perfect place to start. Sweet and savory with a mild kick and plenty of citrusy zing, it's great alongside your favorite meat or fish, as the base of a burrito bowl, or on its own as a snack or light lunch.

1. Preheat the oven to 400°F. Line a large baking sheet with parchment paper.

2. Arrange the cubed sweet potatoes on the prepared baking sheet in an even layer. Drizzle with 1 tablespoon of the olive oil, add a pinch of salt, and toss to coat. Roast for 25 minutes until tender, turning them once halfway through the cooking time. Let cool to room temperature.

3. Heat the remaining 1 tablespoon olive oil in a large skillet over medium heat. When the oil is hot and shimmering, add the corn kernels and cook for 5 to 6 minutes or until lightly browned. Remove from the heat and set aside.

4. In a large bowl, whisk together the ingredients for the dressing. Season with salt to taste. Add the roasted sweet potatoes, corn, black beans, bell pepper, red onion, and cilantro to the bowl. Toss gently to coat. Refrigerate the salad for at least 20 minutes to let the flavors mingle.

5. Serve cold or at room temperature.

THREE-BEAN QUINOA SALAD

Light yet satisfying, this multicolored grain salad is a zesty flavor party that also happens to be ridiculously good for you. The powerhouse trio of edamame, chickpeas, and black beans serves up a hefty dose of fiber, protein, and antioxidants and, as I will continue to remind you throughout this book, quinoa is a Dude Dieter's best bud. This is one of those dishes that tastes even better after a day or two in the fridge, so it's a great make-ahead option for tailgating, barbecues, and busy weeknights.

1. Combine the quinoa and water in a small saucepan and bring to a boil. Lower to a simmer, cover the saucepan with a lid, and cook for 14 minutes, or until all of the liquid has been absorbed. Let the quinoa rest, covered, for 5 minutes, then fluff with a fork. Set aside.

2. Meanwhile, combine the red onion, garlic, lemon juice, olive oil, salt, and pepper in a large bowl. Let the mixture stand for 10 minutes or until the onions have softened slightly.

3. Drain and rinse your beans. When it comes to the chickpeas, I like to remove the skins. To do this, place the drained chickpeas between two sheets of paper towel and rub lightly. This will loosen the skins, which you can then pick off and discard. (This is optional, but it's really not that difficult. Just do it.)

4. Add the chickpeas, black beans, edamame, cooked quinoa, parsley, and scallions to the bowl with the dressing. Toss to combine.

5. Cover and refrigerate your salad for at least half an hour to let the flavors get friendly with each other. Serve cold or at room temperature.

½ cup uncooked quinoa, rinsed and drained

¾ cup water

½ medium red onion, minced

3 garlic cloves, minced

Juice of 1 large lemon

2 tablespoons extra-virgin olive oil

¾ teaspoon kosher salt

¾ teaspoon freshly ground black pepper

One 15-ounce can black beans, drained and rinsed

One 15-ounce can chickpeas, drained and rinsed

1 cup shelled edamame (If using frozen edamame, thaw according to the package directions.)

¼ cup packed fresh flat-leaf parsley leaves, finely chopped

3 scallions, finely chopped

> **YOU DO YOU:** FEEL FREE TO MAKE THIS SALAD WITH WHATEVER WHOLE GRAINS YOU HAVE ON HAND AND EXPERIMENT WITH YOUR FAVORITE BEANS—PINTO. KIDNEY. AND CANNELLINI ARE ALL EXCELLENT IDEAS.

JALAPEÑO-CHEDDAR SKILLET CORNBREAD

SERVES 8—10

Ahhhhh, cornbread. The most beloved and dangerous of the "invisible sides." Adding a hunk of cornbread to a giant plate of barbecue or a bowl of chili is often an afterthought, like grabbing a spoon, which makes sense given the fact that many dudes use it to shovel said barbecue and chili into their mouths. The problem with this carb-y utensil is that it can pack just as many calories and fat grams as the meal itself.

The good news is that with just a few simple tweaks, this fan favorite can be made over to support your Dude Dieting efforts. Just swap a mix of heart-healthy olive oil and yogurt for the usual butter, dial back the sugar, and use whole-wheat flour in place of white. The resulting skillet-crisped cornbread is sweet, spicy, and perfectly moist, with just enough sharp cheddar to satisfy your perpetual need for cheese.

1 cup yellow cornmeal

1 cup whole-wheat flour

1 teaspoon kosher salt

2 teaspoons baking powder

1 large egg

⅓ cup nonfat plain yogurt

1 cup 2 percent milk

4 tablespoons extra-virgin olive oil, divided

¼ cup honey

¾ cup grated sharp cheddar cheese, divided

⅓ cup pickled jalapeño rounds, finely chopped

1. Place a 12-inch ovenproof skillet (preferably cast iron) in the oven. Preheat the oven to 375°F.

2. In a large bowl, whisk together the cornmeal, flour, salt, and baking powder. In a separate bowl, whisk the egg, yogurt, milk, 3 tablespoons of the olive oil, and the honey. Pour the wet ingredients over the dry ingredients and mix with a spatula *just* until combined. Do NOT overmix the batter, dudes! A few small lumps are totally fine. Fold in ½ cup of the cheddar and the chopped jalapeños.

3. Using oven mitts, very carefully remove the hot skillet from the oven and place it on the stovetop. Add the remaining 1 tablespoon of olive oil to the skillet and swirl to coat the bottom and sides of the pan. (Watch out—the oil may spit a little!) Pour in the cornbread batter, and sprinkle the remaining ¼ cup cheddar on top. (Feel free to add a few decorative jalapeño rounds while you're at it.) Bake the cornbread for 20 minutes, or until the top is golden brown and a tester inserted in the center comes out clean.

4. Let your cornbread cool for at least 10 minutes before slicing.

AVOCADO-DIJON COLESLAW

6 cups shredded green cabbage (about half a medium head of cabbage, core removed)

2 cups shredded carrots

1 small jalapeño, thinly sliced (optional)

Freshly ground black pepper

FOR THE DRESSING:

1 ripe medium-size avocado, pitted and peeled

2 tablespoons Dijon mustard

2 tablespoons apple cider vinegar

¼ teaspoon kosher salt

¼ cup extra-virgin olive oil

At its core, coleslaw is cabbage salad, which is a beautiful thing. Cabbage has killer detoxifying and cancer-fighting powers, and it can help improve the health of your digestive tract. However, slathering the vegetable in mass quantities of creamy dressing negates all of those glorious health benefits, and a single cup of the mainstream mayo-laden stuff can clock in at over 300 calories and 20 grams of fat. You may as well eat French fries, dudes—but please don't. Instead, take this unbelievably flavorful slaw for a spin. Bright and tangy with a kick of heat, it gets its creaminess from a Dijon-spiked avocado vinaigrette, making it as kind to your bod as it is to your taste buds.

1. In a large bowl, combine the cabbage, carrot, and jalapeño (if using).

2. Place the ingredients for the dressing in the bowl of a food processor (or high-speed blender), and process until smooth, scraping down the sides of the bowl/blender once or twice if necessary. With the motor running, slowly drizzle in the olive oil. Continue processing until the mixture is silky smooth.

3. Add the dressing to the slaw and toss to coat. Season with freshly ground black pepper to taste. Serve immediately.

JUST THE TIP: IF YOU HAVE A LARGE FOOD PROCESSOR WITH A SHREDDING ATTACHMENT, MAKE YOUR LIFE EASIER AND USE IT TO SLICE THE CABBAGE AND CARROTS. YOU CAN ALSO BUY PREPACKAGED COLESLAW MIX IF YOU LIKE. (NO JUDGMENT.)

smashed potatoes with garlic and thyme

SERVES 4

2 pounds baby red potatoes (about 16 potatoes)

3 tablespoons extra-virgin olive oil

1 tablespoon finely chopped fresh thyme leaves

3 garlic cloves, minced

½ teaspoon freshly ground black pepper

1 teaspoon kosher salt

Flaky sea salt, such as Maldon, for serving (optional)

I like to think of these potatoes as a cross between garlicky steak fries and fancy Tater Tots, but without the deep-fried guilt or safety hazards of either. As such, I dedicate these crispy little nuggets to potato-loving dudes everywhere. Try them alongside Grilled Flank Steak (page 157) or Magic Fauxtisserie Chicken (page 103) the next time you need a meat-and-potatoes fix.

1. Put the potatoes in a medium saucepan and add enough cold water to cover by at least 2 inches. Bring to a rolling boil over high heat. Once boiling, reduce the heat slightly so that the water is gently boiling, and cook for about 20 minutes, or until the potatoes can be easily pierced with the tip of a sharp knife. Drain and let cool for 10 minutes (or until you can comfortably handle them).

2. Meanwhile, preheat the oven to 425°F. Line a large baking sheet with parchment paper and set aside.

3. In a small bowl, combine the olive oil, chopped thyme, garlic, and pepper.

4. Arrange the cooled potatoes on the lined baking sheet in rows, leaving about 2 inches between each one. Using a potato smasher or the bottom of a glass, gently smash the potatoes into ½-inch-thick cakes. They will be craggy and jagged, and some may even break apart in places. Don't worry about it.

5. Spoon or brush a little of the olive oil mixture onto each potato. Carefully lift up the bottom of the potatoes to let a little of the oil get on the undersides. Sprinkle all of the potatoes with kosher salt. Roast for 20 to 25 minutes or until golden brown and crispy. Serve hot garnished with flaky sea salt (if you like), and experience the magic.

YOU DO YOU: ONCE YOU MASTER THE SMASHED POTATO TECHNIQUE. GET CREATIVE WITH THE SEASONING. A HANDFUL OF IDEAS TO CONSIDER: ROSEMARY AND PARMESAN. OREGANO AND LEMON PEPPER. A CAJUN OR BARBECUE SPICE RUB. AND PLAIN OLD SEA SALT WITH A FEW DASHES OF WHITE VINEGAR ADDED JUST BEFORE SERVING.

VEGETABLE SOBA NOODLES
WITH PEANUT SAUCE

SERVES 4—6

8 ounces buckwheat soba noodles

1 teaspoon dark sesame oil

¾ cup shelled edamame (If using frozen edamame, thaw according to the package directions.)

¾ cup shredded carrots

1 small red bell pepper, seeded and very thinly sliced

3 scallions, white and light green parts only, thinly sliced

¼ cup fresh cilantro leaves, finely chopped

FOR THE PEANUT SAUCE

¼ cup chunky peanut butter

Juice of 1 lime

2 tablespoons low-sodium soy sauce

1 tablespoon dark sesame oil

1 tablespoon sriracha sauce

1 tablespoon honey

1 garlic clove, grated or finely minced

1 to 2 tablespoons warm water

Logan once lived on this recipe for almost a week when I was out of town, and he still describes these creamy, spicy noodles with the type of breathy reverence usually reserved for cheesesteaks, jam bands, and Philadelphia sports teams. Hot or cold, they really are *that* good. For an all-out Asian inspired feast, serve them with Thai Chicken Meatballs (page 123) or Fiery Pork and Pineapple Skewers (as pictured on page 160).

1. Bring a large pot of water to a boil. When boiling add the soba noodles and cook for 4 to 5 minutes or just until tender. (Be careful, dudes, most packages will tell you to cook the noodles for 6 minutes, which will turn them into complete mush.) Drain the noodles immediately and rinse them well with cold water to keep them from sticking together. Transfer to a large bowl and add the sesame oil. Toss gently to coat.

2. In a medium bowl, whisk together all the ingredients for the peanut sauce except the water. Add the water, 1 teaspoon at a time, until the sauce is smooth and pourable.

3. Add the peanut sauce to the soba noodles and toss gently to coat. Add the edamame, carrot, bell pepper, and scallions and toss again.

4. Serve the noodles warm, at room temperature, or cold, garnished with the cilantro.

KNOWLEDGE BOMB: BUCKWHEAT PROVIDES MORE PROTEIN PER SERVING THAN ANY OTHER GRAIN EXCEPT OATS. MAKING SOBA A SUPER FILLING AND ENERGIZING NOODLE OPTION. TRY TOSSING SOBA NOODLES WITH DIFFERENT SAUCES. AND ADDING THEM TO SOUPS AND STIR-FRIES FOR A TASTY NUTRIENT BOOST.

SAUTÉED ASPARAGUS WITH BACON

I'm tempted to wax poetic about the many wonders of this simple sauté, but I'll restrain myself. After all, a dissertation on the flavor nuances of garlicky spring asparagus seems sort of unnecessary and pretentious when I know you're only interested in one thing . . .

There's lots of crispy bacon in this asparagus, dudes. (You're welcome.)

1. Slice the asparagus on the diagonal into 1-inch pieces, leaving the tips whole. Set aside.

2. Heat a large skillet or sauté pan over medium heat. When hot, add the bacon and cook for 5 to 6 minutes or until browned and crispy. Using a slotted spoon, transfer the bacon to a small bowl, leaving the grease in the pan. (That's right, you're going to cook the asparagus in the bacon grease.)

3. Add the shallot and garlic to the skillet and cook for 1 minute or until softened slightly, then add the asparagus, salt, and pepper. Cook until the asparagus is just tender, 8 to 10 minutes. Add the vinegar and cook for 30 seconds more. Return the bacon to the skillet and toss to combine. Remove from the heat and serve immediately.

2 bunches (about 1½ pounds) medium asparagus, woody ends removed

3 slices bacon (preferably with no added nitrates), sliced crosswise into ¾-inch pieces

1 small shallot, minced

2 garlic cloves, minced

½ teaspoon kosher salt

¼ teaspoon freshly ground black pepper

1½ teaspoons balsamic vinegar

JUST THE TIP: TO REMOVE THE TOUGH AND FIBROUS "WOODY ENDS" ON YOUR ASPARAGUS. SIMPLY BEND EACH SPEAR BACK AND FORTH ABOVE THE WHITE PART OF THE STALK UNTIL IT BREAKS. THE SPEARS WILL NATURALLY BREAK WHERE THE WOODY PART ENDS AND THE FRESH. TENDER ASPARAGUS BEGINS.

MANLY MEDITERRANEAN SALAD

When asked to describe his salad preferences, Logan has always been pretty succinct: *More good shit, less lettuce.* This Mediterranean miracle meets the criteria and then some. A hearty mix of chopped fresh vegetables, buttery chickpeas, and salty feta tossed with an oregano-laced lemon dressing, it's a quick and crowd-pleasing recipe that performs equally well as a side, light meal, or snack.

1. In a large bowl, whisk together all the ingredients for the dressing. Add the salad ingredients and toss to combine.

2. Cover and refrigerate for at least 15 minutes before serving to let all the awesome flavors mingle. Serve cold or at room temperature.

KNOWLEDGE BOMB: CHICKPEAS (AKA GARBANZO BEANS) ARE INCREDIBLY HIGH IN PROTEIN AND FIBER. AND STUDIES HAVE SHOWN THAT PEOPLE WHO EAT THEM AS PART OF THEIR REGULAR DIET CONSUME FEWER OVERALL CALORIES. NEEDLESS TO SAY, THE DUDE DIET ENDORSES CHICKPEAS.

1 red bell pepper, seeded and diced

½ English cucumber (aka seedless cucumber), diced

¼ medium red onion, thinly sliced

1 cup grape tomatoes, halved from pole to pole

One 15-ounce can chickpeas, drained and rinsed

3 ounces feta cheese, cut into ½-inch cubes

¼ cup fresh flat-leaf parsley leaves, finely chopped

FOR THE DRESSING
Juice of 1 lemon

1 tablespoon extra-virgin olive oil

1 large garlic clove, grated or finely minced

¾ teaspoon dried oregano

½ teaspoon kosher salt

¼ teaspoon freshly ground black pepper

SHAVED BRUSSELS SPROUTS WITH RED PEPPER AND PECORINO ROMANO

SERVES 4

1 pound Brussels sprouts (about 3 cups whole sprouts), washed well, stems and any ugly outer leaves removed

2 tablespoons extra-virgin olive oil

½ teaspoon kosher salt

1 teaspoon crushed red pepper flakes

Juice of ½ lemon

¼ cup freshly grated pecorino Romano cheese

Brussels sprouts are a divisive vegetable—you either love them or hate them. But I've found that most haters were traumatized by boiled sprouts during their formative years and are still haunted by the mushy texture and rotten egg smell. If you happen to be one of those poor souls, I feel for you, but it's time to face your tiny cabbage fears and give these shaved sprouts a fighting chance. Their spicy, lemon-scented deliciousness is a total revelation, and since Brussels sprouts have the highest cancer-fighting potential of all cruciferous vegetables (even more than kale), I'm praying you'll see the light.

1. Slice the sprouts in half lengthwise, and then slice them very thinly crosswise. (On the off chance that you have a mandoline slicer, you can definitely use it to speed things up.)

2. Heat the olive oil in a large skillet over medium-high heat. When the oil is hot and shimmering, add the sprouts in an even layer and cook, undisturbed, for 2 to 3 minutes so that they get a nice little char going on the bottom.

3. Add the salt and red pepper flakes to the sprouts and cook for another 2 minutes, stirring periodically, just until tender. Stir in the lemon juice and cook for 1 minute more.

4. Transfer the sprouts to a serving plate or bowl and top with the grated cheese. Serve warm or at room temperature.

> YOU DO YOU: PECORINO ROMANO IS A SHEEP'S MILK CHEESE WITH A SHARP, SALTY FLAVOR. IT'S WIDELY AVAILABLE IN MOST GROCERY STORES, BUT PARMESAN, ASIAGO, AND GRANA PADANO ARE ALL GREAT SUBSTITUTIONS.

CAULIFLOWER PUREE WITH Parmesan AND CHIVES

SERVES 4—6

The first time Logan tried this cheesy cauliflower puree, he practically licked his plate before commenting, "These potatoes taste different, but I dig it." When I admitted that they were not actually potatoes at all, something unexpected happened. Instead of retracting his compliment and sulking over having been tricked into eating a half head of cauliflower, he broke into a Cheshire cat grin and said, "SWEET. I feel so healthy now! Can I have the rest of yours?"

If that's not a ringing endorsement, I'm not sure what is.

1. Combine the cauliflower florets and chicken broth in a medium saucepan and bring the liquid to a boil. Lower to a simmer, cover the saucepan with a lid, and cook for 15 to 20 minutes or until the cauliflower is tender. Please keep an eye on it, dudes—you want it to be tender but not completely falling apart.

2. Using a slotted spoon, transfer the cauliflower to a blender or food processor. (No slotted spoon? No problem. Simply drain the cauliflower in a colander.) Puree until silky smooth.

3. Transfer the puree to a bowl (or the saucepan if you're not serving it immediately). Stir in the Parmesan, salt, and chives, and season with freshly ground pepper to taste. Serve warm.

2 small heads cauliflower, cored and broken into florets (about 7 cups)

2 cups low-sodium chicken broth

¼ cup freshly grated Parmesan cheese

¾ teaspoon kosher salt

3 tablespoons finely chopped fresh chives

Freshly ground black pepper

KNOWLEDGE BOMB: WHILE POTATOES AREN'T INHERENTLY BAD FOR YOU, MASHED POTATOES REQUIRE COPIOUS AMOUNTS OF BUTTER AND MILK (OR WORSE, CREAM) TO DEVELOP THE SMOOTH TEXTURE AND COMFORTING FLAVOR YOU KNOW AND LOVE. CAULIFLOWER PUREE, HOWEVER, IS SO NATURALLY FLAVORFUL AND SILKY THAT IT DOESN'T NEED SUCH FATTY ENHANCEMENTS TO TASTE AMAZING. EVEN WITH THE PARMESAN CHEESE, SERVING THIS RECIPE IN PLACE OF MASHED POTATOES WILL SAVE YOU HUNDREDS OF CALORIES PER MEAL.

CHIPOTLE MASHED SWEET POTATOES WITH GOAT CHEESE

2 large sweet potatoes (1¼ to 1½ pounds each)

1 tablespoon honey

1 chipotle pepper canned in adobo sauce, finely chopped (If you're sensitive to spice, seed the pepper first.)

1 teaspoon adobo sauce from the chipotle can

½ teaspoon kosher salt, plus extra if needed

⅛ teaspoon ground cinnamon

3 ounces goat cheese, crumbled, divided

1 tablespoon finely chopped fresh cilantro leaves (optional)

If you're more of a hands-off cook, this is your fantasy side. Just throw a couple of sweet potatoes in the oven, and do your thing for an hour or so while they roast. Once the spuds are done, mash them up with a drizzle of honey, a fiery chipotle pepper, and some creamy goat cheese. Boom, done. (I'm talking 5 minutes of actual work here.)

Feel free to serve this mash six sexy ways to Sunday, but I highly recommend piling the potatoes into bowls and smothering them with 1-Hour Pulled Pork (page 74), which you can simmer on the stovetop while the sweet potatoes roast. Just be sure to mentally prepare yourself for the associated flavor fireworks.

1. Preheat the oven to 425°F. Line a baking sheet with aluminum foil.

2. Pierce the skin of each sweet potato all over with a fork and place them on the prepared baking sheet. (Don't go too crazy—six good stabs should do it.) Bake for 1 hour to 1 hour and 15 minutes or until very tender when pierced with the tip of a sharp knife. Let the potatoes cool slightly.

3. When the potatoes are cool enough to handle, remove their skins. (They should peel right off.) Transfer the flesh to a medium bowl, add the honey, chipotle pepper, adobo sauce, salt, and cinnamon, and mash with a fork until very smooth. Using a spatula, gently fold in three-quarters of the cheese. (It will melt slightly, but there's no need to incorporate it completely—little pockets of goat cheese are bomb.)

4. Taste and season with a little extra salt if necessary. Serve warm, garnished with the remaining one-quarter cheese and the cilantro (if using).

JUST THE TIP: ROASTING THE SWEET POTATOES GIVES THEM THE BEST FLAVOR. BUT YOU CAN MICROWAVE THEM IF YOU'RE IN A HURRY. PIERCE THE POTATOES AS DIRECTED. PLACE THEM ON A PLATE. AND MICROWAVE FOR 8 TO 12 MINUTES ON HIGH. TURNING THEM OVER ONCE HALFWAY THROUGH.

Garlic-Ginger Snap Peas

5 cups sugar snap peas

1 tablespoon dark sesame oil

3 garlic cloves, minced

1 tablespoon peeled and minced fresh ginger

2 tablespoons low-sodium soy sauce

2 teaspoons honey

Freshly ground black pepper

If there was ever a green vegetable side dish to get fired up about, this is it, dudes. Sweet and gingery with an addictive crunch, these flavor-blasted peas are super-quick to make and impossible to screw up. The only labor-intensive aspect of the recipe is removing the string from each pea pod—which shouldn't take you more than 10 minutes—and you'll be well rewarded for the effort.

1. Start by prepping your snap peas. Each pod has a little string attached to it that you'll need to remove. To do this, just snap off one of the pointy ends of the pod and pull lightly on the attached string. The string should peel right off.

2. Heat the sesame oil in a large skillet over medium-high heat. When the oil is hot and shimmering (but not smoking!), add the snap peas and cook for 3 to 4 minutes or until crisp-tender. Add the garlic, ginger, soy sauce, and honey and cook for 1 minute more.

3. Transfer the snap peas to a serving bowl and season generously with freshly ground black pepper.

YOU DO YOU: CAN'T FIND SNAP PEAS OR SIMPLY DON'T LIKE THEM? TRY SUBBING GREEN BEANS. BLANCH THE GREEN BEANS IN BOILING WATER FOR 2 MINUTES UNTIL BRIGHT GREEN. IMMEDIATELY PUT THEM INTO A BOWL OF ICE WATER TO STOP THE COOKING, AND DRAIN. THEN FOLLOW THE RECIPE AS WRITTEN.

caprese quinoa cakes

All the summer flavors of a Caprese salad wrapped up in a crispy little quinoa fritter? Win. Crush the cakes alongside your favorite grilled meat or fish, or try them over a pile of mixed greens when you're in the mood for something light.

1. Combine the quinoa and vegetable broth in a small saucepan and bring to a boil. Lower to a simmer, cover the saucepan with a lid, and cook for 14 minutes, or until all of the liquid has been absorbed. Let the quinoa rest, covered, for 5 minutes, then fluff with a fork. Transfer the grains to a medium bowl and let cool for at least 10 minutes.

2. Meanwhile, start your balsamic reduction. Pour the balsamic vinegar into a small saucepan and bring to a boil. Reduce the heat to low and simmer for 10 minutes or until it becomes thick and syrupy. Cover with a lid and set aside until ready to use.

3. Drain any excess juice from the chopped tomatoes and add them to the cooled quinoa along with the basil, garlic, mozzarella, egg, flour, salt, and pepper. Stir until everything is very well combined.

4. Line a baking sheet with parchment or wax paper. Using your hands, gently mold ¼-cup measures of the quinoa mixture into patties, roughly 2 inches in diameter, and place them on the prepared baking sheet. You should have 12 cute little cakes.

5. Heat 2 tablespoons of the olive oil in your largest nonstick skillet over medium heat until shimmering (but not smoking!). Using a thin metal spatula, carefully transfer half of the cakes to the pan. Let them cook, undisturbed, for 4 minutes or until you can see that they are golden brown around the edges. (If you try to move them before

½ cup uncooked quinoa, rinsed and drained

¾ cup low-sodium vegetable broth

⅓ cup balsamic vinegar

1 cup grape or cherry tomatoes, finely chopped

½ packed cup fresh basil leaves, finely chopped, plus extra for serving

1 large garlic clove, grated or finely minced

½ cup grated fresh mozzarella

1 large egg, lightly beaten

¼ cup whole-wheat flour

¾ teaspoon kosher salt

¼ teaspoon freshly ground black pepper

4 tablespoons extra-virgin olive oil

this happens, the cakes will fall apart. That will be on you, dudes.)
Carefully, but confidently, flip the cakes over and cook for another 3 to
4 minutes on the opposite sides or until browned and crispy. Transfer
to a platter or serving dish. Add the remaining 2 tablespoons of olive
oil to the pan and repeat the process to cook the remaining cakes.

6. Serve the quinoa cakes drizzled with the balsamic reduction (you
may need to reheat it for 30 seconds to loosen it up) and sprinkled with
a little extra chopped basil.

ROASTED BROCCOLI WITH FONTINA AND GARLICKY BREAD CRUMBS

SERVES 4 GENEROUSLY

1¼ pounds broccoli florets (about 8 cups)

3 tablespoons extra-virgin olive oil, divided

½ teaspoon kosher salt, divided

Freshly ground black pepper

3 garlic cloves, minced

3 tablespoons whole-wheat panko bread crumbs

¼ teaspoon crushed red pepper flakes (optional)

2 ounces (½ cup) grated Fontina cheese

Like cauliflower, roasting has a magical transformative effect on broccoli, and the addition of creamy Fontina and toasted garlicky bread crumbs makes for a savory, awesomely textured side that's packed with essential vitamins and minerals. I like to think of it as steamed broccoli with Velveeta's svelte Italian cousin. Everyone wants a piece . . .

1. Preheat the oven to 425°F. Line a large baking sheet with parchment paper.

2. Place the broccoli florets in a large bowl. Drizzle with 2 tablespoons of the olive oil and sprinkle with ¼ teaspoon of the kosher salt and a few cranks of freshly ground black pepper. Toss to coat. Arrange the broccoli in a single layer on the prepared baking sheet. (Try not to overlap the florets, or they'll steam instead of crisping up.) Roast for 13 to 15 minutes or until tender and lightly browned in spots.

3. While the broccoli is roasting, heat the remaining 1 tablespoon olive oil in a small skillet over medium heat. When hot, add the garlic and cook for about 2 minutes until golden brown. (Be very careful not to burn your garlic! If it looks like it's browning too quickly, turn down the heat.) Stir in the remaining ¼ teaspoon kosher salt, the bread crumbs, and red pepper flakes (if using). Cook for 2 minutes or until the bread crumbs are nicely toasted and have darkened a shade in color. Remove from the heat.

4. Sprinkle the broccoli with the Fontina and the garlicky bread crumbs. Roast for 5 minutes more until the cheese has melted and is bubbling. Serve warm, making sure to scrape up any magical crispy cheese from the baking sheet.

YOU DO YOU: FONTINA IS A SEMISOFT CHEESE WITH A BUTTERY, SLIGHTLY NUTTY TASTE. YOU SHOULD BE ABLE TO FIND IT IN THE CHEESE DEPARTMENT OF MOST MARKETS, BUT PROVOLONE, GOUDA, AND MOZZARELLA ARE ALL GREAT SUBSTITUTES.

BACK-POCKET RECIPES

Using your Dude Diet knowledge to make smarter choices when dining out (or ordering in) is all well and good, but cooking at home is the true cornerstone of long-term health and weight loss. Making a meal yourself is the only way to have 100 percent control over what you're putting in your body, so flexing your culinary muscles on the reg is an absolute must if you're serious about cleaning up your diet. No ifs, ands, or buts.

While none of the recipes in this book are overly challenging, I recognize that you may not always have the motivation for a major market haul or the patience to tackle a seemingly exotic feast for the first time. That's where this chapter comes in. From life-changing techniques for cooking chicken breasts and fish to a better bowl of pasta and soul-warming stew, these easy, reliable meals are what I like to call "back-pocket recipes." They're the culinary building blocks and fallback staples that will bolster your kitchen confidence and keep you on the nutritional straight and narrow under even the most trying circumstances. (Read: Quickie dankness for unplanned game-day celebrations, romantic encounters, and those busy weeknights when exhaustion and extreme hunger tempt you to throw caution to the wind and rendezvous with your favorite Chinese deliveryman.) Consider them your Dude Diet safety net.

The following recipes aren't just simple, they're also incredibly flexible and should be modified according to what you happen to have on hand. (Throw the veggies lingering in your crisper into your Go-To Frittata [page 258]! Make Spinach Pesto [page 260] with almonds instead of walnuts! Build your fantasy Tortilla Pizza [page 263]!) However, in order to pull them off with the intended ease, you will actually have to have some ingredients *on hand*. Consider this a friendly reminder to keep your kitchen stocked with at least a handful of the essentials (review the full list on page 12) and to pick up a few proteins, like chicken breasts, eggs, or fresh fish, on a weekly basis.

To minimize your time in the kitchen each week and help set you up for Dude Diet domination, I recommend doubling or tripling down on some of these recipes when you can. Make a bunch of Idiotproof Chicken Breasts (page 257) on a Sunday and add them to salads, pastas, and casseroles throughout the week, or whip up an extra-large Sausage and Peppers Skillet (page 267) so that you can have leftovers for breakfast with an egg on top. Freeze a second batch of Smoky Black Bean Chicken Stew (page 270) for impromptu entertaining and nights when you just can't be bothered to cook anything fresh. I could go on, but you get the point.

Success is 90 percent planning, 10 percent execution, dudes. Be a planner.

IDIOTPROOF CHICKEN BREASTS

Boneless, skinless chicken breasts, aka BS breasts, are often dismissed as dry, stringy, and tasteless, which is ridiculous. These dismal descriptors are due to the fact that most people fear undercooked poultry and tend to overcompensate, cooking their chicken well beyond the point of no return. But that's about to change, dudes. This idiotproof method gives BS breasts an image overhaul, eliminating "is it done?" anxiety and producing tender, juicy goodness every single time.

The only tricky aspect of this technique is that it requires a significant amount of blind trust. You cannot, *under any circumstances*, lift the lid on the pan while the chicken cooks. It will be tempting to peek, but you must resist the urge. I promise that when you finally lift the lid, you'll have perfect chicken breasts, ready to be added to everything from salads to burrito bowls or served with the sexy sides of your choice.

Two 8-ounce boneless, skinless chicken breasts

Kosher salt

Coarsely ground black pepper

1 tablespoon olive oil

1. Pat the chicken breasts dry with paper towels and season both sides generously with salt and pepper.

2. Heat a large skillet or sauté pan over medium-high heat. When hot, add the olive oil and swirl to coat the bottom of the pan. Lower the heat to medium and add the chicken breasts. Cook for 1 minute, then flip the breasts over. Reduce the heat to low, cover the pan with a tight-fitting lid, and cook for 10 minutes. DO NOT LIFT THE LID.

3. After 10 minutes, turn off the heat and let the chicken sit, covered, for an additional 10 minutes. Again, DO NOT LIFT THE LID. Resist the urge.

4. After the full 20 minutes, remove the lid. Boom, done. (Your chicken will be cooked, but if you're still nervous, you can check it with an instant-read thermometer to make sure it has an internal temperature of least 165°F.)

GO-TO Frittata

6 large eggs

1 teaspoon hot sauce of your choice, such as Cholula (optional)

Pinch of kosher salt

1 teaspoon extra-virgin olive oil

1 link spicy chicken sausage, diced

½ red bell pepper, seeded and thinly sliced

½ small yellow onion, thinly sliced

1 garlic clove, minced

⅓ cup grated Monterey Jack cheese

¼ cup salsa of your choice

1 tablespoon chopped fresh cilantro leaves (optional)

Frittatas make quick and easy anytime meals, and they're the most delicious way to use up whatever random ingredients happen to be hanging out in your fridge. Once you nail the technique, you'll be able to create an endless variety of eggcellent creations, but this recipe is a great starting point. The killer combo of sautéed sausage, peppers, and onions never disappoints, and melted Jack cheese, salsa, and fresh cilantro give this protein-packed frittata a little Southwestern flair. If you're willing to go the extra mile, I recommend getting some Chipotle Guacamole (page 111) involved.

1. In a medium bowl, whisk together the eggs, hot sauce, and salt. Set aside.

2. Preheat the broiler on high.

3. Heat the olive oil in a 10-inch nonstick, ovenproof skillet over medium heat. When the oil is hot and shimmering, add the sausage and cook for about 3 minutes or until lightly browned. Add the bell pepper, onion, and garlic and cook for 3 to 4 minutes or until the vegetables are just tender.

4. Pour the eggs into the pan and cook for about 3 minutes until the eggs are beginning to set. Sprinkle with the cheese and cook for another 2 minutes until your frittata is almost set, but the top is still a little bit runny.

5. Place the skillet under the broiler. Broil for 1 to 2 minutes or until the cheese has melted and the top of the frittata is puffed up and very lightly browned.

6. Loosen the frittata from the pan with a spatula and slide it onto a cutting board. Slice in half (or quarters), transfer to two plates, and top with salsa and cilantro if you like.

> JUST THE TIP: IF YOU DON'T HAVE AN OVENPROOF SKILLET (OR YOU SIMPLY DON'T WANT TO MESS WITH THE BROILER), FINISH THE FRITTATA ON THE STOVETOP. SIMPLY LOWER THE HEAT TO MEDIUM-LOW, POP A LID ON THE PAN, AND COOK UNTIL THE FRITTATA IS COMPLETELY SET.

PENNE WITH SPINACH PESTO

12 ounces brown rice penne (I like Jovial brand), or whole-grain penne of your choice

FOR THE PESTO
3 packed cups baby spinach

⅓ packed cup fresh basil leaves

3 garlic cloves, peeled and smashed

½ cup raw walnuts

2 tablespoons fresh lemon juice

¾ teaspoon kosher salt, plus extra if needed

½ teaspoon freshly ground black pepper, plus extra if needed

¼ cup extra-virgin olive oil

FOR SERVING (OPTIONAL)
Freshly grated Parmesan cheese

Crushed red pepper flakes

This is one of the few bowls of pasta you can be proud of, dudes. Brown rice penne has far more health benefits than its white flour counterpart, and the fresh pesto is a nutritional heavy hitter. Spinach serves up twice as much fiber as other greens and is full of disease-fighting antioxidants, potassium, and blood sugar–regulating phytochemicals, and the walnuts deliver a solid dose of necessary omega-3s. You can whip up the pesto in roughly the same amount of time it takes to heat a jar of store-bought sauce—and it tastes infinitely better—so save the excuses and work this recipe into your regular rotation ASAP.

The occasional vegetarian meal won't kill you (I swear), but if you're truly offended by the lack of meat, bulk up your penne with diced Idiotproof Chicken Breasts (page 257) or some browned chicken or turkey sausage.

1. Bring a large pot of salted water to a boil.

2. Meanwhile, place the spinach and basil in the bowl of a food processor (or high-powered blender) and pulse a few times until coarsely chopped. Add the garlic, walnuts, lemon juice, salt, and pepper and process until the mixture forms a relatively smooth paste, scraping down the sides of the bowl a few times if necessary. With the motor running, slowly pour in the olive oil and process or until the pesto looks uniform. Taste and season with a little extra salt and pepper if necessary.

3. Cook the penne al dente according to the package directions. Drain, reserving about a ¼ cup of the pasta's cooking water.

4. Return the penne to the pot. Add the pesto and 2 tablespoons of the reserved pasta water and toss to coat. (If the pesto is too thick, add a little more of the cooking water.)

5. Transfer the pasta to bowls and serve warm. Top with a responsible amount of freshly grated Parmesan and a sprinkling of crushed red pepper flakes if you like.

JUST THE TIP: IF YOU'RE COOKING FOR ONE (OR TWO) AND DON'T WANT PASTA LEFTOVERS, MAKE HALF THE AMOUNT OF PENNE, AND SAVE THE EXTRA PESTO TO JAZZ UP FUTURE MEALS. IT'S AN AWESOME ADDITION TO EVERYTHING FROM SCRAMBLED EGGS TO SALADS AND STEAK.

Big Pineapple Tortilla Pizza

MAKES 1 personal pizza

On those days when you're considering crushing an entire pizza solo, whip out a skillet and take this personal pie for a spin. It's light, topped with a sweet and savory combo of pineapple and turkey bacon, and guaranteed to hit the spot without throwing you into a shame spiral. Plus, it can be ready in 20 minutes. Logan's been known to spend twice that long building his fantasy pizza on the Domino's app . . .

2 slices turkey bacon

2 teaspoons extra-virgin olive oil

One 10-inch whole-wheat tortilla or wrap

¼ cup marinara sauce

⅓ cup shredded part-skim mozzarella cheese

¼ cup finely chopped pineapple

¼ teaspoon crushed red pepper flakes (optional)

3 fresh basil leaves, stacked, rolled, and thinly sliced (aka chiffonade)

1. Cook the turkey bacon in a skillet over medium heat until browned and crispy, about 4 to 5 minutes per side. Transfer to a paper towel–lined plate and let cool for 2 to 3 minutes, then chop into small pieces.

2. Preheat the broiler on high.

3. Heat a large ovenproof skillet over medium-high heat. When hot, add the olive oil and swirl to coat the bottom of the skillet. Place the tortilla in the skillet and cook for 30 seconds to 1 minute or until it puffs up slightly and the underside is lightly browned.

4. Reduce the heat to medium-low. Quickly spread the marinara sauce on the tortilla in an even layer. Sprinkle with the cheese and top with chopped pineapple, the chopped, cooked turkey bacon, and red pepper flakes (if using).

5. Transfer the skillet to the broiler and broil for 2 to 3 minutes or until the cheese has melted and is bubbling, and the edges of the tortilla are dark brown. (Pay attention, dudes—things can go from brown to burnt very quickly!)

6. Using oven mitts, remove the skillet from the broiler, loosen the bottom of the tortilla from the skillet with the tip of a knife, and slide it onto a cutting board. Sprinkle with the basil. Slice your 'za into 6 triangles and get after it.

Parchment Salmon
AND VEGETABLES

1 small zucchini, sliced into ¼-inch rounds

1 small shallot, thinly sliced

6 cherry or grape tomatoes, halved from pole to pole

2 teaspoons extra-virgin olive oil, divided

2 teaspoons balsamic vinegar, divided

Kosher salt

Freshly ground black pepper

One 6- to 8-ounce skinless salmon fillet, about 1 inch thick

2 to 3 fresh basil leaves, chopped (optional)

This one goes out to the dudes that appreciate a good piece of fish but aren't sure how to cook it at home. Whatever your fears may be—undercooking, overcooking, stink, etc.—this technique will lay them all to rest. Just drizzle salmon and fresh veggies with olive oil and balsamic vinegar, seal them in parchment paper, and toss the package in the oven for 20 minutes. When you rip open the paper, you'll find a flawless piece of fish over expertly steamed veggies. No mess, no guesswork, no fishy-smelling kitchen.

The recipe makes a single perfectly portioned meal, but you can easily assemble multiple packets at a time, so keep it in mind for stress-free date nights, family dinners, and entertaining. If salmon isn't your jam, apply the same technique—known in fancy culinary circles as *en papillote*—to cook almost any firm white fish of a similar thickness.

1. Preheat the oven to 375°F. Fold a 15 x 16-inch piece of parchment paper in half. Open the parchment paper back up and place it on a baking sheet.

2. Arrange the zucchini, shallot, and tomatoes on one side of the parchment paper near the fold. Drizzle with 1 teaspoon of the olive oil and 1 teaspoon of the vinegar, and season generously with salt and pepper.

3. Rinse the salmon under cold water and pat dry with paper towels. Season the fillet with salt and pepper, and place it on top of the vegetables. Drizzle with the remaining 1 teaspoon olive oil and 1 teaspoon vinegar.

4. Fold the parchment paper over the fish. Starting at the top crease, make small overlapping folds to seal the edges of your "package" in a half-moon shape. (It doesn't have to be beautiful, dudes, but please make sure it's tightly sealed.)

5. Bake for 20 minutes or until the paper has puffed up and browned slightly and your salmon has cooked through.

6. Transfer the packet to a plate, open it up (careful, there will be some steam!), and garnish with the fresh basil if you have it.

Sausage AND Peppers Skillet

Early in our courtship, Logan invited me over for a romantic dinner and wooed me with several Coors Lights and a version of this classic skillet. We've eaten it countless times since, and although I've taken some liberties with the original recipe (i.e., using a responsible amount of chicken sausage, swapping farro for white rice, and omitting the bottle of hot sauce), it will always be Logan's "signature dish." He looks forward to receiving your fan mail.

1. Cook the farro according to the package directions. Drain and set aside.

2. Meanwhile, heat the olive oil in a large skillet over medium-high heat until shimmering. Add the sausage and cook for 5 minutes or until lightly browned. (It doesn't have to be super-brown, dudes, it's going to keep browning once you add the veggies.)

3. Add the bell peppers, onion, garlic, oregano, salt, and red pepper flakes (if using) and cook for 8 to 10 minutes or until the vegetables have softened and lightly browned.

4. Add the balsamic vinegar, reduce the heat to medium, and cook for 1 minute more. Stir in the farro and remove the skillet from the heat.

5. Divide the deliciousness between two bowls and top each with Parmesan and chopped fresh herbs if you've got them.

> YOU DO YOU: I LIKE THE SLIGHTLY CHEWY TEXTURE OF FARRO FOR THIS SKILLET. BUT FEEL FREE TO USE WHATEVER WHOLE GRAIN YOU HAVE ON HAND—BROWN RICE, QUINOA, AND BARLEY ARE ALL GREAT SUBS.

½ cup pearled or semipearled farro

1 tablespoon extra-virgin olive oil

3 mild or sweet Italian chicken sausage links, thinly sliced at a slight angle

1 red bell pepper, seeded and thinly sliced

1 yellow bell pepper, seeded and thinly sliced

1 medium yellow onion, thinly sliced

3 garlic cloves, minced

¾ teaspoon dried oregano

½ teaspoon kosher salt

¼ teaspoon crushed red pepper flakes (optional)

2 tablespoons balsamic vinegar

FOR SERVING (OPTIONAL)
2 tablespoons grated Parmesan cheese

2 tablespoons chopped fresh flat-leaf parsley or basil leaves

TURKEY MELT WITH SPINACH AND MUSHROOMS

2 teaspoons extra-virgin olive oil

8 ounces baby bella or cremini mushrooms (about 2 cups), thinly sliced

1 small shallot, minced

2 garlic cloves, minced

¼ teaspoon kosher salt

¼ teaspoon freshly ground black pepper

2 packed cups baby spinach

½ pound thinly sliced low-sodium turkey breast

4 slices whole-grain sandwich bread (I like a good seeded loaf, but you do you.)

4 teaspoons Dijon mustard

¾ cup grated Gruyère cheese (Gouda, sharp cheddar, and provolone are also great.)

Most dudes have a soft spot for sandwiches, which is understandable. Sandwiches are comforting and convenient, and they involve the three most beloved dude foods: meat, cheese, and bread. While a sandwich can be a well-balanced meal, there seems to be a widespread misconception that *all* sandwiches are healthy. I'm not sure where this myth originated, but I'd venture that Subway has something to do with it, as I've heard a few dudes defend their less-than-slimming sandos with the claim, "Michael Phelps crushes foot-longs all day!" That's a valid argument if you're planning to adopt an Olympic athlete's training schedule, but until then, please rethink your sandwich choices.

When it comes to building a smarter sandwich, stick to whole-grain bread, vegetables, lean meats, a reasonable amount of cheese, and light condiments, as demonstrated by this epic turkey melt. Loaded with protein and a full serving of veggies, it will keep your bod fueled and satisfied without roughing up your waistline. Sadly, I can't say the same for a meatball sub . . .

1. Heat the olive oil in a large skillet or sauté pan over medium heat. When the oil is hot and shimmering, add the mushrooms, shallot, garlic, salt, and pepper, and cook for 5 minutes or until the mushrooms are soft and lightly browned. Add the spinach and cook just until wilted, about 1 minute. Transfer to a bowl and set aside.

2. Microwave the turkey breast for 15 to 20 seconds until slightly warm (Nothing is worse than biting into a hot sandwich with a cold center.)

3. Time to assemble your sandos! Spread one side of each slice of bread with a teaspoon of mustard. Sprinkle each of two slices with a quarter of the cheese. Top with half of the mushroom mixture and half of the turkey, and sprinkle with the remaining cheese. Close the sandwiches with the remaining two slices of bread, Dijon side down (duh).

4. Wipe out the pan used for the mushrooms and return it to the stovetop. Heat the pan over medium heat. When hot, add the sandwiches to the pan, cover with a lid, and cook for 3 minutes or until the undersides are golden brown. Carefully flip the sandwiches, cover again, and cook for another 2 to 3 minutes or until the opposite sides have browned and the cheese has melted. Slice the sandwiches in half and serve immediately.

smoky black bean CHICKEN STEW

Two 15-ounce cans black beans, drained and rinsed

1 tablespoon extra-virgin olive oil

1 red bell pepper, seeded and diced small

1 medium yellow onion, finely chopped

3 garlic cloves, minced

1 tablespoon smoked paprika

2 teaspoons dried oregano

1 teaspoon kosher salt

1 teaspoon ground cumin

1 chipotle pepper canned in adobo sauce, finely chopped

1 tablespoon adobo sauce from the chipotle can

1 teaspoon honey

2 cups low-sodium chicken broth

1 pound boneless, skinless chicken breasts, halved crosswise

Juice of ½ lime

Keep a few extra cans of black beans in stock during the cooler months so you can simmer this smoky, soul-warming stew on short notice. With an ingredient list that's mostly pantry staples, about 20 minutes of hands-on time, and almost no cleanup, it's the ideal emergency option for busy weeknights, last-minute game-day celebrations, and everything in between. Since stew also happens to be one of those boss creations that tastes even better after a day or two of chilling in the fridge, leftovers are something to be stoked about.

1. Place the black beans in a large bowl and roughly mash them with a fork. (Some whole beans are totally fine, dudes.) Set aside.

2. Heat the olive oil in a medium Dutch oven or soup pot over medium heat until shimmering. Add the bell pepper, onion, and garlic and cook for 3 minutes or until the onion is translucent and the pepper has softened slightly. Stir in the paprika, oregano, salt, and cumin, and cook for 1 minute more until toasted and fragrant. Add the mashed black beans, chipotle, adobo sauce, honey, and chicken broth and bring to a simmer. Once simmering, add the chicken breasts and cover with a lid. Simmer for 15 minutes until the chicken is cooked through.

3. Carefully transfer the chicken to a cutting board. Shred the meat with two forks, then return it to the stew. Turn off the heat and stir in the lime juice.

4. Ladle the stew into bowls. Garnish with some fresh toppings if you're feeling festive.

YOU DO YOU: I LIKE TO DRESS UP THIS STEW WITH DICED AVOCADO, A DOLLOP OF NON-FAT GREEK YOGURT, AND PLENTY OF CHOPPED CILANTRO. BUT THE GARNISH POSSIBILITIES ARE ENDLESS. CHEESE LOVERS SHOULD DEFINITELY TRY ADDING SOME CRUMBLED GOAT CHEESE TO THEIR BOWLS—THE CREAMY TANG ADDS AN UNEXPECTED (AND INSANELY) DELICIOUS TWIST.

Grown-up Beans on Toast

Regardless of differences in language, sports, and beer selections, when it comes to feeding themselves, the international dude community tends to favor the same things—comfort and convenience. So, while "beans on toast" may have British origins, the recipe's simplicity has universal appeal: Heat up can of beans. Pour on toast.

I've elevated things a tiny bit here, ramping up the flavor with some fresh ingredients, and working in a little more protein and fiber, but the extra steps are pretty painless. All you need to transform basic bachelor grub into a full-blown rustic feast is hearty whole-grain bread and a few minutes to simmer beans and browned chicken sausage in a simple tomato sauce. Finish your toast with a sprinkling of grated Parmesan and chopped herbs if you have them, and congratulate yourself on being such a culinary ace. You may use a British accent if you like. (Logan usually does.)

1. Heat the olive oil in a medium skillet or sauté pan over medium heat. When the oil is hot and shimmering, add the chicken sausage and cook for 4 to 5 minutes until lightly browned. Add the onion and garlic and cook for about 2 minutes or until the onion has softened and the garlic is fragrant, then stir in the tomato paste, oregano, paprika, salt, and red pepper flakes (if using). Cook for 2 minutes more.

2. Add the beans, crushed tomatoes, and chicken broth and bring to a boil. Reduce the heat to low and cook for 10 minutes to let those comforting flavors combine. (If your beans seem too thick, just add a little more chicken broth or water.)

3. Toast your bread. Smother each piece with a quarter of the bean mixture and top with Parmesan and parsley if you've got them. Serve immediately.

> YOU DO YOU: IF YOU CAN'T FIND (OR DON'T LIKE) CANNELLINI BEANS, GREAT NORTHERN BEANS OR NAVY BEANS WILL ALSO WORK.

2 teaspoons extra-virgin olive oil

2 links Italian chicken sausage (sweet or spicy), diced

½ small yellow onion, finely chopped

2 garlic cloves, minced

2 teaspoons tomato paste

1 teaspoon dried oregano

¾ teaspoon smoked paprika

¼ teaspoon kosher salt

¼ teaspoon crushed red pepper flakes (optional)

One 15-ounce can cannellini beans, drained and rinsed

One 14.5-ounce can crushed tomatoes

¼ cup low-sodium chicken broth or water

4 slices whole-grain bread

FOR SERVING (OPTIONAL)
¼ cup shaved Parmesan cheese

2 tablespoons chopped fresh flat-leaf parsley leaves

CHRONIC COCKTAILS

Making smarter solid food choices is one critical component to Dude Diet success, but regulating your liquid consumption is an equally, if not more, important piece of the puzzle. Given the average dude's love for booze and sugary soft drinks, the number of calories imbibed on a weekly basis can be truly mind-blowing. The worst part is that most don't fully grasp the dangers of downing a casual six-pack, ordering White Russians as an aperitif, or double-fisting tropical drinks on warm-weather getaways. The entire dude community seems to be operating under the happy illusion that they consume far fewer liquid calories than they actually do.

I'm sure it's wonderful to exist in this glorious world of bottomless beers and c-tails, but consuming a day's worth of calories at the bar crushes both your liver and your waistline. In case you didn't know, metabolizing fat is one of your liver's most important jobs. Alcohol distracts the liver from this critical task by forcing it to focus on eliminating boozy toxins, causing your body's fat-burning ability to plummet. So, if you hit the gym after work and then go ham at happy hour, you're not only gaining back every calorie burned (and then some), you are actually slowing the rate at which your body burns calories to begin with. Bad news for those of you working on your beach bod.

I'd also like to point out that excessive boozing tends to have some rather disturbing food-related consequences. Alcohol lowers your inhibitions, especially when it comes to your diet, and the more you drink, the more likely you are to wake up cuddling an empty pizza box or covered in Taco Bell wrappers. Not to mention the fact that hangovers can compel even the most diligent Dude Dieters to self-medicate with gallons of Gatorade and more shameless feasting.

Luckily, the prescription for these alcohol-related problems is simple: *Quit drinking.*

PSYCH.

I'm messing with you guys! Such a Draconian approach to boozing is both unrealistic and potentially damaging to your social life. All I ask is that you wise up when it comes to the nutrition facts of your favorite adult beverages and drink a little more responsibly (i.e., stop chugging margaritas the size of your head). The following guidelines should help.

The Dude Diet Boozing Guidelines

- MODERATION, MODERATION, MODERATION. Unless you've got something to celebrate, limit yourself to 1 to 2 alcoholic beverages per day, *max*. And you should (almost) never be drinking more than 14 in a single week. If you're willing to go the extra Dude Diet mile, dry out during the workweek. (The lbs practically fall off when you cut out wine with dinner and weeknight beers on the couch.)

- KNOW (AND RESPECT) ALCOHOL SERVING SIZES. There are 12 ounces (1 bottle) of beer, 5 ounces of wine, and 1.5 ounces (1 shot) of hard liquor in a single serving. Many bars and restaurants will give you at least 1.5 servings of alcohol in your cocktail or wine glass, so think long and hard before ordering an extra round.

- SLOWWWW DOWN. I know "it tastes so good once it hits your lips," but chugging drinks Frank the Tank–style is a recipe for disaster, both physically and behaviorally. Not only does drinking more slowly and mindfully help moderate your caloric intake and your buzz, it also allows you to appreciate the deliciousness of your booze.

- LIGHTEN UP YOUR BREWS. Beer is practically its own food group in most dudes' diets, and while I'd never dream of asking you to live a brew-free existence, making smart selections is non-negotiable. If you're only sipping on one (or maybe two), feel free to indulge in a 200-calorie IPA, but on occasions when you plan to down "frat sodas" at a high volume, LIGHT beer is the way to go. I know some of you may feel a little soft ordering a light beer, but I promise it's well worth the momentary discomfort in the long run. Especially if you're single. (When it comes to meeting a potential mate, it's usually best to lead with your personality, not your beer belly.)

• **GO CLEAR.** Clear liquors like vodka, silver tequila, gin, and light rum tend to have slightly fewer calories than darker spirits like whiskey, brandy, and dark rum, but more importantly, they contain fewer congeners. Congeners are toxic compounds that are formed when alcohol is fermented, and they have been shown to exponentially increase the severity of your hangovers.

• **SIDELINE THE SUGAR.** Adding extra sugar to your booze in the form of granulated sugar, flavored syrups, store-bought mixers, soda, and processed juices sends your cocktail's calorie content through the roof and tends to cause particularly painful hangovers. Sugar also masks the flavor of alcohol, so sweet cocktails are typically consumed dangerously fast. Unless The Dude himself—as in, *The Big Lebowski*—is your ideal body type, I recommend drinking your liquor straight or mixing it with water, club soda, or a squeeze of fresh citrus.

• **WINE IS NOT A "MAGICAL HEALTH ELIXIR."** I know that wine seems lighter than beer, and you've probably read somewhere that red wine contains antioxidants and promotes heart health and longevity, but neither of those things gives you license to down it with abandon. A single serving of vino has an average of 125 calories, dudes. Moderation and pacing rules still apply.

• **HYDRATE.** And I'm not just talking about chugging from the sink before bed—you need to stay hydrated *while* imbibing, dudes. Alternating every alcoholic beverage with a glass of high-quality H2O helps you stay sober *and* keeps you feeling full, which drastically reduces your chances of both late-night feasting and morning after misery.

Now that you're familiar with The Dude Diet's boozing rules, I'm hoping it's safe to unleash you on the chronic cocktails in this chapter. Created for those days when a light beer or vodka soda simply won't cut it, the following libations are made with natural flavors and minimal added sugar to keep your caloric intake (and hangover) in check. Cheers.

JUST THE TIP: TRY SERVING THIS TEA WARM DURING THE COOLER MONTHS. IT'S QUITE THE TAILGATE CROWD-PLEASER. AS WELL AS A SURPRISINGLY EFFECTIVE COLD REMEDY.

TWISTED LEMON-MINT ICED TEA

Logan doesn't do so well in the heat. He gets tense and irritable at temperatures above 75 degrees, which means there's a lot of cursing and sweating once summer hits its suffocating stride in NYC, as well as an unspoken ban on all physical contact outside of heavily air-conditioned spaces. (I learned this the hard way when I tried to hold his hand one particularly balmy summer night, and he screamed, "Are you insane?!!" in the middle of Sixth Avenue.)

While Logan is a particularly sweaty case, he's not the only dude that suffers from this special brand of seasonal affective disorder. Luckily, there are a couple of tried-and-true ways to beat the heat: (1) Eat more salads and veggie-heavy meals (this will help you stay hydrated), and (2) Keep this bourbon-spiked iced tea on hand at all times. Minty, slightly sweet, and unbelievably refreshing, it's the perfect pitcher cocktail to sip on all summer long.

To stay cool *and* keep a clear head, make a virgin batch and add bourbon to individual cocktails as needed.

6 cups filtered water

6 black tea bags

1 cup fresh mint leaves, packed

½ cup fresh lemon juice

6 tablespoons honey

2 cups bourbon

FOR GARNISH (OPTIONAL)
1 lemon, sliced into thin rounds

Fresh mint sprigs

1. Bring the water to a boil in a medium saucepan. Once boiling, remove from the heat and add the tea bags and the 1 cup of mint leaves. Cover and steep for 10 minutes.

2. Meanwhile, heat the lemon juice and honey in a small saucepan over medium heat. Simmer for 2 to 3 minutes, swirling the saucepan occasionally or until the honey has completely dissolved. Set aside.

3. Once the tea has steeped, strain it into a large pitcher, discarding the mint and tea bags. Mix in the lemon-honey syrup and refrigerate the tea until completely cool, about 2 hours.

4. Stir the bourbon into the cooled tea. Add lemon slices and fresh mint to the pitcher for extra flair.

5. Serve in tall glasses (or mason jars) with plenty of ice.

rosemary GIN FIZZ

8 ounces gin

2 ounces fresh lemon juice

2 ounces Rosemary Simple Syrup

12 ounces club soda

4 sprigs fresh rosemary

FOR THE ROSEMARY SIMPLE SYRUP

½ cup honey

½ cup water

5 sprigs fresh rosemary

There are certain occasions that call for a slightly more sophisticated beverage, and this one's a good go-to. Booze-forward and refreshing with an herbal twist, it's a winning year-round cocktail that looks sexy as hell in a highball or rocks glass. The rosemary-infused simple syrup will set you back about 30 minutes, but it couldn't be easier, and you can store it in the fridge for up to 2 weeks.

P.S. If you haven't already, please consider investing in a few decent cocktail glasses. A gin fizz in an NFL mug doesn't have quite the same effect.

1. First make the Rosemary Simple Syrup: Combine the ingredients in a small saucepan and bring to a boil. Cook for 1 minute, swirling the pan occasionally or until the honey is completely dissolved. Turn off the heat, cover the saucepan, and let it sit for 30 minutes to infuse. Strain the syrup into a mason jar or airtight container and refrigerate until ready to use. You'll have about 1 cup syrup.

2. Add the gin, lemon juice, and simple syrup to a cocktail shaker with ice and shake well.

3. Strain into 4 highball or rocks glasses with ice and top with club soda. Garnish each with a rosemary sprig and get your fizz on.

YOU DO YOU: GIN HATERS CAN SUBSTITUTE VODKA FOR AN EQUALLY REFRESHING. IF SOMEWHAT LESS COMPLEX. SIP.

JALAPEÑO MULE

¾ teaspoon finely chopped jalapeño (with seeds)

2 ounces vodka

1 ounce fresh lime juice

3 ounces non-alcoholic ginger beer (I recommend Fever-Tree or Barritts.)

1½ ounces club soda

FOR GARNISH (OPTIONAL)
Lime wedge
Seeded jalapeño rounds

If you like your booze with a little kick, this jalapeño-infused play on the classic Moscow Mule is right up your alley. A generous squeeze of lime juice cuts the sweetness of the ginger beer, and a splash of club soda lightens things up. To make this cocktail for a crowd, simply shake up a big batch of the fiery vodka base (the proportions are pretty easy to multiply), strain it into a pitcher or punch bowl, and stir in the ginger beer and soda come party time.

1. Add the jalapeño, vodka, and lime juice to a cocktail shaker with ice. Shake well.

2. Strain into a copper mug or tall glass with ice. Stir in the ginger beer and top with club soda.

3. Garnish with lime wedges and a couple of jalapeño rounds.

JUST THE TIP: GINGER BEER IS NOT THE SAME AS GINGER ALE! GINGER BEER HAS A MUCH STRONGER GINGER FLAVOR AND IS LESS CARBONATED AND LESS SWEET THAN GINGER ALE. MOST MAJOR MARKETS TEND TO KEEP IT IN STOCK (USUALLY WITH THE SODAS), SO YOU SHOULDN'T HAVE TOO MUCH TROUBLE TRACKING IT DOWN.

MANHATTAN SMASH

MAKES **1 cocktail**

This lighter, fruitier twist on a Manhattan packs a punch, but it won't knock you out quite like the classic cocktail. That's a good thing, dudes. As we discussed, impaired judgment tends to have unfortunate pizza-related casualties.

Take advantage of fresh sweet cherries when they're in season, and sub frozen cherries during the cooler months.

1. Muddle the cherries and lemon juice in a mixing glass. (No need to pulverize the cherries, you just want to break them down and release some of their juices.) Stir in the whiskey and vermouth.

2. Transfer to a rocks glass and fill the glass up with crushed ice. Top with a splash of club soda.

½ cup fresh or frozen sweet cherries, pitted (If using frozen cherries, you'll need to let them thaw first.)

1 teaspoon fresh lemon juice

2 ounces rye whiskey

1½ ounces sweet vermouth

Club soda

JUST THE TIP: ALWAYS USE A PINT GLASS OR A STURDY PLASTIC TUMBLER FOR MUD-DLING AND MIXING COCKTAILS TO PREVENT BREAKING A NICE GLASS. BETTER SAFE THAN SORRY.

Grapefruit Beergarita

Since most dudes are in the "beer makes everything" better camp, I'm guessing I don't have to sell you on the beauty of a beer floater on your marg. But if you're skeptical, I promise that beer, tequila, and lots of fresh citrus play very well together, and you'll love the boozy but balanced flavor of this trashed up margarita. Pink grapefruit gives the drink an awesome tangy sweetness, but feel free to fiesta with other fruit juices and purees if you like. Blood orange, mango, and strawberry are particularly exciting alternatives.

1. Start by rimming your glass. Pour a little kosher salt into a small shallow dish. Moisten the rim of your favorite cocktail glass with a lime wedge and dip it in the salt.

2. Add the grapefruit juice, tequila, lime juice, and agave (if using) to a cocktail shaker with ice. Shake well.

3. Strain into the rimmed glass with ice. Top with beer and party on.

Kosher salt for rimming the glass

Lime wedge for rimming the glass

2 ounces fresh-squeezed pink grapefruit juice

1½ ounces tequila reposado

1 ounce fresh lime juice

1 teaspoon pure agave syrup (optional)

2 ounces Mexican beer, such as Corona or Modelo

KNOWLEDGE BOMB: THIS BEERGARITA IS ON THE LIGHTER SIDE BECAUSE IT'S MADE WITH NOTHING MORE THAN FRESH FRUIT JUICE. GOOD TEQUILA. A LITTLE AGAVE. AND A SPLASH OF BEER. RESTAURANT VERSIONS OF THE COCKTAIL ARE MOST DEFINITELY NOT DUDE DIET APPROVED. SO DON'T GO POURING FULL BEERS INTO YOUR OVERSIZED DIVE BAR MARGARITAS AND CONSIDERING THEM "DIET DRINKS."

Frozen Rosé Sangria

MAKES **1 pitcher** / **6 cocktails**

1 bottle dry rosé wine (You want something light pink.)

2 cups frozen peaches

1½ cups frozen strawberries

1 cup frozen mango

Juice of 1 lime

1 tablespoon honey

FOR GARNISH (OPTIONAL)
Fresh mint sprigs or sliced fresh strawberries

I'd like to take a moment to warn you about an especially dangerous category of adult beverages that Logan affectionately refers to as "boat drinks." These are your standard umbrella cocktails (i.e., piña coladas, daiquiris, and frozen margs), and while delicious, they're loaded with artificial flavors, refined sugar, calories, and fat. Just as a point of reference, the average piña colada contains more calories than a Big Mac. Would you crush multiple Big Macs while frolicking half-naked on the beach?

(That was a rhetorical question.)

I would never ask you to give up boat drinks altogether—especially since some of my favorite memories of Logan involve him splashing around with one in hand—but the sugary store-bought mixes have got to go. Instead, blend a better-for-you beverage like this sangria, which gets its frosty sweetness from frozen peaches, strawberries, mango, and a drizzle of honey. It's not quite as light on calories as some of the other cocktails in this chapter, so I don't recommend chugging the entire pitcher solo, but you can at least feel good about the lack of additives and the fact that you're getting almost a full serving of fruit in each glass. Vitamins with your booze are always a plus.

1. Place all the ingredients for the sangria in a blender and puree until smooth.

2. Pour the sangria into a pitcher or directly into glasses. Serve garnished with fresh mint or strawberry slices.

> YOU DO YOU: NOT A "ROSÉ ALL DAY" TYPE? TRY A DRY WHITE WINE INSTEAD. PROSECCO ALSO WORKS WELL IF YOU'RE INTO BUBBLES.

WATERMELON MOJITO

⅓ cup fresh mint leaves

½ ounce (1 tablespoon) fresh lime juice

4 ounces Watermelon Juice (see below)

2 ounces light rum

Club soda

FOR GARNISH (OPTIONAL)
Fresh mint sprig
Lime round

FOR THE WATERMELON JUICE
2 cups cubed seedless watermelon

When it comes to Dude Diet–friendly cocktail mixers, watermelon juice gets two very enthusiastic thumbs up. It's light on calories and sugar but heavy on flavor, vitamins (especially vitamins C and A), and lycopene, a powerful antioxidant that fights disease and inflammation. And since watermelon is more than 90 percent water, its nutrient-rich juice is supremely hydrating and full of electrolytes, which may help keep your hangover at bay. Based on these thrilling facts, I move to make this watermelon mojito the dude community's new poolside c-tail of choice.

As Logan always says, real men drink pink cocktails. Spread the word.

1. First make the Watermelon Juice. Place the watermelon in a blender and blend until smooth. Strain through a fine-mesh strainer. (Yes, you can use a pasta strainer if that's all you have.) You'll have about 1½ cups juice.

2. Gently muddle the mint leaves and lime juice in a cocktail shaker. Add the watermelon juice, rum, and a couple of ice cubes. Shake well.

3. Strain into a glass with ice, and top with a splash of club soda. Garnish with a sprig of mint and a lime round.

JUST THE TIP: THE WATERMELON JUICE CAN BE MADE UP TO 2 DAYS IN ADVANCE AND STORED IN AN AIRTIGHT CONTAINER IN THE FRIDGE.

PINEAPPLE REFRESHER

For those who tend to treat their hangovers with a little hair of the dog, this lip-smacking tropical treat is just what the Dude Diet doctor ordered. Fresh pineapple boasts high quantities of bromelain, an enzyme that reduces inflammation, promotes immunity and digestion, relieves muscle pain, and helps detoxify your body. Combine that magic with stomach-settling ginger, hydrating coconut water, and a splash of vodka for the "scaries," and you've got quite the detox/retox elixir on your hands. Bottoms up.

1. First make the Pineapple Puree: Throw the pineapple chunks in a blender and puree until smooth. You'll end up with about 1 cup puree.

2. Place all the ingredients for the refresher in a cocktail shaker with ice. Shake well.

3. Strain into a tall glass with ice. Garnish with lime rounds if you're feeling extra fresh.

3 ounces pure coconut water

2 ounces Pineapple Puree (see below)

1½ ounces vodka

1 ounce fresh lime juice

1 teaspoon peeled and finely chopped fresh ginger

Thinly sliced lime rounds (optional)

FOR THE PINEAPPLE PUREE
2 cups fresh pineapple chunks

YOU DO YOU: THIS ALSO MAKES AN EXCELLENT "MOCKTAIL" FOR THOSE THAT ARE OFF THE SAUCE. SIMPLY REPLACE THE VODKA WITH EXTRA COCONUT WATER.

SWEETNESS

Reflecting on dudes and their relationships with sugar, I'm reminded of a rather telling experience at my local nail salon. I was mid-manicure, enjoying the tranquility of the salon's atmosphere, only to have it abruptly shattered by a series of high-pitched, agonized screams and a stream of choice expletives. Panicked, I made eye contact with the lady at the front desk, who pointed to one of the treatment rooms and mouthed "first back wax" through tears of silent laughter. When the poor dude in question finally emerged from his torture chamber, the manager offered him a cookie from a jar next to the register. He took six "to ease the pain."

While the specifics vary, this tale of pain and cookies is a common one. From back wax recovery to managing work stress and all the unpleasant things in between, sugar is many dudes' panacea drug of choice. And given its awesome short-term effect on the brain, it's a tough one to quit. Everyone loves a good sugar high, amiright?

As you may know, it's also common to celebrate special occasions with sugar. I'm all for a piece of birthday cake, a couple of Christmas cookies, or a Super Bowl sundae, but when you find yourself "celebrating" everyday things like getting to work on time or finding a boss parking spot? Check yourself before you wreck yourself. The side effects of both self-soothing and celebrating with sugar are less than sweet.

We've already covered the many dangers of excessive refined sugar consumption, but in case you need a little refresher, it suppresses your immune system, fucks up your insulin and hormone levels, and increases the rate of fat deposition in fat cells. In short, too much sugar makes you sick, moody, and flabby, and regulating your intake is a must. Pay closer attention to what you put in your mouth on a day-to-day basis, and do your best to eliminate (or at least limit) the most sugar-heavy items. Remember, dudes, refined sugars aren't just found in typical "dessert-y" foods—they're in everything from bagels to ketchup and Gatorade. Be aware. (And when in doubt, Google.)

Looking to make serious Dude Diet strides? Try cutting out refined sugar altogether for at least two weeks to help kick your cravings for the stuff. If you're more of a savory than sweet type, dialing back the sugar shouldn't be overly difficult. (You've likely got bigger, cheeseburger-shaped fish to fry when it comes to maintaining your health.) However, those of you with a serious sweet tooth have a bit of a bumpy road ahead. Detoxing from refined sugar can get weird, and you should be prepared to experience some unpleasant withdrawal symptoms, including headaches, fatigue, and mood swings. If you're anything like Logan, you will be tempted to throw in the towel at some point and bum-rush the nearest vending machine or tray of baked goods just to get a fix. *Resist the urge.* I promise that if you can power through the pain of the first few days of a detox, you'll find that your burning desire for sugar subsides pretty quickly. (Many people report fewer cravings after just three days sans refined sugar.) Stress-busting workouts, fresh fruit, and meals high in mood-boosting omega-3s like Parchment Salmon and Vegetables (page 264) and Asian Kale Salad with Chia-Crusted Tuna (page 178) will also help take the edge off.

Once you've kicked your more serious cravings and can happily function without regular sugary pick-me-ups, it will be safe to treat yourself on occasion. When you do, please employ all of the Dude Diet decision-making skills you've honed thus far—i.e., do not attack a gallon of ice cream or eat your weight in Snickers—and opt for more responsible indulgences like the smarter sweets in this chapter.

The following pages contain a variety of sweetness, from breakfast-y items and snacks to more traditional desserts like crumble and cookies. All are made with mostly wholesome ingredients and as little refined sugar as possible, but not every recipe is created equal on the nutrition front—some should be consumed with more restraint than others. (A daily Coconut-Lime Chia Pudding or Cherry Garcia "Milkshake" is cool, a slab of Double Chocolate Pound Cake is not.) A good rule of thumb to follow is this: If there is refined sugar listed in the ingredients (i.e., cane or brown sugar), stick to a single serving once or twice a week to keep your Dude Dieting efforts on track.

Carrot Cake Cupcakes with Maple-Cream Cheese Frosting

1⅓ cups grated carrots

1 large egg

1 large egg white

⅓ cup unsweetened applesauce

½ packed cup light brown sugar

2 tablespoons honey

½ cup liquid coconut oil

1 cup plus 2 tablespoons all-purpose flour

1 teaspoon ground cinnamon

¼ teaspoon ground dried ginger

¼ teaspoon fine-grain sea salt

1¼ teaspoons baking soda

¼ cup golden raisins (optional)

½ cup chopped walnuts, divided (optional)

(cont.)

If you've made it to this point in the book, the following knowledge bomb may seem redundant, but I'm going to go ahead and drop it anyway just to be safe: *Carrot cake is not "healthy" because it contains a vegetable.* In fact, most carrot cake is so loaded with fat it makes brownies and cookies seem like responsible, upstanding treats in comparison. The handful of grated carrots in this dessert isn't going to magically shield your belly or moobs from its disastrous effects.

Not to worry, dudes, I've clearly got your cake-loving backs. These chronic cupcakes deliver all the moist, spiced carrot goodness you live for, but thanks to a slimmed-down ingredient list and built-in portion control, they won't send your (rapidly improving!) bod into a tailspin.

1. Preheat the oven to 350°F. Line a standard muffin tin with 12 paper or foil liners.

2. In a medium bowl, whisk the carrots, whole egg, egg white, applesauce, sugar, and honey for 1 minute. (Whisking will warm up the mixture so the coconut oil doesn't solidify when you add it to the mix.)

3. Slowly whisk in the coconut oil.

4. In a separate bowl, sift together the flour, cinnamon, ginger, salt, and baking soda. (You can use a fine-mesh pasta strainer for this if that's all you have.)

5. Add the dry ingredients to the wet ingredients in two parts, stirring just until combined. (Try not to overmix; you want these cupcakes to be light and fluffy.) Stir in the raisins and half of the chopped walnuts (if using).

FOR THE FROSTING

8 ounces cream cheese, softened

¼ cup nonfat plain Greek yogurt

3 tablespoons pure maple syrup

1 teaspoon pure vanilla extract

6. Spoon the batter into the cupcake liners, filling each one about two-thirds full. Bake for 16 to 17 minutes or until a tester inserted into the center of the cupcakes comes out clean. Transfer to a wire rack to cool completely.

7. Meanwhile, whip up the frosting. Place all the ingredients for the frosting in a medium bowl and beat with an electric hand mixer until well combined. (Yes, you can flex your muscles and use a regular old whisk if you don't have a hand mixer.) Refrigerate the frosting until ready to use.

8. Spread each cooled cupcake with a heaping tablespoon of frosting. Garnish with the remaining chopped walnuts (if using).

JUST THE TIP: THE CUPCAKES CAN BE STORED IN THE FRIDGE. BUT MAKE SURE TO LET THEM RETURN TO ROOM TEMPERATURE BEFORE SERVING. (THE TEXTURE OF COLD CUPCAKES IS SUBPAR.)

PUMPKIN-BANANA BREAD

There also appears to be some serious confusion in the dude community surrounding baked goods that contain fruit. I've heard many an argument that an oversize blueberry muffin, apple doughnut, or hunk of banana bread is healthy because "it has fruit," and "fruit is good for you!" While both of those statements are technically true, the insane quantities of butter, refined sugar, and flour mixed with said fruit definitely aren't doing you any nutritional favors.

Sure, the occasional bakery treat is acceptable (whatsup, No-Cal Sunday?), but when it comes to feeding your day-to-day cravings, I recommend a thick slice of lightened-up pumpkin-banana bread. This warmly spiced loaf is made with heart-healthy coconut oil, a good amount of whole-wheat flour, and significantly less sugar than the classic recipe, but it's every bit as comforting and addictive. I promise.

1. Preheat the oven to 350°F. Coat an 8 x 4-inch loaf pan with cooking spray and set aside.

2. In a medium bowl, whisk together the flours, cinnamon, nutmeg, salt, and baking soda. Set aside.

3. Place your bananas in a separate large bowl. Using a potato masher or a large fork, mash the bananas well. You want them to be pretty smooth, but a few lumps are fine. Whisk in the pumpkin puree and coconut oil, and then add the sugar, honey, and egg. Whisk until smooth.

4. Add the dry ingredients to the wet ingredients and mix just until incorporated.

5. Pour the batter into the prepared loaf pan and sprinkle with the chopped pecans (if using). Bake for 50 minutes to 1 hour or until a wooden skewer or the tip of a sharp knife inserted into the center comes out clean.

6. Let your bread cool in the pan for 10 to 15 few minutes, then transfer it to a wire rack to cool completely. Slice and serve.

¾ cup all-purpose flour

¾ cup whole-wheat flour

1 teaspoon ground cinnamon

⅛ teaspoon ground nutmeg

⅛ teaspoon fine-grain sea salt

1 teaspoon baking soda

2 large very ripe bananas

1 cup 100 percent pure pumpkin puree, such as Libby's

½ cup liquid extra-virgin coconut oil

½ packed cup light brown sugar

2 tablespoons honey

1 large egg, lightly beaten

⅓ cup chopped pecans (optional)

CARAMELIZED PEACH
CRISP SUNDAES

SERVES 4

Peach season is short and this show-stopping sundae plays hard to get most of the year, so take advantage while you can (read: July and August). Roasting ramps up the fruit's natural sweetness and softens it to the point that each caramelized bite practically melts in your mouth. The peaches are killer with their syrupy, bourbon-tinged pan juices alone, but topped with a scoop of vanilla ice cream and your favorite crunchy granola? Out of control. Even the fruity dessert haters will want in.

1. Preheat the oven to 400°F.

2. Melt the butter in a large ovenproof skillet over medium heat. When it's melted and frothy, whisk in the bourbon, sugar, lemon juice, cinnamon, and water. Bring to a boil, then add the peaches, cut side down.

3. Transfer the skillet to the oven and roast for 20 to 25 minutes or until the peaches are very tender.

4. Divide the peach halves among four bowls or plates, and top each with a small scoop of ice cream and 2 tablespoons of the granola. Drizzle each sundae with the syrupy pan juices and serve immediately.

JUST THE TIP: SUB GREEK YOGURT FOR ICE CREAM AND SERVE THIS AS A FANCY WEEKEND BREAKFAST.

2 tablespoons unsalted butter

2 tablespoons bourbon

2 packed tablespoons light brown sugar

1 teaspoon fresh lemon juice

¾ teaspoon ground cinnamon

¼ cup water

4 ripe but slightly firm peaches, halved and pitted

1 cup vanilla ice cream or frozen yogurt

½ cup Quinoa Crunch Granola (page 46), or granola of your choice

SWEETNESS 303

COCONUT-LIME CHIA PUDDING

One 13.5-ounce can light coconut milk

½ cup nonfat plain Greek yogurt

¼ cup finely shredded unsweetened coconut

5 tablespoons chia seeds

3 tablespoons fresh lime juice

3 tablespoons honey

FOR SERVING (OPTIONAL)
Diced mango
Sliced almonds

Chia's miraculous gelling capabilities are put to work in this nutrient-dense "pudding" made with coconut milk, shredded coconut, lime, and a little Greek yogurt for creaminess and extra protein. The unique texture—which is more tapioca-like than Snack Pack smooth—may weird you out at first, but chances are you'll love it more and more with each tart-sweet bite.

The best thing about this stuff is that it requires less than five minutes of hands-on prep. Then you just stick it in the fridge for a few hours (or overnight) while the chia seeds do their thing, mix it up, and—BOOM—sweet superfood breakfasts, snacks, or desserts for days! Sliced almonds and mango add to the pudding's "lime in the coconut" tropical vibe, but don't be afraid to experiment with different mix-ins. Variety is the spice of Dude Diet life.

1. Combine all the ingredients in a medium bowl. Cover tightly with plastic wrap and refrigerate for at least 4 hours or overnight to let the chia seeds work their gelling magic.

2. Give the pudding a good stir, then spoon it into bowls or glasses. Serve topped with mango and sliced almonds or fruit/nut toppings of your choice.

JUST THE TIP: STORE YOUR PUDDING IN INDIVIDUAL JARS OR PLASTIC CONTAINERS FOR GRAB-AND-GO BREAKFASTS AND SNACKS.

NUTTY CHOCOLATE BROOKIES

1/3 cup unsweetened 100 percent cocoa powder (not Dutch-process)

1/2 cup pure cane sugar

3 tablespoons liquid extra-virgin coconut oil

1 tablespoon water

1/2 teaspoon pure vanilla extract

1 large egg

1/4 cup whole-wheat flour

1/4 teaspoon fine-grain sea salt

1/4 teaspoon baking soda

3/4 cup chopped walnuts

1/4 cup dark chocolate chips

Part brownie, part cookie, these beautiful walnut-studded babies rock the best qualities of both—I'm talking intense chocolaty flavor with slightly fudgy middles and perfect, chewy edges. And since they're made with whole-wheat flour, coconut oil, and a much more reasonable amount of sugar than your average baked goods, the occasional indulgence won't derail your Dude Diet progress. Just one should hit the sweet spot.

1. Preheat the oven to 350°F. Line a large baking sheet with parchment paper.

2. In a medium bowl, combine the cocoa powder, sugar, coconut oil, water, and vanilla. Add the egg and stir vigorously until the batter becomes smooth and slightly shiny.

3. In a separate bowl, whisk together the flour, salt, and baking soda. Add this mixture to the cocoa mixture and stir just until incorporated. Fold in the walnuts and chocolate chips, making sure everything is well combined.

4. Scoop heaping tablespoons of the dough onto the prepared baking sheet, leaving about 2 inches between each one. You should have enough for exactly 12 brookies. (Rubbing your tablespoon with a little coconut oil before scooping the batter will make this process easier.) Using damp fingers, smooth the scoops around the edges if necessary to make sure your brookies come out round(ish).

5. Bake for 11 minutes, or just until the brookies are set. Let cool on the baking sheet for 10 minutes. (You MUST wait the full 10 minutes, dudes. The brookies will be very soft coming out of the oven, and they need time to firm up.) Transfer to a wire rack to cool completely.

YOU DO YOU: IF YOU'RE ALLERGIC TO NUTS OR SIMPLY DON'T LIKE THEM. YOU CAN EITHER LEAVE THEM OUT. OR REPLACE THEM WITH 1 CUP CRISPY BROWN RICE CEREAL. THE LATTER YIELDS A DELIGHTFULLY CHEWY TREAT. ALMOST LIKE A MACAROON.

DOUBLE CHOCOLATE POUND CAKE

2 large eggs

¾ cup plus 2 tablespoons pure cane sugar

1 teaspoon pure vanilla extract

⅓ cup liquid extra-virgin coconut oil

⅓ cup unsweetened applesauce

1 cup unsweetened almond milk

1½ cups whole-wheat flour

⅓ cup unsweetened 100 percent cocoa powder (not Dutch-process)

1½ teaspoons instant espresso powder (optional)

1¼ teaspoons baking soda

½ teaspoon fine-grain sea salt

1 teaspoon apple cider vinegar

½ cup dark chocolate chips

FOR SERVING (OPTIONAL)
12 ounces fresh raspberries

My dad was the original sugar-loving dude in my life, and while I've caught him "tasting" cookies and sneaking late-night ice cream more times than I can count, the man's true soft spots are chocolate and cake. This one's for him.

1. Preheat the oven to 350°F. Spray an 8 x 4-inch loaf pan with cooking spray and set aside. (You can also grease the pan with coconut oil if you like.)

2. In a large bowl, whisk the eggs, sugar, and vanilla until pale yellow and fluffy. Whisk in the coconut oil, applesauce, and almond milk. Set aside.

3. In a separate bowl, sift together the flour, cocoa powder, espresso powder (if using), baking soda, and salt. (You can use a fine-mesh pasta strainer for this.)

4. Little by little, whisk the dry ingredients into the wet ingredients until well incorporated. Whisk in the vinegar. (It will lighten the color of the batter slightly. Magic!) Stir in the chocolate chips.

5. Pour the cake batter into the prepared pan and bake for 55 minutes or until a tester inserted in the center of the cake comes out clean. (Pay attention to timing, dudes, you don't want to overbake this chocolate masterpiece.)

6. Let the cake cool in the pan for at least 15 minutes, then transfer it to a wire rack to cool completely.

7. Slice the cake into responsible portions and serve topped with fresh raspberries.

YOU DO YOU: PREFER CHOCOLATE CUPCAKES? LINE A MUFFIN TIN WITH CUPCAKE LINERS AND FILL EACH ONE THREE-QUARTERS OF THE WAY FULL WITH THE BATTER. BAKE FOR 15 TO 17 MINUTES UNTIL A TESTER INSERTED IN THE CENTER OF THE CUPCAKES COMES OUT CLEAN. (YOU SHOULD HAVE ENOUGH BATTER FOR 10 TO 12 CUPCAKES.) THEY'RE GREAT ON THEIR OWN OR WITH A LITTLE DOLLOP OF MAPLE-CREAM CHEESE FROSTING (SEE PAGE 298).

YOU DO YOU: THESE PARFAITS ARE BOMB WITH ALMOST ANY TYPE OF BERRY, AS WELL AS PEACHES, NECTARINES, AND CHERRIES. CHOCOHOLICS MAY WISH TO USE CHOCOLATE GRAHAM CRACKERS.

NO-BAKE STRAWBERRY CHEESECAKE PARFAITS

To write a cookbook for dudes without cheesecake would be like writing a children's book without a happy ending—just plain wrong. So here's your cheesecake happy ending, dudes. I know it looks slightly different than what you're used to, but that's a good thing. Baking a cheesecake is a pain in the ass, and the boatload of fat and sugar in most recipes will spike your insulin levels faster than a yard-long piña colada. These personal parfaits, lightened up with Greek yogurt and a little honey, are a much better call. They've got all the sweet, tangy flavor and graham cracker crunch of your favorite dessert, and once you have everything prepped and ready to go, assembly takes less than 10 minutes.

Cheesecake looks good on The Dude Diet. You do, too.

5 sheets graham crackers (10 squares)

8 ounces cream cheese, softened

1 cup nonfat plain Greek yogurt

3 tablespoons honey

1 teaspoon fresh lemon juice

½ teaspoon pure vanilla extract

16 ounces strawberries, hulled and diced

1. Place the graham crackers in a ziplock food storage bag. Seal the bag, removing as much air as possible. Gently pound the crackers a few times with a rolling pin (or any other heavy object you have on hand) to crumble. (Don't go too crazy—a few chunks are awesome.) Pour the graham cracker crumble out into a bowl and set aside.

2. Place the cream cheese, yogurt, honey, lemon juice, and vanilla in a food processor (or high-speed blender). Process until very smooth, scraping down the sides of the bowl a few times if necessary.

3. Now set up a little assembly line with the graham cracker crumble, filling, and strawberries. Line up four of your finest glasses. (You'll need glasses that hold at least 8 ounces, dudes.) Add 1 heaping tablespoon of the graham cracker crumble to each glass. Top the crumble with ¼ cup of the filling, and then 2 heaping tablespoons of the diced strawberries. Repeat the layers a second time.

4. Cover the parfaits with plastic wrap and refrigerate for at least 1 hour until well chilled. Serve topped with the remaining graham cracker crumble.

CHOCOLATE-ALMOND "COOKIE DOUGH" BITES

MAKES 18—20 bites / SERVES 6—8

I started making these bites for myself years ago and was hooked on their chewy, chocolaty awesomeness and insane nutrition benefits from the get-go. Their Dude Diet potential didn't even cross my mind until months later, when I came home late one night to find a surprisingly zen Logan on the couch. As it was more than an hour past his usual feeding time, I'd expected him to be in the early stages of a hunger-induced rage blackout. Instead, the dude smiled up at me and said, "I ate a couple of those dank cookie dough balls in the fridge and I feel great. I'm not even hungry!" Once I realized that these protein and fiber-packed energy bites (and not actual cookie dough) had saved the day, I was pumped. Double batches have been kept on hand for emergency snacking, dessert, and the occasional breakfast on the fly ever since.

1 cup old-fashioned rolled oats (not quick-cooking!)

$2/3$ cup smooth almond butter

$1/3$ cup honey

2 tablespoons chia seeds

$1/2$ teaspoon pure vanilla extract

$1/4$ teaspoon kosher salt

$1/3$ cup finely chopped dark chocolate or dark chocolate chips (at least 70 percent cocoa)

1. Place the oats in a food processor (or high-speed blender) and pulse a few times until they resemble a coarse flour.

2. Transfer the oat "flour" to a medium bowl and add the almond butter, honey, chia seeds, vanilla, and salt. Stir vigorously with a wooden spoon or spatula until the ingredients are very well combined. (This will take some upper-body strength, dudes. Give it all you've got.) Stir in the dark chocolate.

3. Roll tablespoon-sized amounts of the mixture into balls and place them on a plate or parchment paper–lined baking sheet. Refrigerate for at least 30 minutes to firm up. (The bites can be stored in an airtight container in the fridge for up to 1 week.)

cherry Garcia "MILKSHAKE"

1½ cups frozen sweet cherries

1 frozen banana

¼ cup nonfat plain Greek yogurt

½ cup unsweetened almond milk (or milk of your choice)

1 tablespoon unsweetened 100 percent cocoa powder

FOR SERVING (OPTIONAL)
1 tablespoon dark chocolate shavings

If Ben and Jerry are members of your regular wolf pack, this sweet shake is about to change your life and bod for the better. I'm clearly playing fast and loose with the term "milkshake" here given the lack of ice cream involved, but I swear this frosty chocolate-cherry delight tastes every bit as creamy and indulgent as the name suggests. It's blended with exclusively good-for-you ingredients, so feel free to crush one anytime a craving strikes.

1. Place all the ingredients except the chocolate in a blender and blend until smooth.

2. Pour into a tall glass and top with chocolate shavings.

JUST THE TIP: FROZEN BANANAS ELIMINATE THE NEED FOR ICE AND ADD AMAZING CREAMINESS TO SMOOTHIES. KEEP A ZIPLOCK BAG OF PEELED BANANAS IN YOUR FREEZER TO HAVE ON HAND FOR THIS RECIPE AND ANY OTHER BLENDED CREATIONS YOU DREAM UP.

APPLE-BLUEBERRY SKILLET CRUMBLE

FOR THE TOPPING

⅔ cup old-fashioned rolled oats (not quick-cooking!)

½ cup plus 1 tablespoon whole-wheat flour

⅓ packed cup light brown sugar

⅛ teaspoon fine-grain sea salt

½ cup chopped walnuts

½ teaspoon pure vanilla extract

⅓ cup liquid extra-virgin coconut oil

3 tablespoons nonfat plain Greek yogurt (I strongly recommend Fage brand for its thick texture.)

FOR THE FILLING

2 cups fresh or frozen blueberries

2 teaspoons cornstarch

1 tablespoon extra-virgin coconut oil

Don't be fooled by the length of the recipe, dudes—this rustic fruit crumble requires minimal hard work and zero culinary skill. Just cook a bunch of diced apples in a skillet with a few basic pantry ingredients, stir in the blueberries, and smother the whole thing with a simple nut and oat topping. After a short stint in the oven, you'll have a glorious, bubbling, shareable dessert on your (oven-mitted!) hands. Take that sweet skillet for a victory lap.

1. Preheat the oven to 375°F.

2. In a medium bowl, combine the oats, flour, sugar, salt, and walnuts. Add the vanilla, coconut oil, and yogurt. Mix with your hands until all the ingredients are incorporated and the mixture is crumbly. (Clumps are a good thing.) Cover and refrigerate until ready to use.

3. Place the blueberries and cornstarch in a large bowl and toss to combine. Set aside.

4. Heat the coconut oil in a large ovenproof skillet over medium heat. When the oil is hot and shimmering, add the apples, maple syrup, lemon juice, ginger, cinnamon, and salt and cook for 10 to 12 minutes or until the apples are soft (but not mushy!). Turn off the heat and stir in the blueberries.

5. Crumble the topping in an even layer over the fruit in the skillet. Bake for 25 to 30 minutes or until the top is lightly browned and the juices are bubbling.

6. Let your crumble cool for at least 10 minutes before serving. (Seriously, it will be scary hot!) Serve with Greek yogurt or a reasonable amount of vanilla ice cream.

> JUST THE TIP: IF YOU DON'T HAVE AN OVENPROOF SKILLET, DON'T PANIC. COOK THE FILLING IN A LARGE SAUTÉ PAN, THEN TRANSFER IT TO A BAKING DISH, ADD THE TOPPING, AND BAKE AS DIRECTED.

6 Granny Smith apples (you can also use a combination of apples if you're feeling adventurous), peeled, cored, and diced into ½-inch pieces

2 tablespoons pure maple syrup

1 tablespoon fresh lemon juice

1 teaspoon peeled and grated fresh ginger

1 teaspoon ground cinnamon

⅛ teaspoon fine-grain sea salt

Oatmeal-Chocolate CHUNK Cookies

In a perfect world, I'd sit around feeding Logan chocolate chip cookies all day just to bask in the pure, unadulterated joy he radiates while eating them. Obviously this is a selfish fantasy (and a Dude Diet disaster), but I occasionally indulge it on a smaller scale with a couple of these healthier oatmeal cookies. With a base of antioxidant-rich dark chocolate, whole-wheat flour, and high-fiber rolled oats to balance the sugar, these chewy favorites induce full-blown cookie euphoria without the usual crash (or bellyache). Make sure not to overbake them, dudes. Unlike your bod, they're best on the softer side.

¾ cup whole-wheat flour

½ teaspoon ground cinnamon

¼ teaspoon kosher salt

½ teaspoon baking soda

½ cup firmly packed dark brown sugar

½ cup liquid coconut oil

1 large egg, at room temperature

½ teaspoon pure vanilla extract

1½ cups old-fashioned rolled oats (not quick-cooking!)

One 3.5-ounce bar dark chocolate, chopped into small pieces

1. Preheat the oven to 350°F. Line two baking sheets with parchment paper and set aside.

2. In a medium bowl, whisk together the flour, cinnamon, salt, and baking soda.

3. In a separate bowl, whisk together the sugar, coconut oil, egg, and vanilla until smooth.

4. Slowly add the dry ingredients to the wet ingredients and mix with a spatula or wooden spoon until well combined. Stir in the oats and chopped chocolate.

5. Scoop heaping tablespoons of the cookie dough onto the prepared baking sheets, leaving about 2 inches of space between each one. Gently flatten the top of each with the palm of your hand. If the sides are messy, use damp fingers to smooth them out. (No need to be a perfectionist, but I assume you like round cookies?)

6. Bake for 11 minutes. The cookies will look very soft, but they will firm up as they cool. (You *really* don't want to overbake these, dudes!)

7. Let the cookies cool on the baking sheets for 5 full minutes, then transfer them to a wire rack to cool completely.

YOU DO YOU: IF YOU PREFER A FRUITIER OATMEAL COOKIE. SUB RAISINS OR DRIED CHERRIES FOR THE CHOCOLATE.

GLAZED BANANAS with RUM CREAM

3 large ripe but still firm bananas

1 tablespoon unsalted butter (You can also use coconut oil if you like.)

2 tablespoons pure maple syrup

¼ teaspoon ground cinnamon

⅛ teaspoon ground nutmeg

FOR THE RUM CREAM
¼ cup cold heavy cream

3 tablespoons nonfat plain Greek yogurt (I recommend Fage brand for thickness.)

1½ teaspoons spiced rum (Regular dark rum will also work.)

1½ teaspoons pure maple syrup

FOR THE TOPPING
2 tablespoons chopped raw almonds

2 tablespoons unsweetened flaked coconut

Every dude needs one impressive and idiotproof dessert recipe in his back pocket, and this is it. These kick-ass caramelized bananas are a revamped version of traditional Bananas Foster, which involves sautéing bananas with butter, sugar, and spices, before dousing them in rum and lighting the whole shebang on fire. I axed the fancy flaming step here for obvious safety reasons, adding a splash of spiced rum to the yogurt-laced cream instead. The sprinkling of toasted coconut and almonds may seem a little precious, but the crunch factor is clutch. Don't skip it.

1. Start with the rum cream. Place the heavy cream in a medium bowl and whisk vigorously until soft, fluffy peaks form. (If you have an electric hand mixer, you may want to use it to speed things up.) Add the yogurt, rum, and maple syrup and whisk to combine. Cover and refrigerate until ready to use.

2. Moving on to the topping! Heat a small skillet over medium-high heat. (Don't put any oil in the pan, dudes.) When hot, add the almonds and coconut and cook for 1 to 2 minutes, shaking the pan occasionally, until the coconut is golden brown. Transfer to a small bowl and set aside.

3. Slice your bananas in half crosswise, then slice each of the halves in half lengthwise. (Just to be clear, you should have 12 banana pieces total.)

4. In your largest nonstick skillet, melt the butter over medium heat. Whisk in the maple syrup, cinnamon, and nutmeg. Bring to a simmer and immediately add the bananas. Cook for 2 minutes, shaking the pan occasionally or until the bananas are slightly softened and coated in glaze.

5. Divide the bananas among four small plates or bowls. Top with the rum cream and sprinkle with the almond-coconut topping. Serve immediately.

JUST THE TIP: SINCE THIS RECIPE ONLY CALLS FOR A VERY SMALL AMOUNT OF COCONUT. YOU'RE GOING TO HAVE LOTS LEFT OVER. STORE THE FLAKES IN THE FREEZER AND ADD THEM (TOASTED OR UNTOASTED) TO YOGURT. FRESH FRUIT. SMOOTHIES. CEREAL. AND GRANOLA. THEY'RE ALSO GREAT SPRINKLED ON SALADS. CURRIES. AND STIR-FRIES FOR A LITTLE SWEETNESS AND TEXTURE.

Dark Chocolate Power Bark

Four 3.5-ounce dark chocolate bars (at least 70 percent cocoa), chopped into small pieces

¾ cup Quinoa Crunch Granola (page 46), or granola of your choice

¾ cup dried tart cherries

¼ cup chopped pecans

Loaded with powerful antioxidants and chemical compounds that boost your mood, improve brain function, and help fight heart disease, dark chocolate is shockingly good for you (in moderation). Dressed up with crunchy whole-grain granola, chopped pecans, and tart cherries—all of which boast their own set of badass health benefits—this bark is a deliciously responsible way to satisfy your sweet tooth, and I've yet to find a dude that doesn't dig it. In fact, Logan and his friends are known to raid the freezer for "the hippie chocolate" on game days. It's apparently far less painful to watch the Eagles screw the pooch with homemade chocolate bark in hand . . .

1. Line a large baking sheet with aluminum foil or parchment paper.

2. Place the chocolate in a large microwave-safe bowl. Microwave in 20-second intervals, stirring after each one, until the chocolate has completely melted, about 2 minutes.

3. Pour the melted chocolate onto the prepared baking sheet and smooth it out with a spatula until it's about ⅛ inch thick. Evenly sprinkle the granola, cherries, and pecans over the chocolate.

4. Let the bark stand at room temperature for 3 hours until set, or pop it in the fridge for 30 minutes. (I'd go with the latter if I were you.) Peel off the foil or parchment paper, and break the bark into whatever size pieces you'd like. Refrigerate in an airtight container for up to 1 week, or stash it in the freezer for all eternity.

> **YOU DO YOU:** YOU CAN MAKE THIS BARK YOUR OWN BY MIXING UP THE TOPPINGS. BUT PLEASE EXERCISE DUDE DIET DISCRETION. STICK TO WHOLE-GRAIN CEREALS AND PRETZELS. NUTS. SEEDS. AND DRIED FRUIT.

322 THE DUDE DIET

ACKNOWLEDGMENTS

Julie Will, thank you for being such an encouraging, thoughtful editor to this (mildly neurotic) first-time author. I feel so lucky to have worked on this project with you. Milan Bozic and Leah Carlson-Stanisic, thank you for making *The Dude Diet* look unbelievably badass from cover to cover. (It's so much cooler than I could have ever imagined!) And to the entire team of brilliant individuals at Harper Wave that made this book possible, thank you for all of your hard work. I have endless respect and appreciation for each of you.

Matt Armendariz, I adore you as a photographer and as a person. Your beautiful photographs brought *The Dude Diet* to life, and I feel beyond #blessed to have collaborated with you on this book. Thank you. Marian Cooper Cairns, thank you for working your unique brand of styling magic and making my food look so damn good. Your talent (and taste in Pandora stations) is inspiring. Alexis, Byron, and Laura—hey, you guys!! Thank you for rounding out *The Dude Diet* dream team and for making every day on set a total blast.

Thank you, thank you, thank you to each and every member of *The Dude Diet*'s recipe-testing family. This book's deliciousness is a result of your fearless culinary experimentation and thoughtful feedback, and I'm eternally grateful for your service. (You da best.) An extra-special, supersize thank-you to Kay Cochran, Jan Lehmann-Shaw, Kaycie Allen, Mary Curran, Alex Morris, Emily Ballard, Rebecca Kasper, Calia Battista, Aleia Bucci, Emily Smith, Anna Kelley, Nia Bowling, Natalie Burns, Janel Thompson, and Sarah Shattuck. You guys tested an ungodly number of recipes, and I'm forever in your debt. For real.

To my WME peeps, you guys rock. Eve Attermann, thank you for believing in *The Dude Diet* since day one and for guiding me through every step of this crazy process. Meghan Mackenzie, thank you for helping make this book a reality. And, Josh Pyatt, thanks for sticking with me—I really think this is gonna be our year. . . .

Mom (don't cry), I am bursting with gratitude for the woman that you are. Thank you for believing in me more than I believe in myself, for helping me face my fears, and for always inspiring me to be well-dressed! my best, and most authentic, self. You're my hero, and I love you. Dad, thank you for opening so many doors, for passing along your incredible work ethic, and for telling it like it is. I love you, and I couldn't be more proud to be your daughter. Olivia, thank you for being the most supportive and loving sister a girl could ask for. Elliot, gracias for the grassroots PR and for perpetually keeping me on my toes with your startling intelligence and sparkling wit. (I hope this acknowledgment helps you snag a nice lady friend.)

Fifi Knott, thank you for being my person and my biggest cheerleader. Annie Blaine, thank you for being the most patient human alive and talking me off the ledge every other day since I inked this deal—I owe you big-time. (You shall receive the first fur coat in the entourage!) To my girls—Annabel, Daphne, Lara, and Starr—thank you for not kicking me out of the group despite the fact that I only talked about this book for two years straight. You are the smartest, funniest, prettiest people I know, and I'm so thankful for your unconditional support. To *all* of my friends, old and new, thank you for lighting up my life. I love you.

Thank you to the loyal readers of *Domesticate ME!* This book wouldn't have been possible without your support (seriously—I included some of your more complimentary e-mails in my book proposal), and I will never, ever forget that. Virtual koala hug.

And last, but obviously not least, I'd like to thank the Dude himself. Logan, thank you for being my creative muse, my better/hairier half, and the most wonderful, supportive, and hilarious dude I know. I still shudder at the thought that I might have ended up with some muscled dude that ate exclusively clean, whole foods, and I thank my lucky stars for our Parisian meet cute every single day. Thank you for providing a bottomless well of Dude Diet inspiration, for allowing me to chronicle your nutritional confusion in print, and for your willingness to laugh at yourself (and me) always. You are hands down the best thing that has ever happened to me, and I love you more than words could possibly express.

INDEX

ABOUT THE AUTHOR

After graduating from Harvard in 2009, Serena Wolf followed her passion for food to Le Cordon Bleu Paris, receiving her cuisine diploma in 2011. Since then, she has put her culinary skills (and sense of humor) to work as a private chef, culinary instructor, food writer, recipe developer, and blogger extraordinaire at Domesticate-Me.com. Serena's work has been featured on *The Dr. Oz Show*, Martha Stewart Radio, the *Huffington Post*, Elle.com, Shape.com, Self.com, People.com, and FoodandWine.com, as well as many other well-known publications and media outlets. She lives in New York with her dude.